Nordic Gothic

INTERNATIONAL GOTHiC

The Series' Board of General Editors

Elisabeth Bronfen, University of Zurich, Switzerland
Steven Bruhm, University of Western Ontario, Canada
Ken Gelder, University of Melbourne, Australia
Jerrold Hogle, University of Arizona, USA (Chair)
Avril Horner, Kingston University, UK
William Hughes, Bath Spa University, UK

The Editorial Advisory Board

Glennis Byron, University of Stirling, Scotland
Robert Miles, University of Victoria, Canada
David Punter, University of Bristol, England
Andrew Smith, University of Sheffield, England
Anne Williams, University of Georgia, USA

Previously published
Neoliberal Gothic: international Gothic in the neoliberal age Edited by Linnie Blake and Agnieszka Soltysik Monnet
Monstrous media/spectral subjects: imaging Gothic from the nineteenth century to the present Edited by Fred Botting and Catherine Spooner
Globalgothic Edited by Glennis Byron
The Gothic and death Edited by Carol Margaret Davison
Suicide and the Gothic Edited by William Hughes and Andrew Smith
EcoGothic Edited by Andrew Smith and William Hughes

Nordic Gothic

Maria Holmgren Troy, Johan Höglund,
Yvonne Leffler and Sofia Wijkmark

Manchester University Press

Copyright © Manchester University Press 2020

While copyright in the volume as a whole is vested in Manchester University Press, copyright in individual chapters belongs to their respective authors, and no chapter may be reproduced wholly or in part without the express permission in writing of both author and publisher.

Published by Manchester University Press
Oxford Road, Manchester M13 9PL
www.manchesteruniversitypress.co.uk

British Library Cataloguing-in-Publication Data is available

ISBN 978 1 5261 2643 6 hardback
ISBN 978 1 5261 6395 0 paperback

First published by Manchester University Press in hardback 2020

This edition first published 2022

The publisher has no responsibility for the persistence or accuracy of URLs for any external or third-party internet websites referred to in this book, and does not guarantee that any content on such websites is, or will remain, accurate or appropriate.

Typeset by Toppan Best-set Premedia Limited

Series editor's preface

Each volume in this Series contains new essays on the many forms assumed by – as well as the most important themes and topics in – the ever-expanding range of international 'Gothic' fictions from the eighteenth to the twenty-first century. Launched by leading members of the International Gothic Association (IGA) and some editors and advisory board members of its journal, *Gothic Studies*, this Series thus offers cutting-edge analyses of the great many variations in the Gothic mode over time and all over the world, whether these have occurred in literature, film, theatre, art, several forms of cybernetic media, or other manifestations ranging from 'Goth' group identities to *avant garde* displays of aesthetic and even political critique.

The 'Gothic Story' began in earnest in 1760s England, both in fiction and drama, with Horace Walpole's efforts to combine the 'ancient' or supernatural and the 'modern' or realistic romance. This blend of anomalous tendencies has proved itself remarkably flexible in playing out the cultural conflicts of the late Enlightenment and of more recent periods. Antiquated settings with haunting ghosts or monsters and deep, dark secrets that are the mysteries behind them, albeit in many different incarnations, continue to intimate what audiences most fear in both the personal subconscious and the most pervasive tensions underlying Western culture. But this always unsettling interplay of conflicting tendencies has expanded out of its original potentials as well, especially in the hands of its greatest innovators, to appear in an astounding variety of expressive, aesthetic and public manifestations over time. The results have transported this inherently boundary-breaking mode across geographical and cultural borders into 'Gothics' that now appear throughout the world: in the settler communities of Canada, New Zealand and Australia; in such post-colonial areas as India and Africa; in the Americas and the Caribbean; and in East Asia and several of the islands within the entire Pacific Rim.

These volumes consequently reveal and explain the 'globalisation' of the Gothic as it has proliferated across two-and-a-half centuries. The General Editors of this series and the editors of every volume, of course, bring special expertise to this expanding development, as well as the underlying dynamics, of the Gothic. Each resulting collection, plus the occasional monograph, therefore draws together important new studies about particular examples of the international Gothic – past, present or emerging – and these contributions can come from both established scholars in the field and the newest 'rising stars' of Gothic studies. These scholars, moreover, are and must be just as international in their locations and orientations as this Series is. Interested experts from throughout the globe, in fact, are invited to propose collections and topics for this series to the Manchester University Press. These will be evaluated, as appropriate, by the General Editors, members of the Editorial Advisory Board, and/or other scholars with the requisite expertise so that every published volume is professionally put together and properly refereed within the highest academic standards. Only in this way can the International Gothic Series be what its creators intend: a premiere world-wide venue for examining and understanding the shape-shifting 'strangeness' of a Gothic mode that is now as multi-cultural and multi-faceted as it has ever been in its long, continuing and profoundly haunted history.

Contents

List of figures								page ix
Acknowledgements							x

    Introduction							1

1 The past that haunts the present: the rise of Nordic Gothic 11
    Yvonne Leffler & Johan Höglund

2 Two Nordic Gothic icons: Hans Christian Andersen and
    Selma Lagerlöf							29
    Maria Holmgren Troy & Sofia Wijkmark

3 Swedish Gothic and the demise of the welfare state		47
    Sofia Wijkmark

4 Nordic Gothic crime: places and spaces in Johan Theorin's
    Öland quartet series						65
    Yvonne Leffler

5 'The Chosen Ones': Sara B. Elfgren and Mats Strandberg's
    teenage witch trilogy						84
    Maria Holmgren Troy

6 Nordic troll Gothic							103
    Sofia Wijkmark

7 Indigenous hauntings: Nordic Gothic and colonialism		125
    Johan Höglund

8   Lost (and gained) in translation: Nordic Gothic and
    transcultural adaptation   147
    Maria Holmgren Troy

9   Nordic Gothic new media   169
    Johan Höglund

Appendix: Nordic Gothic fiction   191
Bibliography   195
Index   205

List of figures

7.1 The ghost of Evelina urging Eddie on in his project of vengeance (SVT/Canal+, 2016, *Idjabeaivváš/Jour Polaire/Midnight Sun/Midnattssol*). 141
7.2 Eddie urging the viewer to seize the spear and take back Sápmi (SVT/Canal+, 2016, *Idjabeaivváš/Jour Polaire/Midnight Sun/Midnattssol*). 142
9.1 The gaming interface of *Alan Wake* (Remedy Entertainment, 2010, *Alan Wake*). 174
9.2 Six running to avoid the long arms of the janitor in *Little Nightmares* (Tarsier Studios, 2017, *Little Nightmares*). 179
9.3 Six feeding off a gnome that has attempted to hand her the sausage that lies ignored to the left (Tarsier Studios, 2017, *Little Nightmares*). 180
9.4 The recognisably Swedish house where Daniel can be assumed to live in *Year Walk* (Simago, 2013, *Year Walk*). 182
9.5 Karen entering one of the derelict Viking settlements on the island in *Through the Woods* (Antagonist, 2016, *Through the Woods*). 185
9.6 Karen approaches the site where Erik is about to sacrifice Espen to the Fenris Wolf. The jagged mountains in the background are the wolf's gigantic, open jaws (Antagonist, 2016, *Through the Woods*). 187

Acknowledgements

First, we would like to thank the editor of the International Gothic Series, Jerrold E. Hogle, who encouraged the idea of this book from the very beginning. His support and advice have made the journey towards a finished book much less Gothic than it otherwise could have been. Since, on the whole, the conception of the book, as well as the writing of it, has been a pleasurable and intellectually stimulating collaborative venture, the authors/editors are also very grateful to each other, not least for being the Nordic Gothic 'dream team'. Special thanks go to Yvonne for organising a number of workshops for us in Gothenburg; to Johan for treating us to a workshop in a Gothic castle in Växjö; and to Sofia and Maria for taking the main responsibility for contacts with the series editor and Manchester University Press, as well as for getting the manuscript together at the end. We also thank everyone who has offered comments on our papers on Nordic Gothic at different international conferences during the past few years.

Maria Holmgren Troy and Sofia Wijkmark are grateful to *Magnus Bergvalls Stiftelse* for travel grants that supported research trips to the British Library in 2018. They would also like to thank KuFo, the Research Group for Culture Studies at Karlstad University, for financial as well as intellectual support. Troy wishes to acknowledge the former editor of *American Studies in Scandinavia* for granting permission to reprint excerpts from an article that appeared in that journal in 2016 (48:1). As always, she is also grateful for Mark Troy's support, patience and good cheer. Wijkmark wishes to acknowledge Makadam förlag for granting permission to reprint excerpts from an article published in the Swedish anthology *Norrlandslitteratur: Ekokritiska perspektiv* (2018), edited by Peter Degerman, Anders E. Johansson and Anders Öhman.

Johan Höglund wishes to thank *Magnus Bergvalls Stiftelse* for the funding in 2015 that enabled important preliminary research. He also extends his thanks to the members of the Nordic Colonialism Cluster of the Linnaeus University Centre for Concurrences in Colonial and Postcolonial Studies for their valuable comments and encouragement. Finally, he is immensely grateful to his family Cissi, David, Agnes, Edith and Hilda for bearing with him during the completion of this project. You are the best.

Introduction

Defining 'Nordic Gothic'

In the Nordic countries, Gothic fiction has become increasingly pervasive and popular in the past few decades and invaded all cultural registers – popular, highbrow, children's and young adult fiction – and contemporary Nordic Gothic has been well received by critics and general audiences, both nationally and internationally. In view of this, it is striking that Nordic Gothic remains a more or less unexplored territory in the internationally extensive field of Gothic Studies. Addressing this dearth of knowledge, *Nordic Gothic* traces Gothic fiction in the Nordic region from its beginnings in the nineteenth century, with a main focus on the development of Gothic from the 1990s onwards in literature, film, TV series and electronic games. This volume thus aims to give an overview of contemporary Nordic Gothic fiction, to provide a number of case studies and in-depth analyses of individual narratives and productions, and to study these narratives and productions in relation to transnational developments and cross-fertilisations. The intention is to create an understanding of a ubiquitous but under-researched cultural phenomenon: Nordic Gothic.

Here, it is necessary to first define what 'Nordic' and 'Gothic' mean. Of these two concepts, strangely enough, Gothic is perhaps the least elusive, despite its long and complex theoretical history. Most contemporary critics agree that Gothic is a continuously productive, transhistorical genre characterised by a certain affect or effect of terror or horror, by a dark and often uncanny atmosphere, and by a specific ideological endeavour: the interrogation of enlightenment rationality as a potentially destructive patriarchal, colonial and anthropocentric, yet anti-human force.[1] For the purpose of this book, it is unnecessary to have a more rigid and narrow definition. Rather, we want to stress what Jerrold E. Hogle has dubbed 'Gothic's essentially betwixt-and-between nature', its heterogeneity and transgressiveness.[2] At the same time, it is important to be aware of the conventions of the Gothic novel always lurking in the background, sometimes transformed into something else, sometimes appearing in their original shape as hauntings from the past. *Nordic Gothic* deals with texts that relate to the Gothic in different ways; while some can be defined as typically Gothic, others are better described as inspired by the genre or examples of hybrid combinations of genres.

Regarding 'Nordic', it should be observed that this concept has changed substantially over the centuries, as nations, languages, cultures and ethnicities have transformed it and been transformed within it. The Nordic region consists of five separate nation-states, Iceland, Denmark, Sweden, Norway and Finland, and by a number of regions claimed by these nations, including Greenland, the Faroe Islands and Sápmi. While the Danish, Norwegian and Swedish languages have much in common, they are recognised as separate languages and Nordic Gothic can also be produced in a number of other languages spoken in the Nordic region, such as Finnish, Icelandic, Greenlandic, Faroese and the various dialects of the Sámi.

During the past two centuries, the borders of these nations, and the language barriers that they appear to denote, have changed frequently. At the beginning of the nineteenth century, Denmark and Norway belonged to a union that also comprised the colonies Iceland, Greenland and the Faroe Islands. At the time, and until the 1860s, Denmark was still in possession of Schleswig-Holstein and the official languages of the nation were Danish and German. When the Danish-Norwegian union was dissolved in 1814, Norway lost its colonial dominions in the North Atlantic and was forced into a union with Sweden that lasted until 1905. In 1809, Sweden lost possession of what is known today as Finland to Russia, something which turned the Finnish nation into a Grand Duchy until the Russian Revolution in 1917. Yet, Finland remained essentially bilingual and Swedish is still spoken in many parts of the country. In 1810, a French marshal was elected to inherit the Swedish royal throne, strengthening its ties to Napoleonic France and the French language. On Greenland and Iceland, Danish was the official language for a long period, as was Swedish, Norwegian or Finnish in different parts of Sápmi.

To understand the emergence and proliferation of Nordic Gothic, this shifting geographical, political and linguistic context must be taken into consideration. The many and shifting political connections between the nations, and especially Denmark's strong ties to Germany, meant that European literature was often read in either German or French in the nineteenth and early twentieth century. The language situation within Scandinavia also facilitated dissemination of Nordic literature between the Nordic nations. Gothic in Swedish was easily accessible in parts of Norway, Finland and Denmark, while Danish Gothic could be read in Sweden and Norway. Thus, it is possible that the large Swedish-speaking community in Finland would have turned to Swedish Gothic, while the Danish audience may have preferred to read such writers as E. T. A. Hoffmann in the German original.

Since the end of the Second World War, English has been the first foreign language in the Nordic countries and Gothic literature has progressively been read in English, while the import of English language films and games has increased in recent decades. Today, migration into and between nations, and the emergence of strong indigenous movements in Sweden, Norway, Finland and Greenland, are again changing the Nordic cultural and linguistic landscape. New literatures have emerged in the Nordic region, in languages such as Sámi, Arabic and Greenlandic, and in what is sometimes referred to as 'sociolects', social registers employed by certain, often marginalised groups in society. This geopolitical and linguistic history, and the cultural and political tensions that have followed in its wake, deeply inform contemporary Nordic Gothic.

Two Nordic Gothic productions in particular have gained wide-spread international acclaim and have had a significant impact on the Nordic Gothic boom or revival of the early twenty-first century: Lars von Trier's Danish TV series *Riget* (DR, 1994, 1997; *The Kingdom*) and John Ajvide Lindqvist's Swedish novel, *Låt den rätte komma in* (2004; *Let the Right One In*, 2007). Both exhibit distinctive Nordic Gothic traits: created by a Danish filmmaker and a Swedish novelist, these works are set in the Nordic countries and combine critical social realism with supernatural Gothic.

Arthouse film director Lars von Trier's turn to the TV medium and the creation of a Gothic TV series about a haunted hospital proved to be surprisingly popular with TV viewers in Denmark and Sweden, as well as with critics.[3] *Riget* was also successfully presented as a four-hour film at national and international film festivals. In 1995, it won the national Bodil Awards for the best Danish film, best actor, best actress and best supporting actor, and Nils Vørsel won the special award for screenwriting. At the Danish Robert Festival that year, it won the best actor, best actress, best original score, best cinematography, best screenplay and best sound categories. Internationally, it received the award for best film at the Seattle International Film Festival and the director and best actor awards at the Kalovy Vary International Film Festival, where it was also nominated for the Grand Prix – the Crystal Globe. The same year it was screened at cinemas in France and the United States and shown on television in the Netherlands and Germany, where it won the *Grimme-Preis* for Best Series or Mini-Series in 1996. In the Nordic countries, the TV series *Riget* gave a broader audience a sense of what contemporary Nordic Gothic could be, as well as of what could actually be shown on television.

John Ajvide Lindqvist achieved a similar feat in the realm of literature with his debut novel, *Låt den rätte komma in*. Although Gothic was not highly regarded by Swedish literary critics at the time of its publication, this vampire novel managed to win many of them over. Among other national awards, Lindqvist received *Stiftelsen Selma Lagerlöfs litteraturpris* (the Selma Lagerlöf Foundation's literary award) in 2008. At that point, the novel, which became a bestseller in Sweden, had been translated into English, among other languages. Lindqvist had also written the screenplay for the Swedish film adaptation directed by Tomas Alfredson, *Låt den rätte komma in* (2008; *Let the Right One In*), which became an enormous international success and won a great number of high-status film awards across the Nordic countries, Europe and North America. One of Lindqvist's short stories, 'Gräns' (2006; 'Border'), about a troll that works as a customs officer, has also been adapted into a Swedish film: *Gräns* (2018), directed by Ali Abbasi. It has been well received, internationally as well as nationally, and won the *Un certain regard* prize at the Cannes film festival in 2018.

Like earlier Nordic Gothic, contemporary Nordic Gothic productions are clearly influenced and informed by Gothic from outside the region, particularly Anglophone Gothic. For instance, Lindqvist, who is often compared to Stephen King, highlights his admiration for the works of British horror writer and filmmaker Clive Barker. In the case of *Riget*, the main Gothic influences besides the works of Danish Carl Theodor Dreyer are Claude Barma's *Belphegor* (ORTF, 1965), a French TV series about a phantom at the Louvre that von Trier watched as a child, and

David Lynch and Mark Frost's *Twin Peaks* (ABC, 1990–1991), a supernatural crime series. This particular American TV series has also influenced later developments of what is called 'Nordic Noir', a genre of dark crime fiction that has had immense international appeal.

Since the turn of the millennium, a Gothic subgenre to Nordic Noir has emerged. Here, the depiction of a committed crime and subsequent police procedures is complicated by seemingly supernatural activities. The realistic setting and narrative are progressively replaced by Gothic tropes and unreliable perspectives. Although there are obvious references to *Twin Peaks*, contemporary Nordic writers and filmmakers have formed a specific Nordic version of what Yvonne Leffler calls 'Gothic crime'. The stories are set in remote places outside populated urban areas, either in a rural village or the wilderness. The location, particularly if it is untamed nature, is the very source or prerequisite of the crimes taking place. Moreover, in those cases where the crime mystery is eventually solved, the actual existence of supernatural phenomena and creatures is confirmed rather than negated. In recent years, Nordic production teams, and in particular Swedish television, have produced a number of Nordic Gothic crime stories.

Previous research and outline of chapters

Gothic Studies has become a vast and increasingly important international research field during the past three or four decades; however, besides articles and book chapters on certain individual works, Gothic in the Nordic region has hitherto received little scholarly attention – something that *Nordic Gothic* aims to rectify. Most of the previous research has been done in Sweden and mainly on nineteenth century Swedish literature. Among the most important Swedish studies are the dissertations by Yvonne Leffler (1991), Henrik Johnsson (2009) and Sofia Wijkmark (2009).[4] There are no book-length studies on contemporary Swedish Gothic, but Mattias Fyhr's dissertation (2003) on Gothic includes some discussion on late twentieth century Swedish fiction and music.[5] Even less research has been done in the other Nordic countries, but Kirstine Kastbjerg's dissertation on Danish Gothic (2013) from the University of Washington is an important contribution to the Danish field.[6] It has a mainly historical approach, but also includes a final chapter on contemporary novels. In the other Nordic countries, only minor studies have been published on national Gothic. For example, Kati Launis sketches a history of Finnish Gothic in an article from 2013, and two studies on Norwegian fantastic fiction (1998; 2009) include chapters on Gothic fiction from the nineteenth century.[7] Together with Gunnar Iversen's essay on contemporary Nordic horror film (2016), the only studies dealing with the Nordic (or rather Scandinavian) region as a whole are Leffler's essays on Gothic topography in Scandinavian horror fiction (2010; 2013) and female Gothic monsters (2016) and her entry on 'Scandinavian Gothic' in *The Encyclopedia of the Gothic* (2012).[8] Furthermore, Pietari Kääpä's 2014 book on ecology and contemporary Nordic cinema includes a chapter on contemporary Norwegian, Finnish and Icelandic horror films.[9]

By outlining and analysing contemporary Nordic Gothic fiction, as well as providing aesthetic and historical contextualisation, *Nordic Gothic* thus elucidates a widespread but under-researched cultural phenomenon. In Chapter 1 'The past that haunts the present: The rise of Nordic Gothic', Yvonne Leffler and Johan Höglund provide a historical survey of the rise of the Gothic in Nordic literature, film and video games. Leffler and Höglund observe that German, British and French novels around 1800 were quickly translated into the Scandinavian languages, and that they inspired Nordic writers – and, later, film directors – to emulate this tradition but also to adapt the genre to Nordic audiences. The chapter then discusses the evolution of Nordic Gothic during the nineteenth and twentieth century, noting the most important writers and their work. It also describes the emerging scholarship that shows how Nordic canonical authors and filmmakers have been influenced by the Gothic. Finally, it addresses what can be termed the 'Nordic Gothic boom', that can be said to begin in 2004 with Lindqvist's *Låt den rätte komma in*.

Chapter 2, 'Two Nordic Gothic icons: Hans Christian Andersen and Selma Lagerlöf' by Maria Holmgren Troy and Sofia Wijkmark, presents two important forerunners to contemporary Nordic Gothic, Danish Hans Christian Andersen (1805–1875) and Swedish Selma Lagerlöf (1858–1940). The chapter sketches their different literary and historical contexts and touches on translations and adaptions of, or contemporary references to, their Gothic stories and novels. The first part of the chapter focuses on Gothic elements in Andersen's fairy tales 'Den lille Havfrue' (1837; 'The Little Mermaid'), 'Snedronningen' (1844; 'The Snow Queen') and 'De vilde Svaner' (1838; 'The Wild Swans'), and biefly relates the first two to the Disney adaptations of those two tales. The second part of the chapter examines folklore, *fin-de-siècle* and provinciality in the novel *Gösta Berlings saga* (1891; *The Saga of Gösta Berling*). The short stories 'De fågelfrie' (1892; 'The Outlaws') and 'Stenkumlet' (1892;

'The King's Grave') are also briefly discussed as examples of Lagerlöf's use of the forest as a Gothic setting.

In Chapter 3, 'Swedish Gothic and the demise of the welfare state', Sofia Wijkmark examines how contemporary Swedish Gothic relates to the dismantling of the Swedish welfare system, and how the welfare state is described in terms of horror in Lindqvist's novels *Hanteringen av odöda* (2005; *Handling the Undead*) and *Rörelsen. Den andra platsen* (2015; *The Movement. The Other Place*), and Mats Strandberg's novel *Hemmet* (2017; *The Home*). The two authors explore the failures of the welfare state in different ways. Lindqvist's novels often explicitly refer to or quote iconic leaders associated with the welfare state, and *Rörelsen* deals with the murder of Olof Palme in 1986, describing the political climate at the time of his death. The zombie novel *Hanteringen av odöda* addresses the incapacity of the state to take care of the undead, and the story indicates a connection between the awakening of the dead and climate change, reflecting the ecological anxiety of contemporary society. Strandberg's *Hemmet* depicts the consequences of welfare profiteering and can be regarded as what Wijkmark calls 'geriatric Gothic'. The setting is a haunted nursing home and the story combines supernatural horror and social critique with the fear of old age, but also with the fear of having to put a family member in an institution run by a profit-based company.

In Chapter 4, 'Nordic Gothic crime: places and spaces in Johan Theorin's Öland quartet series', Yvonne Leffler examines Gothic crime, that is, the Gothic subgenre of Nordic Noir, where modern crime investigation is obstructed by seemingly supernatural happenings linked to the Nordic location and its history. The internationally recognised Swedish novelist Johan Theorin, Leffler argues, writes within an old Nordic tradition of crime fiction, while simultaneously expanding the importance of setting and Nordic mythology. Yi-Fu Tuan's distinction of place and space is therefore used as a point of departure in the investigation of the return of a fear-provoking past linked to unfamiliar spaces beyond modern society and the tourist attractions on the idyll of Öland.

In Chapter 5, '"The Chosen Ones": Sara B. Elfgren and Mats Strandberg's teenage witch trilogy', Maria Holmgren Troy examines the Swedish young adult novels *Cirkeln* (2011; *The Circle*, 2012), *Eld* (2012; *Fire*, 2013) and *Nyckeln* (2013; *The Key*, 2015). This trilogy, like much contemporary Nordic Gothic, combines supernatural Gothic with critical social realism, and highlights the flaws and failures of the welfare state from a number of teenagers' points of view. It places the story in a particular Swedish geographical and historical setting, while at the same time employing Gothic themes and motifs that have earlier been used in 1990s American films and TV series. The chapter explores the use of multiple focalisation, Gothic plot elements, the place of witchcraft, the school as a Gothic location, doppelgängers and divided selves, and the attraction and dangers of the witches' powers. Despite the elements that it shares with certain American Gothic productions, the trilogy is a distinctly Nordic Gothic production in that it manages to create a plural protagonist, and in the ways in which the geographical and gloomy social setting are used to tie the Gothic elements to particular historical contexts.

In Chapter 6, 'Nordic troll Gothic', Sofia Wijkmark explores the phenomenon of Nordic troll Gothic. She demonstrates how late twentieth and twenty-first century troll fiction can be understood in relation to the concepts of ecogothic and dark ecology, and how the ambiguous character of the troll is used to explore limits and question categories. Nature, especially the forest, is depicted as dark and uncanny and it is sometimes also described as having agency, dissolving the limits between the animate and inanimate. Wijkmark analyses troll stories by Swedish authors Selma Lagerlöf, Kerstin Ekman and Stefan Spjut, and Finnish author Johanna Sinisalo, showing how they make use of both the folklore tradition and the Gothic. The chapter demonstrates, among other things, that the plot is rarely narrated from the point of view of the troll, and that trolls are often depicted as a dying species but also as dark avengers, striking back at humankind.

In Chapter 7, 'Indigenous hauntings: Nordic Gothic and colonialism', Johan Höglund observes that while several studies of Anglophone Gothic have noted the close connection between Gothic and imperialism, very little of the scholarship that exists on Nordic Gothic has considered this dimension. Höglund argues that this should be attributed not only to a general academic reluctance to look beyond Anglophone Gothic, but also to the widespread belief that the Nordic countries remained outside the nineteenth-century colonial project. Referring to several studies that show that the Nordic nations were, in fact, eager participants in the colonial project, Höglund's chapter then discusses a number of late twentieth and early twenty-first century Nordic Gothic texts, with a focus on the fiction of Peter Høeg, Yrsa Sigurðardóttir and Anders Fager, and on the Swedish-French television series *Idjabeaivváš* (*Jour Polaire/ Midnight Sun/Midnattssol*, 2016). Höglund uses these texts to argue that Nordic Gothic, sometimes directly and sometimes furtively, addresses colonial concerns and that this tradition shows the same ambivalence towards the colonial past and present as does international Gothic.

In Chapter 8, 'Lost (and gained) in translation: Nordic Gothic and transcultural adaptation', Maria Holmgren Troy investigates the two most influential examples of contemporary Nordic Gothic, von Trier's TV series *Riget* and Lindqvist's novel *Låt den rätte komma in* and its Swedish film adaptation together with the American adaptations of these Nordic works: Stephen King's *Kingdom Hospital* (ABC, 2004) and Matt Reeves' *Let Me In* (2010). To begin with, the chapter briefly discusses Gothic TV and TV horror and outlines how von Trier, King and Lindqvist have moved between different media. It then goes on to examine some differences between the Nordic and American productions that are related to what Troy calls 'Gothic humour'. In terms of setting, the American adaptations are placed in small American towns rather than the central locations constituted by the Danish capital in *Riget* and the Stockholm suburb in *Låt den rätte komma in*. Whereas the American adaptations thus pertain to King's brand of small-town American Gothic, the Nordic works can be seen as a kind of urban Gothic. The settings, Troy suggests, also make visible ideological differences between the Nordic Gothic works and the American adaptations.

Finally, Chapter 9, 'Nordic Gothic new media' by Johan Höglund, maps and analyses new Gothic media and video games developed in the Nordic region. The chapter first considers what the concepts 'Gothic' and 'Nordic' actually entail when the focus is new media rather than literature or cinema. Following this discussion, the chapter analyses four of the more important and widely disseminated games and considers the interactive stories that they tell in relation to the Nordic geographical, ideological and cultural landscape. The first two, Finnish *Alan Wake* (2010) and Swedish *Little Nightmares* (2017), are well-funded and internationally distributed games made for an international audience. The other two, Swedish *Year Walk* (2013) and Norwegian *Through the Woods* (2016), are independent games that may look for wide dissemination, but that keep much closer to Nordic themes and settings.

Notes

1 R. Hume, 'Gothic versus Romantic: A Revaluation of the Gothic Novel', *PMLA*, 84:2 (1969), pp. 282–9.
2 J. E. Hogle, 'Introduction: The Gothic in Western Culture', in *The Cambridge Companion to Gothic Fiction* (Cambridge: Cambridge University Press, 2002), p. 17.

3 *Riget* 'was primarily funded by DR in cooperation with Swedish Television, but also received the thus far largest support grant – 2.2 million kroner – from the EU media programme, Greco, as well as funding from various Nordic media funds.' J. Stevenson, *Lars von Trier* (London: BFI, 2002), p. 78.
4 Y. Leffler, *I skräckens lustgård. Skräckromantik i svenska 1800-talsromaner* (Göteborg: Göteborgs universitet, 1991); H. Johnsson, *Strindberg och skräcken. Skräckmotiv och identitetstematik i August Strindbergs författarskap* (Umeå: H:ström, 2008); S. Wijkmark, *Hemsökelser. Gotiken i sex berättelser av Selma Lagerlöf* (Karlstad: Karlstads universitet, 2009).
5 M. Fyhr, *De mörka labyrinterna. Gotiken i litteratur, film, musik och rollspel* (Stockholm, Lund: Ellerström, 2003).
6 K. M. Kastbjerg, 'Reading the Surface: The Danish Gothic of B. S. Ingemann, H. C. Andersen, Karen Blixen and Beyond' (PhD dissertation, University of Washington, 2013).
7 K. Launis, 'From Italy to the Finnish Woods: The Rise of Gothic Fiction in Finland', in P. M. Mehtonen and M. Savolainen (eds), *Gothic Topographies: Language, Nation Building and 'Race'* (Farnham: Ashgate, 2013), pp. 169–86; T. Haugen, *Literære skygger. Norsk fantastisk literatur* (Oslo: Landslaget for norskundervisning, 1998); G. K. Omdal, *Grenseerfaringer. Fantastisk literatur i Norge og omegn* (Bergen: Fagbokforlaget, 2009).
8 G. Iversen, 'Between Art and Genre: New Nordic Horror Cinema', in M. Hjort and U. Lindqvist (eds), *A Companion to Nordic Cinema* (Malden: Wiley-Blackwell, 2016), pp. 332–50; Y. Leffler, 'The Gothic Topography in Scandinavian Horror Fiction', in M. Canini (ed.), *The Domination of Fear* (New York: Rodopi 2010), pp. 43–53; Y. Leffler, 'The Devious Landscape of Scandinavian Horror', in Mehtonen, *Gothic Topographies: Language, Nation Building and 'Race'*, pp. 141–52; Y. Leffler, 'Female Gothic Monsters', in *The History of Nordic Women's Literature* (2016), http://nordicwomensliterature.net/article/female-gothic-monsters Accessed 25 January 2019; and Y. Leffler, 'Scandinavian Gothic', in W. Hughes, D. Punter and A. Smith (eds), *The Encyclopedia of the Gothic* (Malden: Wiley-Blackwell, 2012).
9 P. Kääpä, *Ecology and Contemporary Nordic Cinemas: from Nation Building to Cosmopolitanism* (New York: Bloomsbury Academics, 2014).

Yvonne Leffler & Johan Höglund

The past that haunts the present: the rise of Nordic Gothic

There is a long non-realist tradition in Nordic literature and film that goes back to the Romantic period. This tradition frequently employs typical Gothic tropes, it seeks to evoke feelings of terror and horror, and it negotiates, as Gothic is understood to do, the complex tension between the human subject and Enlightenment modernity. Due to a striking reluctance by generations of Nordic literary critics and scholarship to recognise a Gothic tradition in the region, it was not until the late 1980s that the existence of Gothic fiction in the Nordic countries began to be systematically explored through a number of studies by Yvonne Leffler.[1] Since the turn of the millennium, different Nordic writers and aspects of Gothic have been investigated by Scandinavian scholars such as Mathias Fyhr, Henrik Johnsson, Sofia Wijkmark and Kirstine Kastbjerg.[2] Some introductions and surveys of the Scandinavian tradition have also been published.[3] Building on this scholarship, this chapter will trace the Nordic Gothic tradition from its beginnings in the late eighteenth century to the present moment. The aim is to provide a picture of how the Gothic tradition emerged in the Nordic region and to show how Nordic writers, filmmakers and, towards the end of the twentieth century, game producers, make use of Gothic tropes and themes. Several of the authors and filmmakers mentioned in this chapter will be discussed in more detail in other parts of the book.

The rise of Gothic in the Nordic countries

The emergence of Gothic is commonly understood to coincide with the publication of Horace Walpoles's *The Castle of Otranto*, subtitled *A*

Gothic Story, in 1764. The new genre quickly gained momentum until, at the turn of the century, it had spread across Europe, into the United States and many European colonies. Many of these well-known English, German and French novels were available to Nordic readers and some of them were quickly translated into Swedish, Danish and Norwegian. As an example, Matthew Lewis's *The Monk* (1796) was translated and published in sections during 1800–1804 in Sweden.[4] Many of Ann Radcliffe's Gothic novels were translated into Swedish during the first decades of the nineteenth century, as were those by Charlotte Brontë a few decades later. Some of the most popular Gothic novels were also adapted for the theatres. For example, Radcliffe's novel *The Italian* (1794) was staged as *Eleonora Rosalba, eller Ruinerna i Paluzzi* in 1801–1802, followed by François Guillaume Ducray-Duminil's French novel *Victor, ou l'Enfant de la Forêt* (1796) as *Victor, eller skogsbarnet* at the same theatre, Arsenalen in Stockholm, in 1803–1804. The influence of British Gothic is easy to perceive in Danish author Bernhard Severin Ingemann's *Varulven* (1834; *The Werewolf*) and in Victor Rydberg's Swedish serial *Vampyren* (1848; *The Vampire*), both inspired by John Polidori's *The Vampyre* (1819).[5] While Rydberg rewrote and expanded Polidori's story, Ingemann transformed it into a complex story about a werewolf character and the devastating conflict between his bourgeois mask and his sexual drives.

The British writers that belonged to the first phase of Gothic (1765–1820) thus had a considerable impact on Nordic Gothic and helped to inspire the production of similar texts. However, the German and French traditions were arguably just as important and influential. Early Gothic by Ernst Theodor Amadeus Hoffmann, Eugène Sue and Ducray-Duminil were widely read around 1800 and more often translated into Swedish than the British authors were. In particular, Hoffmann's works *Die Elixiere des Teufels* (1815; *The Devil's Elixirs*) and *Der golden Topf* (1814; *The Golden Pot*) influenced many Nordic writers. These writers developed their own kind of Gothic fiction by locating their stories in distinct social and geographical environments, but they also show themselves as unmistakably genre aware by explicitly referring to internationally well-known works. Ingemann's *Sphinxen* (1820; *The Sphinx*) is a rewriting of Hoffmann's *The Golden Pot* about a young protagonist who increasingly confuses dream and reality with the text he is writing. Although there is no evident source text for the Swedish writer Clas Livijn's Gothic-fantastic tale 'Samwetets fantasi' (1821; 'A Fantasy of a Bad Conscience'), it is one of many Nordic stories about a supernatural stalker in the tradition of Hoffmann's *The Devil's Elixirs*. In Livijn's story, a homecoming soldier finds himself followed by a grey man with an axe, who he believes to be connected with his earlier wrongdoing; his former girlfriend was executed for infanticide because he refused to help her when she became pregnant. The pursuer can be interpreted as either an avenging ghost or an image of the soldier's bad conscience and punishing ego. Also, the Swedish writer Erik Johan Stagnelius published several dramas in the Gothic tradition. His drama *Riddartornet* (1821–1823; *The Knight's Tower*) revolves around forbidden passions and incest, with many references to Walpole's *The Castle of Otranto*.[6] The knight, Rheinfels, has imprisoned his unfaithful wife in a desolate tower of his castle to enable him to seduce their daughter Mathilda. The horror reaches its climax when Rheinfels tries to force his daughter to become her mother's murderer.

The motif of the double or doppelgänger was also repeatedly used by Hans Christian Andersen, who is discussed in more detail in Chapter 2. Although his Danish fairy tales and stories are more obviously influenced by Germanic folktales than easily recognisable Gothic fiction, several of his stories stray into clearly Gothic territory. Of particular note is Andersen's short story 'Skyggen' (1847; 'The Shadow'). This is a dark tale of a devious doppelgänger and illustrates the transformation of shadow into body, and how the shadow drains the original body of life.[7] Another version of a gradually stronger double is illustrated in Andersen's 'De røde sko' (1847; 'The Red Shoes'), a cruel story about losing control and blurring the distinction between clothing and body, the ego's willpower and bodily motion, in which the red shoes end up articulating and defining the captive subject and owner of the shoes, the girl.[8] Because of the popularity of his stories, Andersen's work was widely translated and he travelled both within and outside the Nordic region, exerting considerable influence on a number of authors.

As in other European countries, many women writers adjusted the Gothic genre to speak about their own social and geographical context, and the challenges that women faced during the era. The actions take place in a recognisably Nordic environment, often a named location, where local history, myths and customs are important for the plot and Gothic atmosphere. The most prolific and explicitly Gothic author of this period is arguably the Swedish female writer Aurora Ljungstedt. In *Hin Ondes hus* (1853; *The House of the Devil*), about a ghostly house in Stockholm and its afflicted owner, she explicitly refers to Radcliffe's novels about haunted houses.[9] In another story about a man and his evil double, 'Harolds skugga' (1861; 'Harold's Shadow'), she both alludes to Hoffmann's *Die Elexiere des Teufels* (1815) and precedes Robert Louis Stevenson's *The Strange Case of Dr. Jekyll and Mr. Hyde* (1886), in the way that she transforms the motif of the double into a narrative about the civilised and primitive parts of a man's ego.

Fin-de-siècle writing, early filmmaking and interwar Gothic

In Britain, as in many other European nations, the late nineteenth century was a period of fervent colonial expansion into Africa and Asia, but also a time of increasing geopolitical turmoil and, as the century drew to a close, of *fin-de-siècle* anxiety. The emergence of the 'new woman', degeneration fears, class turmoil, economic depressions and competition between colonial empires coloured popular discourse in general and Gothic writing in particular. In fact, Gothic experienced a renaissance, particularly in Britain, at this time. Some seminal Gothic texts that influenced Nordic writers' novels are Stevenson's aforementioned *The Strange Case of Dr. Jekyll and Mr. Hyde*, Bram Stoker's *Dracula* (1897), Florence Maryatt's provocative *Blood of the Vampire* (1897), Edgar Allan Poe's American short horror stories and Arthur Conan Doyle's stories about Sherlock Holmes.[10] Also, many of the most recognised modernist writers, some of whom have been described as Gothic, were translated into Scandinavian languages. The most prominent include Joseph Conrad, Oscar Wilde and Charles Baudelaire, who all had a well-documented impact on Nordic authors. Thus, *fin-de-siècle* writers and the first generation of filmmakers in the Nordic region were influenced by late-Victorian Gothic and the heavily gendered and racialised categories that informed it.[11] It can also be argued that Gothic powerfully influenced the iconoclastic project that much *fin-de-siècle* and modernist writing launched in the Nordic region and beyond.[12]

In contrast to the British and continental European traditions, for a significant time the Gothic works that were published in the Nordic region during the turn of the century were all but erased from Nordic literary history. Even more importantly, when canonical writers in the Nordic region made extensive use of Gothic, it was not recognised or theorised as such, despite obvious references to Gothic tropes in the works and their wide use of affective terror. Yet even a cursory reading of the writers of the era reveals a profound preoccupation with Gothic motifs and discourses. The motif of the male double in combination with avenging ghosts is frequently used in August Strindberg's and Henrik Ibsen's works. In Strindberg's Swedish story *Tschandala* (1889), the male protagonist decides to kill his male companion as he starts to identify with his friends, and in so doing progressively fears to lose what he calls their battle of minds and his individual identity. In *Spöksonaten* (1907; *Ghost Sonata*), Strindberg combines the motif of doubles with that of ghosts and the Nordic *fylgjur*, who drain the living of life and blood. The drama gradually exposes a distorted version of reality where the distinction between life and death is unclear.[13] In Ibsen's Norwegian play *Gengangere* (1881; *Ghosts*), the Nordic motif of '*gengangere*', that is, ghosts returning to take revenge, is used as a metaphor of syphilis in order to highlight the hypocrisy of contemporary bourgeois society. In both Strindberg's and Ibsen's works, the Gothic elements are central to the exposure of evils and social issues in their contemporary society.

While the works of Strindberg and Ibsen are inspired by Gothic discourse, Swedish Nobel laureate Selma Lagerlöf is arguably the *fin-de-siècle* writer that connects most strongly to this tradition. Although her writing will be discussed in more detail in Chapter 2, it should be observed here that she further developed Nordic Gothic into a place-focused genre, in which setting plays a central role and where the landscape is a character taking an active part in the action. *Herr Arnes penningar* (1903; *Herr Arne's Hoard*, 1922) is a thrilling murder and ghost story where the myth of werewolves, in combination with a punishing Arctic landscape, is used to enhance the Gothic atmosphere.[14] Lagerlöf explores various aspects of the return of the past and transgressing boundaries between life and death, human self and monstrous beast, fantasy and reality in stories such as 'Stenkumlet' (1892; 'The King's Grave', 1899) and 'Frid på Jorden' (1917; 'Peace on Earth').[15] Thus, Lagerlöf recurrently uses the Nordic wilderness and local folklore to depict the evil forces in nature and within humankind. Her Gothic style and rural settings inspired other Nordic authors, such as the Norwegian writer Ragnhild Jølsen. Her novel *Rikka Gan* (1904) is a narrative about transgressing boundaries and a haunting past. Just as in many of Lagerlöf's stories, Jølsen's story revolves around a conflict-ridden female protagonist. Here the conventions of Radcliffe's female Gothic and her damsels in distress are more elaborate and are twisted into an eerie story about a woman in pursuit of identity but victimised by her family and the history of her house.[16]

When Gothic began to invade the new art form of cinema during the 1910s and 1920s, Nordic filmmakers were at the forefront with their visualisation of the ambiguous imagery of popular beliefs and Gothic atmosphere on the screen. Benjamin Christensen's Swedish-Danish silent film *Häxan* (1922; *The Witch*) communicates popular ideas about witches, as well as facts about the witch trials that took place in the past. The ghostly visualisation of the ride of the witches inspired Walt Disney's illustration of Modest Mussorgsky's music *Eine Nacht auf dem Kahlen Berge* in his animated film *Fantasia* (1940). Victor Sjöströms's silent film *Körkarlen* (1921; *The Phantom Carriage*) is a *tour de force* that uses the early technique of double exposure to illustrate the world of death and thus highlights the Gothic qualities of Lagerlöf's 1912 novel *Körkarlen* (*Thy Soul Shall Bear Witness*) on which the film was based. The first Nordic vampire movie, Carl Theodor Dreyer's Danish expressionistic film *Vampyr* (1931–1932), is structured as a journey to an isolated island, a settlement beyond time and space at the border of life and death, day and night.[17]

During the interwar years, Gothic also surfaced in Modernist writing, for example, in the Swedish Nobel laurate Pär Lagerkvist's expressionistic writing. The collection *Onda Sagor* (1924; *Evil Tales*) was one of many that clearly aimed to evoke a feeling of terror and deep anxiety at the onslaught of modernity. In the short story 'Far och jag' ('Father and I'), the protagonist walks with his father along railway tracks through a beautiful, pastoral landscape. As evening falls, this landscape becomes uncanny when suddenly an unscheduled train appears, driven by a ghostly and disturbing figure. Like much of Lagerkvists's early work, this story revolves around a deeply felt terror at modernity. His later fiction often draws on the Bible and makes use of archetypal and frequently Gothic tropes such as the scheming dwarf in the eponymous novel *Dvärgen* (1944; *The Dwarf*).

One of the better known and widely read writers of Gothic from this period is Danish Karen Blixen, also known by her pseudonym Isak Dinesen. One of only a few Nordic Gothic writers to write her stories in English, Blixen is best known for her collection *Seven Gothic Tales* (1934). This includes 'The Supper at Elsinore' ('Et familieselskab i Helsingør'), an example of a Gothic ghost story in a specific Danish setting. The detailed description of the town Helsingør and its local history is integrated to heighten the suspense in this story, which deals with a dysfunctional merchant family. Incestuous undercurrents drive the plot and the actions of three siblings whom death cannot part. In the end, the sisters – two old, unmarried women – summon their long-dead and executed brother in the siblings' former secret chamber in their old family home which faces Kronborg, the site of William Shakespeare's Hamlet, in a wintry Helsingør. Their reunion is both a return of the repressed and an atonement of the past and its implicit sins.[18] It is also, as in Lagerlöf's and Jølsen's stories, an eerie tale about female domestic confinement in physical and mental spaces where the sisters' final family reunion with their dead brother, and explicit references to *Hamlet*, details the tyranny of the past.

Gothic and post-war anxiety in the late twentieth century

As in much of the rest of Europe and the West, post-war era fiction and film in the Nordic countries struggled with the sheer horror of the war experience. At this time, realist representations were combined with multifaceted images that employed a fragmented postmodern aesthetic to accommodate the war's darkest aspect. During the post-war period Gothic sometimes furnished a way to speak about the anxiety and sometimes, in its more popular form, it paradoxically became a refuge from the corporeal horror of the past war. Other important developments that left their mark in Gothic were the increasing strength of the Finnish language in Finland, and the beginning of decolonisation movements in Iceland, Greenland and Sápmi. In Finland, S. Albert Kivinen writes short stories inspired by H. P. Lovecraft's Cthulhu mythos, an undertaking shared by Panu Petteri Höglund.[19]

Gothic and horror tropes are also clearly discernible in the oeuvre of one of Scandinavia's most prolific filmmakers, Swedish director Ingmar Bergman. *Det Sjunde Inseglet* (1957; *The Seventh Seal*) is, as Bergman himself admitted, inspired by the powerful Gothic imagery of his Swedish predecessor Sjöström's *Körkarlen*. The violent revenge drama *Jungfrukällan* (1960; *The Virgin Spring*) also plays on terror, a sense of pervading doom, and makes frequent use of Gothic tropes. Bergman's later works make more use of surrealist imagery, repetitive reflections and doppelgängers. The claustrophobic setting in the Swedish archipelago and the thrilling struggle for control and power between two women, a nurse (Bibi Andersson) and her traumatised silent patient (Liv Ullman), turn *Persona* (1966) into a psychological horror drama. The story explores the Jungian concept of 'persona', the themes of duality and doubles, insanity and vampirism, in the depiction of the two women, where smoke and mirrors are used to make their faces double and dissolve in order to turn them into ghostly doubles or different aspects – or personas – of each other.

Vargtimmen (1968; *Hour of the Wolf*), is even more in the tradition of horror film, and also refers to the characters in the earlier film *Persona*. It is about a painter (Max von Sydow) and his wife (Liv Ullman) on a small island, where the painter seeks to be cured from his insomnia but is frequently approached by strange people. What is real and what is his imagination is hard to define and when he is finally attacked by his pursuers or shadows, his wife is left alone in the woods. Just as in Dreyer's films, Bergman's Gothic atmosphere in his early films revolves around transgressions of the individual's physical and psychological integrity, performed by both characters and settings.

As European colonies in Asia, Africa and South America gained independence, islands and territories colonised by the Nordic nation states also began to seek separation from their former colonisers. Iceland gained independence in 1944, and Greenland shed its colonial status in 1953 to become a separate realm of Denmark. The Sámi, inhabiting a territory to the far north, controlled by Norway, Sweden, Finland and Russia, pursued both separate and joint independence movements. While few histories recognise these developments as decolonisation, news media reported frequently on them, and the Arctic – a region that has always received attention from Gothic writers and directors – became the setting for a number of Nordic narratives. Finnish Lapland is explored in *Valkoinen peura* (1952; *The White Reindeer*) by Erik Blomberg. The film is inspired by pre-Christian Sámi mythology and shamanism, and tells the story of a woman (Mirjame Kousmanen) who visits the local shaman. He turns her into a shapeshifting vampiric reindeer, who attracts male herders with tragic results. In the film, the Arctic snowclad landscape provides a sublime backdrop for an uncanny drama about sexual desire and female witchcraft. Sápmi is also the setting of the American-Swedish *Rymdinvasion i Lappland* (1959; *Terror in the Midnight Sun*), a drive-in movie in English for a Swedish audience that shows a strange alien invasion of the Nordic north, complete with egg-head invaders, a gigantic King-Kong-like monster, a young white female in distress and a white, square-jawed male hero. The film is a mash-up of Gothic, sci-fi invasion and the US post-war monster flick that enacts what Fatimah Tobing Rony has referred to as 'ethnographic spectacle'.[20]

As will be discussed in more detail in Chapter 7, Nordic Gothic of the twentieth century increasingly turned to the Arctic region and Sámi concerns. The Swedish writer Kerstin Ekman's first novel *De tre små mästarna* (1961; *Under the Snow*) is an overtly Gothic crime story set in a world that is either all darkness in the winter or all light in the summer. It also hints at a supernatural agency rooted in Sámi religion and practice. At the beginning of the new century, a number of Swedish authors employed Gothic to tell stories about Sápmi and the Sámi, including Matthias Hagberg in *Rekviem för en vanskapt* (2012), Stefan Spjut in *Stallo* (2012) and *Stalpi* (2017), and Mikael Niemi in *Fallvatten* (2012) and *Koka Björn* (2017).

Even when the Arctic is not the focus, the landscape still plays a central role in Nordic Gothic. As Yvonne Leffler has argued, in Nordic Gothic the landscape often takes on the role of the labyrinthine Gothic castle.[21] This can be seen in many of the texts mentioned above, as well as in Kåre Bergstrøm's Norwegian film *De dødes tjern* (1958; *Lake of the Dead*), based on a novel by André Bjerke. Here the horrors are located in the Nordic landscape and a legend that is connected with a specific woodland lake and the evil deeds associated with the place. When six people from Oslo arrive to visit a friend but find him missing and his dog dead in the lake, they decide to stay to solve the mystery, but soon find themselves exposed to the mysterious powers tied to the location and to the lake in particular.

The Gothic Nordic landscape and local folklore are also extensively used by canonical well-recognised Swedish authors, such as the aforementioned Kerstin Ekman. Ekman's historical novel *Rövarna i Skuleskogen* (1988; *The Forest of Hours*) revolves around the small troll Skord, who enters the human world, studies alchemy in Uppsala and travels to the Swedish colony St. Barthelemy. In *Händelser vid vatten* (1993; *Blackwater*), a violent crime scene is visualised through a series of uncanny sensory impressions. The writing of Birgitta Trotzig relies on the symbolic and religious. In many of her short stories, dark forces invade the mind and pervade the landscape. Her novel *Dykungens Dotter: En Barnhistoria* (1985) is loosely based both on Hans Christian Andersens's 'Dyndkongens datter' (1858; 'The Mud-King's Daughter'/'The Marsh King's Daughter') and the Brothers Grimm's 'The Frog King or Iron Heinrich'. It tells a story that converges with the grotesque transformation of the human body and that, at times, appears to seek to paralyse the reader with terror. In addition to these writers, as Matthias Fyhr has argued, Mare Kandre's novels *Bübins unge* (1987; *Bübin's Kid*), *Bestiarium* (1999) and *Aliide, Aliide* (1991) are structured as Gothic romances. Especially in Kandre's stories, the Gothic landscape is used to deepen the psychological portraits of the characters and to endow the text with a symbolic, mythic meaning. In the same tradition of Nordic female Gothic is the Swedish author Maria Gripe, a young-adult writer inspired by Charlotte and Emily Brontë's novels. As has been demonstrated by Carina Lidström, Gripe's *Skuggserie* (1982–1988; *The Shadow series*), where the leifmotif is the shadow, is suffused with Jungian archetypes, as well as with supernatural and Gothic elements.[22]

Throughout the final decades of the twentieth century, a less well-known cadre of Nordic writers produced Nordic versions of widely successful, popular Gothic of the type that Stephen King, Dean Koontz and Clive Barker were writing in the United States and the United Kingdom. Of some significance was the semi-pulp book series *Kalla Kårar* (*Cold Chills*) published by B. Wahlströms bokförlag between 1971 and 1984. This series translated a significant amount of foreign-language Gothic and horror, including works by Fritz Lieber, Richard Matheson, John Wyndham and Graham Masterton. Moreover, Swedish authors Bengt-Åke Cras, Gunnar Dahl and Dagmar Danielsson also produced fiction for the series. Another notable contribution was Helmer Linderholm's collection of Swedish short stories *De ulvgrå* (1972; *The Woolf Grey*), which all revolve around a provincial medical practitioner and his wife, whose background in northern Sweden and Finland seems to have provided her with an uncanny ability to manage challenges from the underworld of Nordic folk mythology. In addition, Åke Ohlmarks, Swedish historian of religion and translator of Tolkien's *The Fellowship of the Ring* trilogy, wrote a number of Gothic novels and short-story collections, including *Gengångare* (1971; *Revenants*) and *Slottsspöken* (1973; *Castle Ghosts*). In the late 1960s, Leif Kranz' formative and popular Gothic thriller series for young adults, *Kullamannen* (1967–1968), was first broadcasted by Swedish Television with several TV repeats. It was also published as a young-adult novel.

In the 1980s, the global success of Gothic-inflected, low-budget slasher and gore films such as *Halloween* (1978), *Friday the 13th* (1980) and *Evil Dead* (1981), spawned a few attempts at new Swedish horror film, including Hans Hatwig's *Blödaren* (1983; *The Bleeder*), Jonas Cornell's *Månguden* (1988; *The Moon God*) and Rumle Hammerich's *Svart Lucia* (1992; *Black Lucia*). The difficulty in raising a reasonable budget for horror films in Sweden led to low production costs – these movies were not well received by critics, nor did they reach big audiences.[23] Danish *Nattevagten* (1994; *Nightwatch*), a Gothic crime story by Ole Bornedal, was more successful, as was Joakim Ersgård's Swedish film *Besökarna* (1988; *The Visitors*) about an urban family's move to a haunted house outside town.

An important breakthrough for Gothic in the Nordic region was Lars von Trier's TV drama *Riget* I-II (1994, 1997; *The Kingdom*). This series is set in an urban environment in the Danish capital Copenhagen, inside a modern hospital built on marshland that calls forth both the powers of nature and an ancient Danish past. Although the hospital is a well-organised workplace, a representation of modern technology and rational clinical medicine, a repressed past that highlights recurrent injustice and inequality in the Danish state emerges. Trier's series also resulted in a US remake, Stephen King's *Kingdom Hospital* (2004), and *Riget* has exerted a tremendous influence on the current generation of writers and filmmakers who have contributed to the production of Nordic Gothic since the turn of the millennium. Both *Riget* and King's US adaptation will be further discussed in Chapter 8.

The final few years of the twentieth century was also when what has been described as 'new media' began to enter homes and offices across the globe. New media includes digital, networked texts and other forms of interactive and performative culture, but is perhaps mostly associated with computer, console and, most recently, tablet and smart-phone gaming. These new media forms have quickly been invaded by Gothic. As Richard Rouse III (2009) has observed, games 'have inhabited the horror genre for almost as long as they have been in existence'.[24] Nordic Gothic also joined the new-media movement during the close of the 1990s and the first decade of the new millennium. However, as discussed in more detail in Chapter 9, this constituted a different development compared to most Nordic Gothic literature and film. Nordic game studios take advantage of games being part of a digital, networked economy and sold on a digital market that, unlike printed books or theatrical film releases, is not dependent on specific geographical locations or distribution of physical objects. In other words, Nordic game manufacturers can, and do, make games for an international, mostly English-speaking market, and sometimes also under licence from some of the major production companies. This means that they are even more sensitive to transnational trends in Gothic and horror than literature and film are, but it does not mean that they necessarily abandon what can be termed the 'Nordic traditions' of Gothic. Although the language used to communicate with the gamer is typically English, these games can still place the gamer within clearly Nordic landscapes and confront her or him with Nordic monsters.

The Gothic revival at the Millennium

It is fair to describe what has occurred in the Nordic countries since the turn of the millennium as a Gothic revival. Many works that belong to this revival have become internationally successful and imitated. The most important text after Danish filmmaker Lars von Trier's TV series *Riget* is arguably John Ajvide Lindqvist's Swedish combination of vampire story and social realist coming-of-age novel *Låt den rätte komma in* (2004; *Let the Right One In*). This novel has been translated into many languages, including English. It was soon adapted into two films: a Swedish-language film directed by Tomas Alfredson in 2008, and an Anglophone remake, *Let Me In*, directed by the American Matt Reeves and released in 2010. *Låt den rätte komma in* and the film adaptations are more closely examined in Chapter 8. About the same time, von Trier launched *Antichrist* (2009), which like many later Nordic horror films, as Gunnar Iversen argues, blurred the boundaries between art cinema and genre film.[25] It starts as a realistic drama about a nameless couple who lose their child in an accident, but turns into an uncanny horror film when the couple try to work through their loss by moving to an old cottage in the woods. Their progressively terrifying hallucinations and violent behaviour end in tragedy and seem to suggest that the local landscape is evil and a place where chaos reigns. Another example of the Gothic revival is Sara Bergmark Elfgren and Mats Strandberg's young-adult or crossover *Engelfors* trilogy (2011–2013), which will be further explored in Chapter 5, as well as the Swedish film adaption of the first part, *Cirkeln* (2015; *The Circle*). These novels were well received both in and outside Scandinavia.

These internationally widely circulated Gothic works illustrate certain distinct ways of using and reformulating the prevalent aspects of Nordic Gothic today. As in Lindqvist's bestselling novels and short stories and the Swedish film adaptations of *Låt den rätte komma in* and 'Gräns' (*Gräns*, 2018; *Border*), many Nordic writers and filmmakers integrate Gothic elements in other genres and discourses. As will be discussed in Chapter 3, Lindqvist continues to use Gothic elements to confront social issues and dismantle cherished ideas about Swedish welfare society in works such as *Hanteringen av odöda* (2005; *Handling the Undead*), *Människohamn* (2008; *Harbour*) and *Lilla Stjärna* (2010; *Little Star*).

The first decade of the twenty-first century was also a time when Nordic Gothic and horror film experienced a renaissance. As Tommy Gustavsson has observed, Nordic horror cinema struggled against both economic and systemic obstacles during the latter half of the twentieth century.[26]

The reluctance of the Nordic film institutes, the Swedish in particular, to fund genre film, meant that it was not until the wide availability of low-cost, digital photography that film makers in the Nordic region were able to make Gothic and horror film. When this technology became widely available a few years into the new millennium, there was an explosion of Gothic and horror film, much of it inspired by American slasher and gore cinema. One example is the first Icelandic horror film ever made, Júlíus Kemp's *Harpoon: Reykjavik Whale Watching Massacre* (2009), which adapts American slasher conventions and explicitly refers to *Texas Chainsaw Massacre*, in order to comment on Iceland's financial crisis in 2008. In the film, a group of international tourists are taken on a whale-watching tour where everything goes wrong. After some misadventures, they are picked up by an Icelandic mother and her two sons on a whaler, but instead of helping the rescued tourists the Icelandic family start to hunt down and kill them one by one, substituting the visitors for whales. Kemp's subversive message seems to be that Iceland's financial collapse reduced native whalers to amusement for disrespectful international tourists, a development that turned these whalers into violent killers.[27]

In line with an international trend, Gothic has entered narratives for children and young adults. Elfgren and Strandberg's aforementioned *Engelfors* trilogy, discussed in detail in Chapter 5, is an example of young protagonists exploring magic powers. Also, in some of these stories, the Gothic castle is replaced by the Nordic wilderness and the landscape is inhabited by mythical creatures recognised from Nordic folktales, as well as various shapeshifters and witches. In Swedish Caroline L. Jensen's *Vargsläkte* (2011; *Wolf Kindred*), for example, Vera discovers that she has inherited her grandmother's ability to assume the shape of a wolf, or rather werewolf, and thereby gains access to new and powerful forces of nature. In numerous witch novels for young readers, such as Lene Kaaberbøl's Danish *Vildheks* (*Wild Witch*) series (2010–), the good witches and female shapeshifters must learn to act as responsible and concerned women capable of cooperation. Thus, they must be guided by their female predecessors in order to learn to distinguish between good and evil and their respective characteristics. In that way, these female coming-of-age stories depict a matriarchal world where women are in charge and set the rules. They maintain a matriarchal power structure founded in ancient Nordic traditions and a strong connection to nature and the regional landscape.

The depiction of untamed nature as a negative and evil place, that is apparent in Selma Lagerlöf's stories and in Ingmar Bergman's films, is also central to much contemporary Nordic Gothic. When the protagonists in Nordic Gothic start losing control over their imagination, there is a fusion between ego and landscape. The landscape becomes a devious place; not just a backdrop to what happens, but an active antagonist in films such as Nicolas Winding Refn's Danish film *Valhalla Rising* (2009). The story takes place in 1000 AD when a mute warrior and his slave board a Viking vessel on Iceland and begin a journey into a land of obscurity. The vessel is engulfed by endless fog before the crew sights a hostile and unknown land where mysterious arrows kill them one by one. The hardships that they must endure soon affect their perception and mental states in a way that makes the spectator believe that they are not attacked by another character or a monster, but by nature itself.

There are a great number of Nordic Gothic and horror films that explore the same Gothic terrain, but through the present moment. In these films, the encounter with nature is an event that dissolves both time and pre-conceived categories. The mythic world of folktale merges with modern everyday life, and species blend into species. The standard formula tells the story of how urbanised people visit snowclad mountainous areas and how such visits become nightmares when the visitors find themselves prey to monstrous hunters. The first example of this subgenre was *Villmark* (2003; *Dark Woods*), Pål Øie's Norwegian version of *The Blair Witch Project*. In Øie's film, two women and two men intend to make a reality TV show set in the Norwegian wilderness, but during filming they find themselves followed by a disturbed killer. In André Øvredal's *Trolljegeren* (2010; *Troll Hunter*), two students and their cameraman set out to make a documentary film about a suspected bear poacher only to discover that he is in fact the only operative of the Troll Security Team, a top-secret branch of the Norwegian government tasked with keeping this primitive and indigenous race under control. In Roar Uthaug's *Fritt vilt* (2006; *Cold Prey*) and Tommy Wirkola's *Død snø* (2009; *Dead Snow*), groups of young city dwellers go to the Norwegian mountains for a vacation, but in both cases the intended winter outing turns into a traumatic experience. In *Fritt Vilt*, the snowboard tourists find themselves trapped in a deserted hotel together with a mad killer. In *Død snø* the skiers are attacked by a group of greedy Nazi zombies, who have stayed in the mountains since the German occupation of Norway during the Second World War. Finally, Alexander L. Nordaas's Norwegian film *Thale* (2012) tells the story of how two cleaners try to scrub the remains of a long-dead man from the floor of a remote cottage in the Norwegian forest. In the cottage, they find an imprisoned female creature named Thale, who is a hybrid between human and a *hulder*, a female forest-creature in Nordic mythology. Gradually, the two men discover that this being has been submitted to experiments by her captor, in a way which, as Höglund argues, is reminiscent of the colonial conquest and eugenic practices that many Nordic states embraced during the early twentieth century.[28] In all these films, the action takes place in the Norwegian wilderness, a normally restful place for recreation, which transforms into an evil place of violence and terror. The same thing occurs in Swedish *Vittra* (2012), a film that merges Nordic folk mythology that is closely tied to the forest with Sam Raimi's *Evil Dead*, as discussed by Höglund.[29]

The first years of the twenty-first century also saw a new generation of writers that walked the fine line that separates Gothic and crime fiction. Of course, this line has been walked by many writers in the past.[30] As will be demonstrated in Chapter 4, the success of Nordic Noir has encouraged a new wave of Gothic crime writing. Many of these locate crime and monstrous actions to the Nordic wilderness, something ancient, barbaric and Other located outside modern urban society, but many of these texts also interrogate a long history of abuse of the people who inhabit these spaces. As discussed in Chapter 7, Danish author Peter Høeg's *Frøken Smillas fornemmelse for sne* (1992; *Miss Smilla's Feeling for Snow*), situates horror both in the wilderness and in the processes by which this space was colonised and modernised. Similarly, Norwegian/Danish writer Kim Leine's *Profeterna i Evighetsfjorden* (2012; *Prophets of Eternal Fjord*), mixes Gothic and crime to retell the history of the colonisation of Greenland by the Danish state. The Swedish author Johan Theorin's novels, such as *Skumtimmen* (2007; *Echoes from the Dead*) and *Nattfåk* (2008; *The Darkest Room*), which are further explored in Chapter 4, as well as Yrsa Sigurðardóttir's Icelandic detective stories, for example *Auðnin* (2008; *The Day is Dark*), are similarly set in remote areas. Also TV series such as Swedish Anders Engström and Henrik Björn's *Jordskott* (2015), Johan Kindblom's and Thomas Tivemark's *Ängelby* (2015) and Måns Mårlind and Björn Stein's *Idjabeaivváš* (also titled *Jour Polaire*, *Midnight Sun* and *Midnattssol* 2016) are located on the outskirts of conventional civilisation, in areas that compromise the stated ideals of today's Nordic society.

Even when the mysteries that these TV crime shows or games describe are solved, the rational account of what happened remains ambiguous. The initially presumed interaction of supernatural powers and creatures known from Nordic popular beliefs is never entirely discredited, and in the end the audience is left uncertain about what really happened. In TV series such as *Jordskott*, or in games such as *Through the Woods*, the revelation does not reinstate a rational and orderly universe. Rather, the further into the narratives the audience or gamer travels, the deeper into pagan mythologies and traditions they get, until these mythologies become part of the universe itself.

The aim of this chapter has been to describe the emergence of Gothic in the Nordic region, to mention the most important texts, and to outline some of the most pertinent developments of Gothic in this part of the world. It is obviously impossible to mention all texts produced in the Nordic region that, in one way or another, make use of the Gothic mode. In this chapter, it has similarly been impossible to provide detailed analysis of the texts that are included. This is the work of the chapters that follow.

Notes

1 Y. Leffler, *I skräckens lustgård: Skräckromantik i svenska 1800-talsromaner* (Göteborg: Göteborg universitet, 1991); Y. Leffler, 'Skräckromantik i svensk romantik', *Nordische Romantik. IASS* 19 (Basel and Frankfurt, 1991), pp. 134–9.
2 M. Fyhr, *De mörka labyrinterna. Gotiken i litteratur, film, musik och rollspel* (Lund: Ellerström, 2003); H. Johnsson, *Strindberg och skräcken. Skräckmotiv och identitetstematik i August Strindbergs författarskap* (Umeå: Bokförlaget H:ström, 2008); S. Wijkmark, *Hemsökelser: Gotiken i sex berättelser av Selma Lagerlöf* (Karlstad University, 2009); K. M. Kastbjerg, 'Reading the Surface: The Danish Gothic of B. S. Ingemann, H. C. Andersen, Karen Blixen and Beyond' (PhD dissertation, University of Washington, 2013).
3 Y. Leffler, 'The Gothic Topography in Scandinavian Horror Fiction', in M. Canini (ed.), *The Domination of Fear*, [At the Interface: Probing the Boundaries, Volume 70] (Amsterdam: Rodopi, 2010), pp. 43–53; Y. Leffler, 'Scandinavian Gothic', W. Hughes, D. Punter and A. Smith (eds), *The Encyclopedia of the Gothic* (Oxford: Wiley-Blackwell, 2012), www.literatureencyclopedia.com; Y. Leffler, 'The Devious Landscape in Scandinavian Horror', in P. M. Mehtonen and M. Savolainen (eds), *Gothic Topographies: Language, Nation Building and 'Race'* (Surrey, England and Burlington, USA: Ashgate, 2013), pp. 141–52; Y. Leffler, 'Female Gothic Monsters', in *The History of Nordic Women's Literature*, http://nordicwomensliterature.net/article/female-gothic-monsters, Publ. 1 December 2016. About the specific Swedish tradition, see M. Fyhr, *Svensk skräcklitteratur 1: Bårtäcken över jordens likrum* (Lund: Ellerström, 2017).
4 The same year as the first volume was printed, Lewis published translations of Danish folk poetry that he had come into contact with through Johann Gottfried Herder's *Volkslieder* (1778), D. H. Thomson in M. G. Lewis, *Tales of Wonder* (Peterborough: Broadview Press, 2010); L. Møller, '"They Dance All under the Greenwood Tree": British and Danish Romantic-Period Adaptations of Two Danish "Elf Ballads"',

in C. Duffy (ed.), *Romantic Norths: Anglo-Nordic Exchanges, 1770–1842* (New York: Palgrave Macmillan, 2016), pp. 129–53.
5 Polidori's story was first published in Swedish in 1823 and attributed to Lord Byron. On how Polidori's story was expanded by Rydberg, see Y. Leffler, 'Vampyrmotivet och erotiken', in B. Svensson and B. Sjöberg (eds), *Kulturhjälten. Viktor Rydbergs humanism* (Stockholm: Atlantis, 2009), pp. 155–68.
6 See Fyhr, *Svensk skräcklitteratur 1*, pp. 161–4.
7 The use of shadow and light in Andersen's 'The Shadow' has been explored by Kastbjerg, 'Reading the Surface', pp. 213–18.
8 Kjastbjerg briefly discusses Andersen's 'The Red Shoes' and the motif of bodily punishment in *Reading the Surface*, pp. 205–6.
9 Leffler, *I skräckens lustgård*, p. 106.
10 Stoker's *Dracula* was published in Swedish as *Mörkrets makter* (1900) and Maryatt's *Blood of the Vampire* was published in Swedish as *Den sköna vampyren* (1900).
11 See P. Brantlinger, *Rule of Darkness: British Literature and Imperialism, 1830–1914* (Ithaca: Cornell University Press, 1988); P. R. O'Malley, *Catholicism, Sexual Deviance, and Victorian Gothic Culture* (Cambridge: Cambridge University Press, 2006); A. Haefele-Thomas, *Queer Others in Victorian Gothic: Transgressing Monstrosity* (Cardiff: University of Wales Press, 2012).
12 See J. P. Riquelme, *Gothic and Modernism: Essaying Dark Literary Modernity* (Baltimore: Johns Hopkins University Press, 2008) and T. L. Norman 'Gothic Modernism: Revising and Representing the Narratives of History and Romance' (PhD dissertation, University of Tennessee, 2012).
13 The theme of identity in Strindberg's *Tschandala* and *Ghost Sonata* has been examined by Johnson, *Strindberg och skräcken*, pp. 141–7, 165–74.
14 For *Herr Arnes Penningar* as a Gothic novel, see Leffler, *I skräckens lustgård*, pp. 153–66.
15 For the use of Gothic conventions in the short stories by Lagerlöf, see Wijkmark, *Hemsökelser*, 2009.
16 About Gothic element in Jølsen's *Rikka Gan*, see H. Howlid Wærp, 'Utover enhver grense – Gotiske trek i Ragnhild Jølsens romancer', in Torgeir Haugen (ed.), *Litterære skygger. Norsk fantastisk litteratur* (Oslo: Cappelen Akademisk Forlag, 1998), pp. 101–21.
17 The Gothic focalisation technique in Dryer's *Vampyr* has been discussed by Y. Leffler, *Horror as Pleasure: The Aesthetics of Horror Fiction* (Stockholm: Almqvist & Wiksell International, 2000), pp. 133–5.
18 About Gothic motifs in Blixen's story, see Kastbjerg, 'Reading the Surface', pp. 253–301.
19 See P. P. Hoglund and S. Albert Kivinen, *The Book of Poison: Stories Inspired by H. P. Lovecraft* (Dundee: Evertype, 2014).
20 R. F. Tobing, *The Third Eye: Race, Cinema and Ethnographic Spectacle* (Durham: Duke University Press, 1996).
21 Leffler, 'The Gothic Topography Scandinavian Horror Fiction', pp. 43–52.
22 C. Lidström, *Sökande, spegling, metamorfos: tre vägar genom Marie Gripes skugg-serie*, Diss. (Stockholm: Symposion Brutus Östlings bokförlag, 1994).
23 See J. Höglund, 'Wither the Present. Wither the Past: The Low-Budget Gothic Horror of Stockholm Syndrome Films', in J. D. Edwards and J. Höglund (eds),

B-Movie Gothic: International Perspectives (Edinburgh: Edinburgh University Press, 2018), pp. 122–38.
24 R. Rouse III, 'Match Made in Hell: The Inevitable Success of the Horror Genre in Video Games', in B. Perron (ed.), Horror Video Games: Essays on the Fusion of Fear and Play (Jefferson: McFarland, 2009), p. 15.
25 G. Iversen, 'Between Art and Genre: New Nordic Horror Cinema', in M. Hjort and U. Lindqvist (eds), A Companion to Nordic Cinema (Malden: Wiley Blackwell, 2016), pp. 332–50.
26 T. Gustavsson, 'Slasher in the Snow: The Rise of the Low-Budget Nordic Horror Film', in T. Gustafsson and P. Kääpä (eds), Nordic Genre Film: Small Nation Film Cultures in the Global Marketplace (Edinburgh: Edinburgh University Press, 2015), pp. 189–202.
27 Iversen, 'Between Art and Genre', pp. 339–41.
28 Höglund, 'Revenge of the Trolls: Norwegian (Post) Colonial Gothic', Edda, 117:2 (2017), pp. 123–6.
29 Höglund, 'Wither the Present', pp. 122–38.
30 Leffler, 'Early Crime Fiction in Nordic Literature', pp. 215–44.

Maria Holmgren Troy & Sofia Wijkmark

Two Nordic Gothic icons: Hans Christian Andersen and Selma Lagerlöf

This chapter presents Gothic aspects in the oeuvre of two iconic Nordic authors: Danish Hans Christian Andersen (1805–1875) and Swedish Selma Lagerlöf (1858–1940). Lagerlöf published her first novel sixteen years after Andersen's death, which means that they published their works in different literary and historical contexts, as will be briefly outlined in this chapter. Nevertheless, they shared an interest in the imaginative or fantastic and, among other things, they both integrated traits and themes from oral traditions such as Nordic ballads and legends in their literature. Often giving the narrator a distinctive voice as storyteller, both authors have at times been denigrated by literary critics who have seen them as 'mere storytellers' rather than major authors, but it has always been difficult to deny the literary value of their writings, as well as their popularity.

By 2018, according to The Hans Christian Andersen Centre in Odense, Denmark, Andersen's tales were available in 160 different languages, while Karen Sanders observes that 'he is listed among the "ten most widely translated authors in the world along with Shakespeare and Karl Marx"'.[1] He travelled widely in Europe and Asia Minor, contributed to genres such as travel writing, drama, autobiography, poetry and fictional prose of different kinds and gained international recognition during his lifetime. Both then and today, he was and is most appreciated as a writer of fairy tales and stories for children or, more accurately, a crossover audience, and the first part of this chapter will focus on three of his most famous fairy tales: 'Den lille Havfrue' (1837; 'The Little Mermaid', 1846), 'Snedronningen' (1844; 'The Snow Queen', 1847) and 'De vilde

Svaner' (1838; 'The Wild Swans', 1846). The first two are the inspiration for two of the most popular Disney films of all time, *The Little Mermaid* (1989) and *Frozen* (2013), and the connection between Nordic Gothic and a global, commercial phenomenon such as Disney is one important reason behind the choice of Andersen's fairy tales for this chapter. What the literal Disneyfication of the two stories has meant for the Gothic content will be briefly addressed below, since the Disney adaptations have had a significant impact on the general public's view of these tales.

Lagerlöf's influence on contemporary Nordic Gothic is obvious in many ways. For example, several of the authors discussed in this book pay tribute to her oeuvre by referring to or quoting it: John Ajvide Lindqvist quotes her famous debut novel *Gösta Berlings saga* in his novel *Människohamn* (2008; *Harbour*, 2011), Johanna Sinisalo quotes 'Bortbytingen' (1908; 'The Changeling', 1923) in *Ennen päivänlaskua ei voi* (2000; *Not Before Sundown*, 2003) and Stefan Spjut refers to her in different ways in *Stallo* (2012). Her stories also appear in anthologies of contemporary Gothic, such as *De odöda. Skräckberättelser av John Ajvide Lindqvist, Johan Theorin, Åke Edwardsson* (2012; The Undead. Gothic Stories by John Ajvide Lindqvist, Johan Theorin and Åke Edwardsson). Furthermore, her Gothic stories have been and remain today continuously adapted to other media such as film, opera, theatre and the graphic novel. The second part of this chapter discusses folklore and the function of place in Lagerlöf's writing, the elements that most clearly reverberate with contemporary Nordic Gothic, and it also points at some typical *fin-de-siècle* traits. The main focus is *Gösta Berlings saga*, but the short stories 'De fågelfrie' (1892; 'The Outlaws', 1899) and 'Stenkumlet' (1892; 'The Kings Grave', 1899) are also briefly examined as examples of her use of the forest as Gothic setting and *fin-de-siècle* motifs.

Hans Christian Andersen: Translation and Disneyfication

Before we turn to the Gothic elements of the fairy tales, we will briefly discuss Andersen in the context of literary history, with special attention to the consequences of translation. Andersen's fairy tales and stories can be placed between romanticism and realism in nineteenth-century literary history. In her 2013 dissertation, Kirstine Kastbjerg argues that his aesthetics from his first publication to his last are also very much related to the Gothic: 'Many of the contradictions apparent in Andersen's work are central to the Gothic: the generic hybridity; the conflict between the supernatural, nostalgic Romanticism and a socially conscious Realism; the constant clash between feeling and reason; an ironic self-awareness accompanied by unapologetic sentimentality; and the battle between high and popular culture that was inevitable in an increasingly democratic age'.[2] In this hybridity, Andersen can be seen as an important forerunner of contemporary creators of Nordic Gothic. As Kastbjerg remarks, 'Andersen's tales always display a strange oscillation between everyday reality and fairy tale'.[3]

That Andersen moves between romanticism and realism is also signalled in the dual way that he designates his short fiction *eventyr* (fairy tales) and *historier* (stories). Kastbjerg comments on this distinction, as well as the shift towards the latter over time: 'Significantly, Andersen's tales, published between 1835 and 1872 and from the outset a wild combination of poetry, fantasy tale and everyday reality, grow increasingly realistic and lose their status as *Eventyr*, meaning both actual fairy tales (*Märchen*) and more fantastic, wondrous tales (*Abenteur*): they are instead designated "*historier*," stories, as they mirror the development towards a more pessimistic realism....'[4] Being involved in the development of American realism as an editor, in an 1871 article Horace Scudder suggests that what he then terms Andersen's 'short stories' should be viewed in the light of this up-and-coming novelistic literary trend: 'Within the narrow limits of his miniature story, Andersen moves us by the same impulse as the modern novelist who depends for his material upon what he has actually seen and heard, and for his inspiration upon the power to penetrate the heart of things; so that the old fairy tale finds its successor in this new realistic wonder-story, just as the old romance gives place to the new novel'.[5] Referring to Andersen's tales as short stories and comparing them to the new realist novels, Scudder thus attempts to give added weight to Andersen's short fiction. Moreover, according to Kastbjerg, 'Andersen, like Hoffmann, represents a Romanticism torn between the traditional fairy tales or *Kunstmärchen* of Universal Romanticism on the one hand, and on the other, a gradual undermining of the mythical, unity seeking premise of those narratives, as Romanticism also points forward to the dissolving – even nihilistic – tendency of modernism, as seen in the fantastic and absurd meta-tales such as *Fodreise* (1829; *A Journey on Foot*) and 'Skyggen' (1847; 'The Shadow', 1848)'.[6] From their two different vantage points, Scudder and Kastbjerg comment on Andersen's two kinds of tale, tracing a move towards realism and, in the latter's case, even towards modernism. The Gothic elements are, however, present in his fairy tales and stories throughout.

Nevertheless, translations can sometimes affect the Gothic content. Studying the English translations of Andersen's fairy tales and stories, Viggo Hjørnager Pedersen concludes that the nineteenth-century translations in English differ due to whether the translator regarded the tales as children's literature or as aimed at both children and adults.[7] Sanders brings up Andersen's 'two central sets of double-articulations that allowed him to address a diverse audience': 1) he aimed 'at both a local (Danish) and a global (world) readership'; and 2) in the fairy tales, he 'addresses the child and the adult simultaneously'.[8] Andersen's fairy tales are thus examples of transnational crossover fiction, although some translations and adaptations have changed them fairly radically to make them less unsettling – which means that the changes have often concerned the Gothic aspects – and thus supposedly more suitable for children. Kastbjerg draws attention to the fact that Gothic elements in Andersen's tales were lost in some English translations, in particular Victorian ones, as well as his quirky, 'witty and ironic style', which according to her has never fully been successfully captured in translation.[9] In general, as Sanders puts it, 'Popular mass culture has recast, some might say bowdlerized, Andersen's fairy tales in what we now know as Disneyfication'.[10]

Gothic elements in 'Den lille Havfrue', 'Snedronningen' and 'De vilde Svaner'

One aspect of Andersen's Gothic can be described as body horror, and 'Den lille Havfrue' is one of his tales that in its original version includes bodily mutilation of a young female protagonist: the little mermaid's tongue is cut out.[11] It also includes the frightening Gothic figure of the sea witch and her horrifying environment. The sea witch's house in 'Den lille Havfrue' is set 'in the midst of a peculiar forest. All the trees and the shrubs were polyps, half animal and half plant. They looked like hundred-headed snakes growing out of the ground. All of their branches were long slimy arms, with fingers like slithery worms, they rippled, joint by joint, from their roots to their very tips. They wrapped tightly around anything in the sea that they could grab and they never let go.'[12] The little mermaid 'saw how each of them was holding something that it had caught. Hundreds of tiny arms were wrapped around it, like strong iron bands. Humans who had perished at sea and sunk into the deep peered out, as white bones, from the arms of the polyps. Rudders and sea chests were held in their grip, the skeletons of land animals, and a little mermaid they had caught and strangled – for her the most terrifying of all'.[13] The mermaid continues and comes 'to a great slimy clearing in the forest where huge fat water snakes romped, showing off their disgusting yellowish-white bellies. In the middle of the clearing a house had been built from the white bones of shipwrecked humans. There sat the sea witch, letting a toad eat from her mouth, the way humans let little canaries eat sugar. She called the hideous fat water snakes her little chickens and let them swarm over her spongy breasts'.[14] Death and the threat of imminent death are everywhere in this passage, which also revels in the disgusting and the grotesque.

The bodily mutilation of the little mermaid is the result of a terrible bargain that she makes with the sea witch in order to be close to the human prince whom she has saved from drowning in a shipwreck, and with whom she has fallen in love. She gives up her life in the sea, which would have lasted for 300 years, as well as her family, in order to gain a pair of legs instead of her fishtail. The price that she must pay also includes constant pain and the loss of her voice. Before granting her wish and cutting out her tongue, the sea witch warns her that giving up her fishtail for a pair of legs 'will feel like a sharp sword passing through you' and 'every step you take will feel like you're treading on a sharp knife and your blood will flow'.[15] Towards the end of Andersen's story the little mermaid, without gaining the soul that the prince's kiss of true love would have bestowed on her, also has to face the horrible choice of either using a knife to kill the prince on his wedding night, after he has married the princess that he wrongly believes saved him from drowning, or being obliterated and thus losing both life and afterlife.

The 1989 Disney version retains few of the Gothic aspects of the tale and features a Hollywood ending with the prince kissing and marrying the mermaid after the sea witch's evil scheme of marrying the prince while assuming the shape of a beautiful woman has failed on their wedding day. The mermaid's soul is never in danger, although she is initially presented as a much more material girl than Andersen's original, who actually cares less about sunken human objects than her sisters do; the Disney mermaid's tongue is not cut off and her voice is restored at the end of the film. Neither does she ever suffer the incessant pain of using her legs and feet that Andersen's *lille havfrue* does. Although frightening, the Disney film's depiction of the sea witch's environment does not match Andersen's in terms of Gothic impact, despite picking up on certain elements of it and, for example, presenting modified versions of the polyps and sea snakes. However, the depiction of the sea witch and her abode is still Gothic enough in Disney's *The Little Mermaid* to warrant a place for the DVD in the section for adults in our public library.

Like 'Den lille Havfrue', Andersen's 'Snedronningen' features a young female protagonist, little Gerda, who is on a mission to save someone for whom she cares deeply: the boy Kai who lives next door. He gets troll splinters in one of his eyes and in his heart and is subsequently taken by the Snow Queen to her palace in Lapland where Gerda finally finds and rescues him after a long and difficult journey. The most Gothic part of Andersen's tale tells the story about the origin of the troll mirror and its pieces. The features and appearances of the trolls are not described, rather the character of the troll is fused with the image of the Devil: 'there was an evil troll. He was one of the very worst; he was the Devil! One day he was in a truly good mood, because he had created a mirror that had the power to make everything good and beautiful reflected in it shrink to almost nothing, while whatever was worthless and loathsome would stand out clearly and look even worse.'[16] The mirror is a great success: 'Everyone who attended troll school – because he ran a troll school – told everyone else that a miracle had occurred. For the first time, they said, it was possible to see how the world and human beings actually looked.'[17] When the trolls have managed to distort the world and the human beings they try to fly up to Heaven to make fun of God and the angels, but the mirror breaks. The pieces of the mirror 'flew around in the wide world, and whenever they landed in someone's eye, that's where they would stay. Then those people would see everything wrong, or only have eyes for what was bad in something, since every little speck of mirror kept the same powers that the whole mirror possessed. Some people even got a little piece of mirror in their hearts, and then it was quite dreadful. The heart would turn into a lump of ice.'[18] The section concludes as follows: 'The Evil One laughed until his belly split, it tickled him so splendidly. But outside, little pieces of glass were still flying around in the air.'[19]

Thus, the troll episode is described using Christian rhetoric and Andersen's troll has little to do with the folklore creature discussed in connection with contemporary Gothic in *Nordic Gothic*. But, as Ármann Jakobsson has observed, since the middle ages the word 'troll' has been used in very diverse contexts,[20] and what really defines a troll is its actions. It is two of the splinters of the troll mirror that set the tale about Gerda and Kai in motion. Disney's *Frozen*, which is allegedly inspired by 'Snedronningen', is a very loose adaptation which has little in common with the original tale in general and which has excluded all Gothic elements that are present in that fairy tale. Trolls appear in the film, but they are benevolent, helpful and thoroughly domesticated.

'De vilde Svaner', so far untouched by Disney, like the other two tales features a young female protagonist. It opens with a king and his twelve children, eleven princes and a princess, who live a good life until the king marries an evil queen. She manages to turn the king against his children, sending away Elisa, the princess, to grow up on a farm and throwing out the princes to fend for themselves in the shape of eleven swans. After Elisa has become a beautiful young woman and returns to the palace, the queen literally besmears her so that her father cannot recognise her and throws her out. Lonely and sad, she wanders and sleeps in the forest, longing for and dreaming about her brothers. An old woman tells her about eleven swans with gold crowns and she finds her brothers who regain their human form during the night while being swans during the day. The brothers carry her across the ocean to the country where they live, after which Fata Morgana tells Elisa in a dream how she can break her brothers' spell: she is to knit eleven long-sleeved shirts with yarn made of nettles that either grow around the cave that she sleeps in or on graves in the churchyard. From the beginning to the end of the work on the shirts, she must keep silent. 'With her delicate hands [Elisa] reached down into the hideous nettles. They were like fire; they burned big blisters into her skin and arms, but this she would gladly endure if she could free her dear brothers. She crushed each nettle with her bare feet and spun the green flax.'[21] Much like the little mermaid, here is a young female protagonist who must endure excruciating pain without being able to explain herself to anyone.

This situation becomes a problem when the king of the land finds her, falls in love with her and brings her to his palace as his bride, 'even though the archbishop shook his head and whispered that the beautiful forest girl was surely a witch.'[22] The king is considerate enough to bring the flax and the finished shirt from the cave, so she can continue her work, but when she runs out of flax starting the seventh shirt she has to pick nettles from the churchyard:

> With fear in her heart, as if she was about to commit an evil deed, she crept out into the moonlight night... She walked down the long lanes out to the deserted streets and over to the churchyard. There she saw, sitting on one of the widest headstones, a group of Lamias, hideous witches. They were taking off their rags, as if they were going to bathe, and then they buried their long, gaunt fingers in the fresh graves, pulled out the bodies, and ate their flesh. Elisa had to pass close by, and they fixed their evil eyes on her, but she recited a prayer, gathered up the burning nettles and carried them home to the palace.[23]

This scene is obviously Gothic with the detailed description of how the naked hideous witches in the churchyard dig up and eat corpses. The archbishop, who has seen Elisa walk to the churchyard and the Lamias, convinces the king to follow her the next time to prove that she is a witch. Elisa continues knitting in the dungeon and on the cart on the way to the pyre where she will be burnt as a witch. When the executioner grabs her she throws the shirts over the swans that have protected her from the mob surrounding the cart: 'There stood eleven handsome princes, but the youngest had a swan's wing in place of one arm, because his shirt of mail was missing a sleeve; she hadn't managed to finish it'.[24] Both Elisa and her brothers are now able to speak and assert her innocence and the tale ends as it started, on a happy note. The bulk of the fairy tale, however, is filled with tension and pain, loss and fear in Gothic fashion and the nettles, the corpse-eating Lamias, the impending burning of Elisa before she has the chance to finish the shirts and the brother with a wing instead of an arm stay with the reader long after the tale is over.

Selma Lagerlöf: Provincial *fin-de-siècle* Gothic

Selma Lagerlöf is one of Sweden's major canonical writers and she was also an important pioneer as a woman: in 1909 she became the first female writer to receive the Nobel prize in literature and in 1914 she was the first woman to become a member of the Swedish Academy. She is also one of the most important Nordic authors of *fin-de-siècle* and early twentieth-century Gothic. Her novels and short stories often explore complex psychological processes by drawing on the features of folktales and other non-realistic genres, and above all she mastered the use of advanced narrative strategies to blur the border between fantasy and fictional reality. To the general public though, she is best known for her only children's book, the enormously popular *Nils Holgerssons underbara resa genom Sverige* (1907; *The Wonderful Adventures of Nils*, 1910), written on commission as a reader for elementary school.

In the late nineteenth century, the Gothic genre had a renaissance of sorts related to the *fin-de-siècle* atmosphere of pessimism and decadence. In Sweden, this Gothic resurgence is more specifically connected to an important moment in Swedish literary history known as the 'shift between the 1880s and the 1890s' – the common denominator is the debut of Selma Lagerlöf. During the 1870s and 1880s, a period known as 'the modern breakthrough', critical realism predominated Scandinavian literature and addressing the problems of modern society was perceived as the author's main task. In a Swedish context, the idea of literature as a vehicle for social criticism became very much associated with a group of young authors and intellectuals known as 'the generation of the 1880s'. With her famous debut novel *Gösta Berlings saga*, published in 1891, Lagerlöf radically challenged this norm. *Gösta Berlings saga* is a rich and multifaceted novel divided into 24 episodic and more or less independent chapters. It is permeated with fantasy and contains a considerable number of Gothic elements such as Faustian pacts with the Devil, doubles, demonic characters and supernatural events – the timing was perfect. At the end of the 1880s the literature of discontent had played out its role and the time was ripe for something new. A few years before Lagerlöf's debut, two authors of a new generation, Verner von Heidenstam and Oscar Levertin, had published a manifesto demanding different aesthetics for the future. Instead of what they condescendingly called 'the dull weather literature' of the generation of the 1880s, the manifesto called for fantasy, romanticism, emotions and poetic expression. *Gösta Berlings saga* became the first work to live up to these demands and has therefore been seen as initiating what literary history has constructed as 'the 90s'.

In the decade after her debut, Lagerlöf produced a number of short stories that can be considered prime examples of Nordic *fin-de-siècle* Gothic, just like the novellas *En herrgårdssägen* (1899; *From a Swedish Homestead*, 1901), a story of madness and redeeming love, and the medieval thriller *Herr Arnes penningar* (1904; *Herr Arne's Hoard*, 1922). The setting is, for the most part, Swedish or Nordic, and Lagerlöf makes use of environments that were familiar to her. For example, *En herrgårdssägen* is set in the province of Dalarna where Lagerlöf lived for many years, while *Herr Arnes penningar* is set on the Swedish west coast where her brother lived. The double is a recurrent motif in *Gösta Berlings saga*, and it continues to be a salient element in her turn-of-the-century fiction: both *En herrgårdssägen* and *Herr Arnes penningar* portray antiheroes with a split character. In the former, a young beautiful student becomes his own bestial double after a mental breakdown, while in the latter, a mercenary solider appears as a werewolf-like assassin, but also a handsome gentleman, seducing the protagonist who witnessed him brutally killing her entire family. It would, however, be unfair to delimit Lagerlöf's Gothic to the turn of the century. Rather, the Gothic genre continued to be a strong influence throughout her literary career – for instance, in *Körkarlen* (1912; *Thy Soul Shall Bear Witness*, 1921), famously adapted for the screen by Victor Sjöström in 1921, in 'Frid på Jorden'

(1917; 'Peace on Earth'), and in the Löwensköld trilogy (*The Löwensköld Ring*, 1925; *Charlotte Löwensköld*, 1925; *Anna Svärd*, 1928).[25]

Gösta Berlings saga

The setting of *Gösta Berlings saga* is the author's own native province Värmland in the 1820s, described as the home of countless eccentric characters and a place where melodrama and fantastic events are part of everyday life. The importance of place is highlighted on the first page of the novel by a map of the northern part of Värmland where the topography is true to life but all names except that of Värmland itself are changed, thus keeping the connection to the actual province but simultaneously endowing it with mythological status. At the centre of the plot is the handsome and irresistible Gösta Berling and the Majoress of Ekeby, Värmland's most powerful woman. Gösta, who is a dismissed minister with a drinking problem, joins a group of cavaliers who live at Ekeby mansion supported by the Majoress. After making a deal with the Devil, they usurp her power and she must roam the roads as a beggar. During this carnivalesque year, the whole province is turned upside down; families are torn apart, madness and passionate feelings reign, nature turns against the humans and supernatural forces are conjured. In certain episodes, figures from Swedish and regional folklore act as characters, and two of these will be examined briefly in the following as examples of the Gothic aspects of the novel.

The episode 'Kevenhüller' describes in a flashback how *skogsfrun* (the lady of the forest) sometimes wanders the streets of Karlstad, the county seat of Värmland, and when meeting her in the main square, the young cavalier Kevenhüller falls under her spell. Many years later, during the chaotic reign of the cavaliers, she turns up at Ekeby as a haunting from the past, and in a desperate attempt to destroy her and free himself from the spell, Kevenhüller sets the whole mansion on fire.

There are many different regional versions of the lady of the forest, but like most folklore creatures she is always ambiguous. She drives men crazy with desire and can lead them astray or bewitch them, but she can also give extraordinary powers to those who help her. The power Kevenhüller is rewarded with for doing her a favour is both a blessing and a curse. His dream is to become an inventor, and the lady of the forest fulfils his dream by giving him extraordinary inventive skills. The drawback is that he will only be able to create one copy of each invention, which is why he wants to be released from the spell: his wish was always to help all humankind. In mid and northern Sweden, the lady of the forest appears as a beautiful, seductive woman with an animal's tail – for example, that of a cow or a horse – and in other parts of the country she is described as having a hollow back, and sometimes as having one human foot and one animal paw or hoof, but she is always a combination of sensual beauty and monstrosity. In Lagerlöf's meticulous version, the folkloristic is mixed with *fin-de-siècle* aesthetics to enhance this ambiguity. Here, the lady of the forest has an air of *femme fatale*, the forcefully sexual and dangerous, possibly lethal, female character so frequent in the literature and art of the late nineteenth century, especially in the Gothic fiction of the period.[26] Her bright green eyes sparkle and she has a red, sweeping fox tail and small, sharp fangs glimmer behind her red lips. She moves smoothly like a wild animal, and is dressed in green silk, wearing a small black viper around her neck.

If Lagerlöf's lady of the forest is both threatening and monstrous, she is nothing compared to the witch of Dovre. In one of the most horrific episodes of *Gösta Berlings saga*, this powerful and fearsome witch descends from her residence in the mountains. She is ancient and incredibly rich, but greedy and comes dressed as a beggar; to deny her what she demands is highly dangerous. Whenever the witch of Dovre appears among humans she has an evil purpose, and this time she comes for Märta Dohna, the decadent countess of Borg. But the worldly, self-indulgent countess is unaware of the witch's malicious abilities and laughingly refuses to give her a juicy brown ham that the maids just brought from the sauna. 'Away with you, beggar hag! ... I would rather give it to the magpies than to someone like you', is her fatal response when the witch asks her for it, and the witch becomes furious.[27] 'She extends her rune-inscribed staff toward the heights and swings it wildly. Her lips utter peculiar words. Her hair stands straight up, her eyes shine, her face is distorted. "It is you that the magpies will eat!" she shrieks at last'.[28] The realisation of the curse becomes a living nightmare for the countess. The scene demonstrates Lagerlöf's masterly use of expressionistic detail to create horrific effect, and the combination of the supernatural and mental breakdown is definitely Gothic:

> From park and orchard they swoop down toward her, dozens of magpies with claws extended and beaks stretched out to peck. They come with howling and laughter. Black and white wings shimmer before her eyes. As in delirium she sees behind this swarm all the magpies of the district approaching, the whole sky full of black and white wings. In the sharp sunlight of forenoon the metallic colors of their wings glisten. Their throats are ruffled up as on angry birds of prey. In

tighter and tighter circles the animals fly around the countess, aiming with beaks and claws at her face and hands. Then she has to flee into the vestibule and close the door. She leans against it, panting with anxiety, while the laughing magpies circle outside.

With that she is also closed off from the sweetness and greenery of summer and from the joy of life. After this, for her there were only closed rooms and drawn curtains; for her, despair; for her, confusion bordering on madness.[29]

As it is also described how the birds soon multiply and how they sit on guard on the rooftop and railing, attacking in a swarm as soon as the countess shows her face in the window, the story is reminiscent of another master of Gothic horror, Alfred Hitchcock, and his film *The Birds* (1963).

The witch of Dovre is depicted as a 'daughter of Finns skilled in magic'; she believes both in 'Thor, the killer of giants, and in powerful Finnish gods [and to her] the Christians are like tame farm dogs before a gray wolf'.[30] During the sixteenth century, Finnish immigrants settled in the Northern forest areas of Värmland. They were called *skogsfinnar*, Forest-Finns, or *svedjefinnar*, due to their practice of *svedjebruk* (slash-and-burn agriculture), and they had a strong cultural identity. For example, through the centuries, they kept not only their language but also their beliefs in old heathen religion and practised shamanism. Hence, they became surrounded by mythical conceptions and were considered to possess the powers of witchcraft. As a minority with foreign habits they could easily be demonised as the Other, as the story clearly demonstrates. The witch of Dovre is thus deeply rooted in the province of Värmland, and the narrator even indicates a factual origin: 'I, who am writing this, have seen her myself'.[31] This comment is obviously first and foremost a narrative strategy but, in an autobiographical story published in 1933, 'Värmländsk naturskönhet' ('The Natural Beauty of Värmland') Lagerlöf describes having an uncanny vision of the witch of Dovre materialising in front of her on a journey to Östmark, a desolate area in the northwestern part of Värmland with a large Finnish community. She associates her with an old beggar woman from the area that she used to be terrified of as a child, since the rumour was that she could bewitch people and make them mad.[32]

The deep forest

A recurrent feature in Lagerlöf's fiction is the use of the forest as a residence of the uncanny, a place of horrific transformations and doublings. Lagerlöf's depictions of the forest have much in common with those of Swedish author Kerstin Ekman, examined later in this book. Ekman often reflects on the forest in her fiction, and she has also dedicated an extensive collection of essays to humankind's relationship to the forest, *Herrarna i skogen* (2007, *The Masters in the Forest*). Her focus is on the Nordic region and she uses Swedish literature as well as scientific sources in her discussion. *Herrarna skogen* can almost be regarded as ecogothic, since it deals so intensely with fear and the uncanny; the forest represents the dangerous and impenetrable, something that humans have always tried to navigate and conquer, and images of the horrors that dwell in the forest are deeply rooted in humanity. In a chapter on Lagerlöf, she points out that in late nineteenth-century Sweden, the forests were still to a large extent vast and desolate: the forest that Lagerlöf refers to is truly deep. Ekman also notes that it is not described with botanical precision; instead it is 'entirely a room for interior transformations'.[33]

Gösta Berlings saga contains one of Swedish literature's most forceful illustrations of the primeval fear of the forest. The episode 'Den stora björnen i Gurlita klätt' ('The Great Bear in Gurlita Bluff') is a veritable catalogue of all the horrors that can be found in the forest, natural as well as supernatural. The natural is, however, not easily separated from the supernatural. Uncanny transformations occur all the time and nothing is reliable:

> The forest is full of unholy animals, possessed by the souls of evil trolls and blood-thirsty scoundrels. Don't trust the brook with the smooth water! Wading in it after sundown is brings sudden illness and death. Trust not the cuckoo who called so merrily in spring! Toward autumn he becomes a hawk with forbidding eyes and gruesome claws! Trust not the moss, not the heather, not the rock; nature is evil, possessed by invisible forces who hate humankind. There is no place where you can safely set your foot. It is strange that your weak race can avoid so much persecution. [34]

The great bear is described as the most horrific of all the animals and, according to the myth, once he has killed a human he can only be killed by a silver bullet. One winter's day, the cavaliers set out to hunt him, but as the story unfolds the image is inverted. When Gösta Berling pulls the rifle trigger and aims at the monstrous bear, he starts to perceive things differently and the message that Lagerlöf conveys is not very subtle: humankind is the true source of horror. Gösta sees how the bear has become, 'blind in one eye from a cut by a cavalier's knife, limping on one leg from a bullet from a cavalier's rifle... alone ever since they killed his wife and carried off his children... a poor, hunted animal, whose life he will not take from him, the last thing he has left, since humans have taken everything else from him'.[35] As is often the case, Lagerlöf's portrayal is ambiguous. Soon the cavaliers understand that the reason why Gösta has not been capable of shooting is because this is 'no ordinary bear' and Gösta has no silver bullet in his rifle.[36]

Supernatural or not, the story of the hunted bear is part of the all-pervading ecological theme of the novel related to the connectedness of everything in the cycle of life. In several episodes Lagerlöf repeats the apocalyptic vision of how human behaviour affects the environment: 'When discord and hatred fill the earth, then dead things too must suffer greatly. Then the wave becomes wild and rapacious as a robber, then the field becomes barren as a miser. But woe to anyone for whose sake the forest sighs and the hills weep!'[37] In this matter, she is clearly an important precursor to contemporary ecogothic.

As Ekman points out, 'the deep forest was the word [Lagerlöf] used for the unplumbed, for the human soul as much as for terrain.'[38] 'De fågelfrie' and 'Stenkumlet', both written the year after the debut with *Gösta Berlings saga*, are good examples of Lagerlöf's use of the forest as the place where the dark and repressed domains of human nature reside, and they are among the most horrific stories of her oeuvre. In both, the Gothic is combined with decadent imagery and motifs in the depiction of characters victimised by their own dark and destructive desires. A medieval Nordic setting, nightmare visions and the use of mythological or folklore allusions enhance the Gothic atmosphere. The original Gothic of the eighteenth and early nineteenth century was often set in the Middle Ages and, thus, 'De fågelfrie' and 'Stenkumlet' hark back to the foundation of the genre and can be regarded as a mixture of original Gothic and *fin-de-siècle* Gothic. But while the setting in the early fiction of iconic authors such as Horace Walpole and Anne Radcliffe was distant not only in time but also in place, Lagerlöf uses a Nordic setting for her medieval stories.

In 'Stenkumlet' the medieval setting is combined with the typically decadent motif of the androgynous couple, represented by two descendants of runaway slaves living together in the forest, the masculine and dominant woman Jofrid and the weak, anaemic and feeble-minded man Tönne. Since they cannot have children of their own, the couple adopts a foster child, but they neglect it and it starves to death. The story enters the realm of Gothic horror as the child returns to haunt its foster parents at night, whining and sobbing, stumbling on small insecure feet outside their little cottage in the forest. Jofrid is portrayed as egotistic and insensitive, and the motif of the double is used to accentuate this aspect of her character. The tomb that has given the story its name is that of an ancient, cruel king, the mythological Atle, and it is located next to the couple's cottage. His ghost appears to Jofrid the first time she visits the cottage as an omen, becoming her dark double as his body of stone mirrors her stone-cold heart. At the end of the story, Jofrid engages in a violent dance of death, and she dies as she stumbles and fall, crushed against the hard rocks of the tomb.

'De fågelfrie' is a complex story of crime, isolation and paranoia set on the Swedish west coast in the period when Christianity was introduced but not yet established. The two protagonists Berg Rese and Tord are outlaws living together in the forest, and Lagerlöf depicts their characters as switching roles and gradually merging together as doubles – the story characteristically ending with the murder of one by the hand of the other.[39] The forest has an important function as a place of isolation and horror. Tord, who is a heathen, is a convicted outlaw for a minor theft that he did not commit, but the Christian Berg Rese has slayed a monk with an axe and this horrible and bloody deed is the driving force of the Gothic plot. The outlaws are persecuted by the village people, but they are also haunted by their own paranoia and the internal conflicts that the killing of the monk has caused. Berg Rese preaches the harsh doctrine of the old testament to Tord, making him realise the severity of Berg Rese's crime. Gradually, the forest becomes an uncanny and ghostly location where dream, hallucination and reality merge together. The apparition of the dead monk, drenched in blood and with a gaping wound in his head from Berg Rese's axe, finally provokes the tragic ending of betrayal and death. The hauntings convince Tord of the necessity to turn his friend in and when Berg Rese understands what has happened he acts out his violent tendencies once again, sinking his axe in Tord's head for betraying him.

The conflict between Christianity and the old Norse religion, the meandering intrigue that it produces, and all the events attached to it are too complicated to account for in this brief analysis. However, the main function of this conflict is as a vehicle for the psychological exploration of a split psyche. The clash between the old and the new belief system causes anxiety and instability and is suitable for the exploration of psychological processes, especially those related to the dichotomy of the civilised and the barbaric so much in focus in the late nineteenth century. The heathen belief is overcome, but only on the surface, and it is related to a fear of the primitive and repressed. In 'De fågelfrie' the double can be understood in relation to the Gothic plot described by William Patrick Day as a failed quest for identity, leading to fragmentation and the metamorphosis of the self into its own double. After an initial state of enthrallment, the outlaws symbolically descend and become entrapped in the Gothic underworld of the forest; they become lost in the circles of their own fears and desires and can never find their way back.[40]

The decadent elements of the story consist, for example, of a lethal *femme fatale* character in medieval disguise, dream sequences combining death and sexuality, and depictions of the forest that mirror the mental decay of the outlaws in imagery that signals artifice and enclosure.[41] For example, a dark tarn in the forest that is central to the plot is described as both artificial and grotesque:

> It was square, with as straight shores and as sharp corners as if it had been cut by the hand of man. On three sides it was surrounded by steep cliffs, on which pines clung with roots as thick as a man's arm. Down by the pool, where the earth had been gradually washed away, their roots stood up out of the water, bare and crooked and wonderfully twisted about one another. It was like an infinite number of serpents which had wanted all at the same time to crawl up out of the pool but had got entangled in one another and been held fast. Or it was like a mass of blackened skeletons of drowned giants which the pool wanted to throw up on the land. Arms and legs writhed about one another, the long fingers dug deep into the very cliff to get a hold, the mighty ribs formed arches, which held up primeval trees.[42]

Dwelling by the tarn, the outlaws have visions and experiences that are both nightmarish and erotic, and the *femme fatale* character appears in the water both as a mermaid and as a sensuous but corpse-like character.

The works of Andersen and Lagerlöf are globally known and continuously translated, retold and adapted into different media. It is, however, only recently that their narratives have been discussed in Gothic terms, although, as indicated above, many of Andersen's most famous stories and fairy tales and Lagerlöf's novels and short stories contain Gothic elements. The ambition of this chapter has therefore been to highlight these two Nordic icons in the context of Nordic Gothic, and as will be demonstrated in the following chapters, witches, trolls and other mythical creatures return in contemporary Nordic fiction.

Notes

1 *H. C. Andersen Centret*. http://andersen.museum.odense.dk/eventyr/start.asp?sprog=dansk. Accessed 18 October 2018; K. Sanders, 'A Man of the World: Hans Christian Andersen', in D. Ringgard and M. Rosendahl Thomsen (eds), *Danish Literature as World Literature* (New York: Bloomsbury, 2017), pp. 91–2.
2 K. M. Kastbjerg, 'Reading the Surface: The Danish Gothic of B. S. Ingemann, H. C. Andersen, Karen Blixen and Beyond' (PhD dissertation, University of Washington, 2013), p. 184.
3 Kastbjerg, 'Reading the Surface', p. 187.
4 Kastbjerg, 'Reading the Surface', p. 183.
5 H. E. Scudder, 'Andersen's Short Stories', *Atlantic Monthly* 36:217 (November 1875), p. 602.
6 Kastbjerg, 'Reading the Surface', p. 182.
7 V. Hjørnager Pedersen, *Ugly Ducklings?: Studies in the English Translations of Hans Christian Andersen's Tales and Stories* (Odense: University Press of Southern Denmark, 2004), pp. 353–4.
8 Sanders, 'A Man of the World', p. 92.
9 Kastbjerg, 'Reading the Surface', pp. 15–17.
10 Sanders, 'A Man of the World', p. 110. Disney adapted Andersen's 'Den grimme Ælling' (1843; 'The Ugly Duck', 1847) into the short animated film *The Ugly Duckling* in 1939. Prior to Disney's *The Little Mermaid* and *Frozen*, the Hollywood musical film *Hans Christian Andersen* (1952), with Danny Kaye as Andersen, popularised the Danish author and his fairy tales, including 'The Ugly Duckling' and 'The Little Mermaid', for a post-Second-World-War international audience.
11 Kastbjerg brings up bodily mutilation of female characters in Andersen's tales including 'Den lille Havfrue', in 'Reading the Surface', pp. 198–204.
12 H. C. Andersen, 'The Little Mermaid', in H. C. Andersen *Fairy Tales*, trans. T. Nunnally, ed. and intro. J. Wullschlager (London: Penguin, 2004), p. 78
13 Andersen, 'The Little Mermaid', p. 78.
14 Andersen, 'The Little Mermaid', p. 78.
15 Andersen, 'The Little Mermaid', p. 79.
16 H. C. Andersen, 'The Snow Queen', in H. C. Andersen *Fairy Tales*, trans. T. Nunnally, ed. and intro. J. Wullschlager (London: Penguin, 2004), p. 175.
17 Andersen, 'The Snow Queen', p. 175.
18 Andersen, 'The Snow Queen', p. 176.
19 Andersen, 'The Snow Queen', p. 176.
20 A. Jakobsson, 'Horror in the Medieval North: The Troll', in K. Korstophine and L. R. Kremmel (eds), *The Palgrave Handbook to Horror Literature* (Cham: Palgrave Macmillan, 2018).
21 H. C. Andersen, 'The Wild Swans', in H. C. Andersen *Fairy Tales*, trans. T. Nunnally, ed. and intro. J. Wullschlager (London: Penguin, 2004), p. 116.
22 Andersen, 'The Wild Swans', p. 118.
23 Andersen, 'The Wild Swans', p. 118.
24 Andersen, 'The Wild Swans', pp. 120–1.

25 For a study of Selma Lagerlöf's *fin-de-siècle* Gothic, see S. Wijkmark, *Hemsökelser. Gotiken i sex berättelser av Selma Lagerlöf* (Karlstad: Karlstad University Studies, 2009). The analysis of 'De fågelfrie' and 'Stenkumlet' are brief summaries of the results of this dissertation. See also Y. Leffler, *I skräckens lustgård: Skräckromantik i svenska 1800-talsromaner* (Göteborg: Göteborgs universitet, 1991), who discusses *Herr Arnes Penningar* in the context of Swedish nineteenth century Gothic.

26 See for example B. Dijkstra, *Idols of Perversity: Fantasies of Feminie Evil in Fin-de-Siècle Culture* (New York: Oxford University Press, 1986).

27 S. Lagerlöf, *The Saga of Gösta Berling*, trans. P. Norlen (New York: Penguin, 2009), p. 246.

28 Lagerlöf, *The Saga of Gösta Berling*, pp. 246–7.

29 Lagerlöf, *The Saga of Gösta Berling*, p. 247.

30 Lagerlöf, *The Saga of Gösta Berling*, pp. 244–5.

31 Lagerlöf, *The Saga of Gösta Berling*, p. 244.

32 Lagerlöf, 'Värmländsk naturskönhet', in *Höst* (Stockholm: Bonniers, 1933), pp. 101–16.

33 '... helt och hållet ett själens omvandlingsrum'. K. Ekman, *Herrarna i skogen* (Stockholm: Bonniers, 2007), p. 322. All translations of quotations from the essay are ours.

34 Lagerlöf, *The Saga of Gösta Berling*, p. 99.

35 Lagerlöf, *The Saga of Gösta Berling*, p. 102.

36 Lagerlöf, *The Saga of Gösta Berling*, p. 103.

37 Lagerlöf, *The Saga of Gösta Berling*, p. 313.

38 '... skogsdjupet... var det ord [Lagerlöf] använde för det opejlade, för människosjäl lika mycket som för terräng'. Ekman, *Herrarna i skogen*, p. 319.

39 On the double and *fin-de-siècle*, see L. Dryden, *The Modern Gothic and Literary Doubles: Stevenson, Wilde and Wells* (Basingstoke: Palgrave Macmillan, 2003); K. Hurley, *The Gothic Body: Sexuality, Materialism and Degeneration at the Fin-de-Siècle* (Cambridge: Cambridge University Press, 1996); A. Schmid, *The Fear of the Other: Approaches to English Stories of the Double (1764–1910)* (Bern: Peter Lang, 1996).

40 W. P. Day, *In the Circles of Fear and Desire: A Study of Gothic Fantasy* (Chicago: University of Chicago Press, 1985).

41 On the mermaid as *femme fatale*, see Dijkstra, *Idols of Perversity*, p. 258.

42 S. Lagerlöf, 'The Outlaws', in *Invisible Links*, trans. P. Bancroft (Boston, 1909), pp. 166–7. Project Gutenberg [EBook #14273].

3

Sofia Wijkmark

Swedish Gothic and the demise of the welfare state

John Ajvide Lindqvist's breakthrough had an enormous impact on Swedish Gothic fiction and on the Swedish reception of Gothic and horror in general. A few years after his debut with the novel *Låt den rätte komma in* (2004; *Let the Right One In*, 2007), it became obvious that the attitude towards Gothic fiction had changed, and that it was about to be accepted not only by the readers but also by the critics. The paraphrasing title of Nicholas Wennö's article from 2009 in the culture section of one of Sweden's leading newspapers, *Dagens Nyheter*, is illustrative: 'Låt fulskräcken komma in' ('Let the Ugly Horror in').[1] Not only did Lindqvist's success change the way that critics and media spoke about the genre, arguably it also paved the way for other writers of Gothic fiction. Lindqvist's approach to the Gothic is distinguished by its combination of supernatural horror and social realism, and Swedish authors such as Madeleine Bäck, Anders Fager, Amanda Hellberg and Mats Strandberg have followed in Lindqvist's footsteps in combining horror and social realism, and sometimes also depicting a welfare state in decline.

In Lindqvist's zombie novel *Hanteringen av odöda* (2005; *Handling the Undead*, 2009), the undead people are locked away by the Swedish government in a residential area called The Heath in a desperate attempt to handle a horrific situation in a rational and bureaucratic manner. A communal space at The Heath is described as follows: 'The courtyard was dominated by the large structure in the centre… it had been planned as a combined laundry, social space and refuse centre. However, there was no water to wash with, no garbage collection, and no desire for social gatherings.'² The quote demonstrates perfectly what this chapter is about. It will focus on contemporary Swedish Gothic as an exploration of the effects of the dismantling of the Swedish welfare system and will examine how the welfare state is portrayed as a site of horror in Lindqvist's novels *Hanteringen av odöda* and *Rörelsen. Den andra platsen* (2015; *The Movement. The Other Place*), and in Mats Strandberg's novel *Hemmet* (2017; *The Home*). First, however, it is necessary to reflect briefly on the concept of the Swedish '*folkhem*', fundamental to the discourse on the Swedish socialist welfare state.³

The *folkhem*, meaning 'people's home', is (or rather was) a famous metaphor in the rhetoric of the Swedish Social Democratic Party, used to describe a state where all people are treated as equals and included in the welfare system. Historically, the idea of a Swedish *folkhem* has come to be intimately associated with the legendary Social Democrat leader Per Albin Hansson (1885–1946), who in 1928 held a speech where he declared his vision that 'the Swedish class society must one day be replaced by the Swedish *folkhem*'.⁴ The vision of the *folkhem* was implemented in the 1930s with a comprehensive political programme of social reforms, which resulted in benefits for the people such as a statutory retirement pension (1935), an annual two-week vacation (1938) and, later on, general health insurance (1955). In short, the economic policy that was the foundation for the idea of the *folkhem* was inspired by Keynesian economics and aimed to reduce unemployment rates and realise a planned economy in order to secure a good standard of living for every citizen, corresponding to the communal income of the labour force. The expansion of the public sector also resulted in a new labour market that would eventually be dominated by women.

Due to the country's minimal involvement in the Second World War, the Swedish economy was relatively intact after the war and the standard of living was therefore able to improve rapidly in the post-war decade. The stereotypical image of the *folkhem* is for many people probably that of a neat and smiling mid-twentieth century (lower middle class/upper working class, heterosexual) family standing in the modern, well-equipped kitchen or the tidy living room of their functional home. However, as Nils Edling has pointed out, the Swedish *folkhem* was not a 'key political concept' during the early reform period. Instead, it was firmly established in Swedish politics during the 1980s as a nostalgic concept describing something that no longer existed: 'the lost *folkhem*'.⁵ Significantly, the notion thus reappeared when the era was already considered over, during a time of financial crisis and political change. In 1976, the Social

Democrats lost the elections and the Swedish government was constituted exclusively by right-wing parties for the first time since 1936.

This is of course by necessity a brief and simplified sketch of the *folkhem* concept and its history. It needs to be emphasised that the *folkhem* has not been for everyone and it is therefore a legitimate question as to whether it has ever really existed. Ethnic minorities such as Romani and Sámi have often been excluded, as well as other marginalised groups. In the following analysis the *folkhem* concept should thus be understood as a nostalgic idea of an era, usually regarded as beginning in the 1930s and ending during the 1970s when the long reign of the Social Democrats was over. The 1980s was a period of increasing neo-liberalism and financial speculation. In 1985, the Bank of Sweden lifted credit regulations, and deregulation led to increased consumption, inflation and ultimately to a financial crisis between 1990 and 1994. In the subsequent decades, the Swedish welfare system underwent significant changes. The Swedish people still enjoy free healthcare and education, but nevertheless, profit-driven companies have made fortunes in the healthcare and education sectors, sometimes with disastrous outcomes for their patients, students or employees, and societal inequalities have increased and become more tangible. This development is explored in different ways by Lindqvist and Strandberg.

Is there room for a zombie in the *folkhem*?

In Lindqvist's fiction, humankind is frequently depicted as a destructive force, while his monsters can develop into ambiguous heroes, or at least into characters that it is possible to sympathise with. Familiar and supposedly safe places that become unfamiliar and frightening also have an important function in his work. As discussed in Chapter 8, in his debut novel *Låt den rätte komma in* the Stockholm suburb of Blackeberg is described as unnatural and uncanny. It has all the facilities: playgrounds, recreational areas and meticulously planned and highly functional apartments. It is in many ways a representation of the *folkhem* project. Yet Blackeberg is also described as lacking history, and without any historical and emotional connection to the place, its inhabitants easily become alienated. They are also lulled into a false sense of security in their well-organised homes in the rationally designed apartment buildings and are therefore ill-prepared for a confrontation with the supernatural and horrific. In addition, as an ironic play with the conventions of vampire fiction, Blackeberg is described as fully secularised: 'You were beyond the grasp of the mysteries of the past; there wasn't even a church. Nine thousand inhabitants and no church.'[6] In part, *Låt den rätte komma in* portrays the less fortunate. A parallel plot to the main narrative of the vampire Eli and the boy Oskar depicts a group of drinking buddies, living more or less on the margins of society: the cat hoarder Göran, 'Karlsson, the only one among them with a "real" job as he himself put it. Larry had taken an early retirement, Morgan worked off and on at an auto scrapyard, and Lacke you didn't know exactly what he did for a living.'[7] The novel is set in 1981 and, as mentioned above, the late 1970s and early 1980s is a period of incipient neo-liberalism in Sweden usually referred to as the last days of the *folkhem*.

Lindqvist's next novel, the zombie narrative *Hanteringen av odöda*, is set in 2002 and is more obviously focused on the welfare state and its shortcomings, as Katarina Gregersdotter has pointed out.[8] As I have demonstrated elsewhere, the social criticism also has an environmental dimension.[9] The Swedish discourse on welfare issues was firmly focused on environmental politics at the turn of the millennium, and this development is significant in understanding the political dimensions of the novel. In the 1990s, Göran Persson, the Social Democrat prime minister from 1996 to 2006, put a new version of the *folkhem* on the agenda called 'the green *folkhem*', focusing on environmental issues which needed to be solved for the future. Persson's environmental politics definitely made a difference, but keeping the vision of the green *folkhem* alive in the long run would prove difficult. Earlier, the *folkhem* equated a higher standard of living; a green *folkhem* would mean quite the opposite. At the time of the publication of *Hanteringen av odöda*, the difficulties had become obvious and, since 2005 was a pre-election year, the vision of the green *folkhem* was continually discussed in the media. At the turn of the millennium, questions of ecology and sustainability had thus been integrated into the ideology of the *folkhem*, but unsurprisingly it had proven challenging for the Swedish people to make the necessary adjustments. The difficulties of realising a vision of a greener living and, related to that on a global scale, the uncanny and 'inconvenient truth' that the environmental catastrophe is here and now, form the backdrop to the novel.[10]

Consumerism and climate change are recurrent topics in *Hanteringen av odöda*. For example, even on the first few pages it is implied that climate change is the reason why the dead are waking up. It is mid-August and Sweden is suffering a heatwave of extreme proportions, and complaints about the weather echo from one character to another: 'This damned weather. It's not natural!'[11] Significantly, one of the protagonists, stand-up comedian David, considers including a joke on the greenhouse effect in his next performance. The thunderstorm that seems to be gathering never erupts, but instead, a high-voltage outburst, described as a reversed power failure, causes all electrical devices to run amok and shortly thereafter the dead start to come alive. Even though his name is never mentioned, the novel is set in 2002 and one can therefore assume that the prime minister appearing to reassure the people that the government has the situation under control is Göran Persson, who dreams of a green *folkhem*. The first chapter also contains a detailed ekphrasis of Duane Hanson's iconic sculpture 'Supermarket Lady' (1969). With her crammed shopping cart, she is easily interpreted as consumerism personified, but to David, who has a picture of the sculpture above the desk in his office as a type of morbid inspiration, she also represents 'Death'.[12]

Lindqvist's zombies are not stereotypical, flesh-eating horror monsters. They are for the most part quite harmless and, as in real life, the majority of the deceased died in old age. The zombies' spark of life is very faint and their consciousness barely there, and the horror of having to face one of the living dead is soon overshadowed by a sense of pity and grief. However, the zombies can become dangerous, especially when forced together in a small area. Nevertheless, the eruptions of violence do not stem from the zombies themselves, but are generated telepathically by the negative and malign thoughts of the living people surrounding them. When the dead come back to life, the concept of solidarity, the ethical foundation of the Swedish Social Democratic Party, faces its ultimate test. The question of solidarity is emphasised by a motto, quoted from a study of the concept by Sven-Eric Liedman, a renowned professor of the history of ideas: 'Solidarity is always directed at "one of us" and "us" cannot refer to everyone… For "we" assumes someone who can be excluded, someone who belongs to the others, and these others cannot be animal or machines, but people.'[13] How are we to categorise the dead coming back to life? Are they 'one of us' or do they belong to the Others? Are they even people? To family members or others with a close relationship to the returning dead of the novel the answer is obvious, at least to begin with. After a while, however, problems are compounded as loved ones do not behave as the living wish.

The Swedish government and various institutions attempt to 'handle' the situation, and the result is indeed depressing. For instance, the well-known strategy of rebranding is used: to neutralise the horror and bring a sense of dignity to the condition, the undead are instead labelled the 'reliving'. After the initial chaos, the undead are transported from hospitals to The Heath, a secluded area where they are supposed to receive proper care. However, rather than being cared for, the 'reliving' are locked away and experimented on. The Heath is a fictitious residential area in the Stockholm region that can be understood as an uncanny metonymic representation of the failed *folkhem*. Its courtyards were constructed in accordance with the vision of the so-called 'Million Programme', a public housing programme implemented by the Social Democrats in the 1960s as a realisation of the *folkhem* ideology. Symbolically, the project was never finished and The Heath remains uninhabited until it is renovated so that the reliving can move in. The environment is sterile and inhumane, and the apartments are described as unhomely imitations of homes. One of the protagonists of the novel, the teenage girl Flora, discusses the situation with her friend and they draw the obvious parallels to concentration camps and guinea pigs. Referring to the legendary Social Democrat leader Tage Erlander, they state that 'society can only be judged… by how it treats its weakest members', and that there 'has never been weaker group than the dead'.[14] Lindqvist often declares that he is not fully at ease with his fiction being labelled social criticism, and in an interview from 2018 he develops his thoughts on the fact that his novels, whether he likes it or not, are interpreted as being more than just plain horror fiction. Interestingly, he uses *Hanteringen av odöda* as an example:

> When I wrote *Hanteringen av odöda*, in which an internment camp for zombies is constructed, many people wondered if this was a criticism of society's treatment of the deviant. But the novel deals with how humans handle zombies, nothing else. I had no intention of writing an allegorical story. At the same time, I understand that the images I hold on to probably have multiple meanings, and that is the reason why I cannot stop thinking about them.[15]

However, there is not necessarily a contradiction between the two interpretations. The novel deals with zombies, but with the ambition of genuinely envisioning a realistic scenario and posing the question of how Swedish society would handle them. In doing so, the novel cannot avoid exposing this society's shortcomings.

Sveavägen, Stockholm, 28 February 1986

The prologue to *Hanteringen av odöda* is essential for understanding the novel in relation to the *folkhem* ideology, and it also leads us on to the next example in this chapter. The location is Sveavägen in Stockholm, exactly on the spot where the Swedish socialist prime minister Olof Palme was assassinated on 28 February 1986, and a man carrying a box of wine toasts the memorial plaque on the pavement: 'Damn it... It's all going to hell, Olof. Down, down and further down.'[16] He then reels on to a nearby graveyard, witnessing the first sign of the awakening of the dead. The assassination of Palme, still unresolved and a collective Swedish trauma, is often regarded as the end of a more innocent era and as 'the shot against the Swedish *folkhem*'. In *Rörelsen*, the death of Olof Palme is the leitmotif. The title, meaning 'the movement' in English, overtly refers to a famous word of guidance from Tage Erlander to his successor Olof Palme. This 1969 speech is quoted as a motto on the first page of the novel: 'Listen to the movement'.[17] The novel is narrated in the first person from a contemporary perspective and is set in Stockholm during the months before Palme's assassination. The 'shot against the Swedish *folkhem*' is thus present as a dark, realistic undercurrent to the supernatural horror plot, and at the end the two are intertwined.

In both *Hanteringen av odöda* and *Rörelsen* formal features are used to create a realistic effect in juxtaposition with their supernatural plots. The first relies on the conventions of fictional documentary, integrating transcripts of interviews from the TV news, scientific lab reports, confidential material from the government and the like, and the latter is a fictitious autobiography. *Rörelsen* tells the story of the 19-year-old John Lindqvist moving into his first apartment in September 1985 and trying to make a living as a magician. As it happens, the apartment is located on Luntmakargatan, only a few steps away from the spot of the assassination. After a while, John realises that something strange is going on in the communal laundry room of the apartment building. A group of neighbours have found a supernatural entity in the shape of black slime that, in exchange for blood, offers access to another dimension where their innermost dreams can be fulfilled. John joins them, but as the months pass this entity changes and eventually it takes human shape. Its shape is fluid and ever changing, and it seems as if the entity projects whatever the person looking at it wants to see. Inexplicably, it sometimes appears as Olof Palme, and at the end of the novel, John witnesses first-hand how the entity, equally inexplicably, kills the prime minister. Thus, the question that in real life still haunts the people of Sweden also goes unanswered in the novel: 'Why? *Why?*'[18]

Rörelsen is a depressing vision of a society shaking at its very foundations, emphasised by the Gothic atmosphere of the novel's urban setting. John's block is characterised by dark streets and narrow passages and his apartment is located in a small shed on a courtyard that is completely overshadowed by the tall surrounding buildings. John therefore has a sense of spending his days in constant twilight. Even taking a shower is described as a Gothic experience: 'The appearance of the room and its location at the very back could create a feeling of claustrophobia while I stood in the bathtub with the weak shower spray trickling over my body. I think it was because of the rock walls. Although I couldn't see them, I could *feel* them around me, their antiquity and weight.'[19] Since his apartment lacks a bathroom, John has to use a shower located next to the haunted communal laundry room that is partially built into the mountain.

The political situation in Sweden at the time of Palme's assassination is a frequent topic of *Rörelsen*. John moves to the apartment one week before Palme and the Social Democrats win the elections and, as a first-time voter, he has politics on his mind. His political consciousness is rather vague, but he intends to vote for Palme: 'I had received my first ballot... and I planned on using it to vote for the Social Democrats. Partially probably because I carried some sort of vague left-wing sympathy with me from home, and partially because the alternatives felt repulsive. Something fishy about right-wing people, while Palme was always Palme.'[20] Two aspects of the Swedish political and social climate of the 1980s are particularly emphasised in the novel. The first is the quite prevalent hatred of Palme, illustrated by a motif on a t-shirt: '*Palmebusters*. A paraphrase of the Ghostbusters logo, inside the red stop sign you could see a long-nosed Olof Palme with an evil appearance instead of a ghost.'[21] Furthermore, while waiting for the election results at the local bar, John overhears a drunk yuppie sharing his opinion on Palme: 'You know, soon all this shit will become Soviet. Spetsnaz units on the streets and submarines in the Baltic Sea and Palme sits there smirking and rubbing his hands while the money goes to the employee funds and disappears to Moscow. Damn.' Continuing, his outburst transforms into an eerie example of dramatic irony: 'If someone offed that swine I'd fucking dance on his grave.'[22] The second aspect visible in the novel concerns general tendencies of the 1980s, personified by the yuppie character:

> There were gyms and sun parlours and Susanne Lanefeldt who hopped around in pastels and you were supposed to shut yourself into your tanned, slimmed skin and realise your potential. Invest in yourself!
> The yuppies had started flashing their Rolexes around Stureplan and the credit market had been deregulated so you could borrow until you dropped. Fittingly

enough, the conversion of rental apartments into co-operatives accelerated, so there was something to buy with the borrowed money.[23]

The point of view here is that of the narrator John, looking back on the decade from a contemporary perspective. He finishes by summarising it as an era of egocentrism and individualism in deep contrast to the collective spirit of the 1970s.

The 19-year-old John also frequently reflects on key socialist concepts such as solidarity and community. A young woman he dates for a while is active in the Social Democratic Youth League (SSU), and that obviously creates the opportunity for political discussions:

> Sofia was involved in the SSU in Sundbyberg. One night… she was at a meeting on… choosing the way forward for social democracy.
> She was quite upbeat when she came home; both the lecture and the discussion afterward had been exciting. In short, these were on the watered-down employee funds as opposed to Meidner's original vision, on the possibilities of collective ownership, on joint accountability leading to greater togetherness and eventually happiness. A wonderful chance that was on its way to being wasted.
> "But," I asked, "can people really be together?"[24]

Thus, John questions whether socialist ideology can ever actually be fully realised, or if a society based on solidarity and community is only a utopian dream.

Geriatric Gothic in the welfare state

Mats Strandberg's novel *Hemmet* can be regarded as a direct comment on the issue of the privatisation of welfare services in Sweden, criticised by the left-wing as 'welfare profiteering', and a recurrent theme in the Swedish political and social debate of the last decade. In Swedish, the title of the novel is doubly significant: the word '*hemmet*' ('the home') is also the common short version for '*ålderdomshem*' ('nursing home' for the elderly), and the novel is set mainly in a nursing home. The novel tells the story of the protagonist Joel returning to his childhood home on the Swedish west coast after many years in Stockholm to move his mother Monika to the nursing home Tallskuggan ('The Pine Shadow') due to her escalating senile dementia. The story is set in the present and Tallskuggan is a typical Swedish post-*folkhem* institution, run by a private company for profit. Significantly, the elderly people are referred to as 'customers' by the unsympathetic supervisor Elisabeth, who is described as being focused only on finances.[25]

It should come as no surprise then, that in Strandberg's novel the Gothic is closely tied to old age.[26] *Hemmet* is a story of occult possession, and Joel's mother Monika is the character functioning as the portal. Her dementia is triggered by a near fatal heart attack; as she regains consciousness, she insists on having met her late husband during this near-death experience and she starts to act confused. She sometimes also claims that her husband has returned to her from the other side, but this is regarded as just another symptom of her dementia. However, when Monika moves to Tallskuggan, strange things start to happen. The nursing home turns into a typical haunted house with the standard attributes of flickering ceiling lights, the television turning on by itself, beds tossing about, scraping sounds in the ventilation system, and a strange fluid seeping through the walls. Gradually, the other patients also start to perceive a supernatural presence and Monika, who is normally very gentle and kind, undergoes significant changes and starts to act out two different personalities. She becomes mean and speaks with an altered, coarse voice. Her behaviour is initially explained as normal for a person with her condition, but when she also reveals knowledge of their deepest and most painful secrets, Joel and his old friend Nina, who works as a nurse at Tallskuggan, start to suspect that they are dealing with something other than dementia. It also becomes evident to the reader that it is not the ghost of her late husband that haunts her but rather an evil, demon-like entity. As the supernatural increasingly takes control, Monika experiences severe seizures and other bodily symptoms, as well as episodes of physically violent behaviour. When she sometimes seemingly regains normal consciousness, she signals that something is wrong and finally Joel finds a hidden handwritten cry for help. Together with Nina he confronts the entity, only to witness Monika committing suicide in a desperate effort to eliminate it. As is typical for this kind of narrative, the novel's ending reveals that supernatural evil cannot be defeated. The entity manages to find a new host, a newborn baby who visits the nursing home with his mother.

Hemmet is in many ways a playful transcultural reworking of American Gothic horror of the 1970s and 1980s in general, those dealing with possession in particular, and the novel pays overt tribute to some of its predecessors. On the bookshelves of Joel's old room nothing has changed since he moved out, those 'eighties editions of Stephen King and Dean R. Koontz are still there'.[27] And when discussing the possibility that they are dealing with the supernatural with his friend Nina, Joel asks her with a laugh if 'they happened to build the home upon an ancient Indian burial ground or something like that', referring to a trope King has used more than once.[28] Furthermore, as demonstrated above, the novel specifically includes all the standard elements and structures of the possession narrative, and one of the most legendary of the genre, *The Exorcist* (William Friedkin, 1973), is an explicit intertext: 'Jokes on scenes from *The Exorcist* are common in the staff room when they have witnessed unusually rapid mood swings and changes of personality, imagined friends suddenly appearing, cascade vomiting.'[29] In her seminal study of late twentieth-century horror film, Carol Clover discusses the possession plot in terms of gender and uses *The Exorcist* as one of her primary examples. She describes the film as generally built around a female character, her body functioning as a portal for the supernatural. However, what seems to be a female narrative often turns out to be so only on the surface, Clover claims, since psychological interest is focused on the male character's internal conflict or life crisis. Clover also identifies the essential binary pair of possession narratives, that of 'white science' (western, rational, male) and 'black magic' (the opposite), as elaborated in 'racial, class and gender terms... some of the most basic social tensions of our times'.[30] In some ways, *Hemmet* follows the pattern outlined by Clover. The possession is indeed gendered feminine and the novel is not a psychological portrait of the possessed woman. Instead, it has a dual focus on her son's psychological struggle with substance abuse, the guilt he feels towards his mother and a lover who died from an overdose, as well as bitterness over a failed musical career, and on his best friend Nina, equally guilt ridden and bitter but for different reasons. However, gender is not the issue here, at least not primarily, and the fact that Joel is gay also complicates the use of a binary model, since it places the male protagonist outside of the patriarchal norm.

    Hemmet is what I would like to call 'geriatric Gothic', and it is a category of social anxiety I would thus like to add age to Clover's list. For, rather than gender, age is the category under scrutiny in Strandberg's possession narrative, although it of course intersects with other thematically subordinate identity markers. In a culture obsessed with youth, ageing – depicted as bodies that are out of control and losing their grip, leaking, drying out and becoming ugly – can be associated with feelings of fear and disgust. Ageing and dying are processes to be contested and repressed and the elderly are among the most vulnerable and powerless in society.[31] *Hemmet* deals with this anxiety and no gruesome details of a body in the final stages of its life are omitted. If *The Exorcist* is mainly a story of another problematic stage in life, namely puberty, and deals with the threat of sexuality taking control over a young woman's body and mind, *Hemmet* deals with the fear of losing control over body and mind at the end of one's life.

'A new home within the home'[32]

As indicated above, the supernatural element is accompanied by the motif of dementia in *Hemmet*. One of the functions of dementia in the novel is that it brings an element of uncertainty into the plot, since the characters initially interpret hauntings as normal symptoms of the disease. However, dementia is also in itself a very potent producer of the uncanny. As Freud pointed out, mental and neurological illnesses can evoke the uncanny in various ways and *Hemmet* can more or less be regarded as an encyclopaedia on the subject.[33] To begin with, dementia transforms the world into a strange and uncanny place for the character suffering from it, especially in the early stage when there are still substantial moments of clarity and reality changes back and forth between the familiar and unfamiliar. The introduction of the novel describes for instance how Monika wakes up on the morning of her move to the nursing home, not remembering why her home has been emptied. Her reaction is that thieves must have taken her furniture. Her reality twists and turns as she realises that if this is the case, they must have been able to move everything but the bed from her bedroom during the night without waking her up. It is also impossible to understand why they bothered to steal family photos. When Joel explains to her what is about to happen, she accuses him of subjecting her to a cruel joke.

Strange forms of repetition are often associated with the uncanny, for instance in the shape of the doppelgänger or as a *déjà-vu* experience, and in *Hemmet* repetitive behaviour is the most frequent device used to portray the uncanniness of dementia. One dimension of the estranged world of memory loss is illustrated by the sad, repetitive act of a 95-year-old woman at the nursing home, who every day tries to call her parents on the phone just to receive the message that the number is no longer in use. When she is reminded of her age, she is struck by the terrible insight that her parents must be dead, a traumatic moment that she must relive over and over again as if for the first time. Another patient is only capable of repeating the same phrase over and over, giving the uncanny impression of automatic processes rather than human behaviour.

Like repetition, automatism is often highlighted as one of the forms that the uncanny takes, and the uncanny effect is created through doubting whether what appears to be human might in reality be a mechanical process or, reversely, with mistaking an automaton for a living creature.[34]

The behaviour of the characters suffering from dementia gives a mechanical impression not only through repetitive actions or repetitive speech, but the characters can also appear as automatons when shifting between a 'normal', conscious self and a state of confusion and memory loss, as if being switched on and off or as though a battery has been discharged. The motif of the automaton corresponds well with the theme of welfare profiteering: putting profit first many times equals depriving the patients of their humanity, treating them like lifeless objects or commodities. In addition, the character can give the impression of being empty, zombie-like: 'Over the years, Nina has seen the gaze of dementia countless times. The emptiness of the eyes. But she has never seen it in someone as close to her as Monika. It is something completely different. It is almost unbearable.'[35] The fictional reality thus appears strange and uncanny, not only to the characters suffering from senile dementia, but of course also to the ones closest to them. Seeing a loved one transformed by the disease, turning into someone else, is a very disturbing experience of the intermingling of the familiar and the unfamiliar that in the novel gradually becomes intertwined with the horror of the supernatural.

The horror of Strandberg's novel is acted out on multiple levels. As a parallel to the supernatural plot and the uncanniness of dementia, runs the socially realistic, but definitely no less horrific plot of spending one's old age at the mercy of a profit-driven company. The point is proven by the character Sucdi, a nurse at Tallskuggan and a refugee from Somalia, one of the most war-ridden countries in the world. Her father has decided to return to his home country, even though his children live in Sweden, and it means that he must move in with distant relatives whom he has met only a few times. 'He doesn't want to depend upon Swedish eldercare when he is no longer capable of taking care of himself', Sucdi declares.[36] Tallskuggan is described as an inhumane environment where the interior is designed and decorated not with the wellbeing of the persons receiving care in mind, but with a focus on efficiency: 'The plastic carpet in the entrance is green, speckled so that spots and marks will be as invisible as possible.'[37] From the beginning, the prison-like atmosphere is highlighted, and by using second-person narration, which in Swedish can be perceived as a direct address to the reader, Strandberg offers the uncanny opportunity to reflect on the possibility of having to call a place like this home:

> The apartments are small and there are not many ways to arrange the furniture. They have small bathrooms, but no kitchens. No hot plates that can be left on. The windows can only be opened a crack. You can lock the door from the inside if you want to, but the staff has keys so that they are always able to get in. In Blocks B and C, facing the woods, the apartments have balconies. They are fenced with chicken wire, so you will not be able to get out that way…
> The new owners are trying to make the staff call you customers, even though you rarely moved here voluntarily.[38]

The company's pursuit of profit is described as cynical: 'When your relatives are offered a place in Tallskuggan they have a week at the most to accept it or not. Things have to move quickly so that the nursing home does not lose money on empty apartments.'[39] Emotions have no place in their directive, and neither does the wellbeing of the elderly.

In many ways, the supervisor Elisabeth becomes the personification of the system in the novel. When discussing where to place Joel's mother, her sentences are 'cut off, effective. Toneless. Emotionless. And why should they be otherwise? Monika Edlund is just another name to her. After this meeting she will not even be that. She will be D6, in short.'[40] Furthermore, it is described how the elderly rarely get out in the open air; the overuse of medication seems to address many of the needs that could have been taken care of by the staff if their schedules were less tight. Elisabeth briefs Nina on Monika's medicines during the morning meeting: '"Nothing strange when it comes to medication", Elisabeth continues. "Trombyl, atorvastatin, metoprolol, ramipril and brilique. Haldol against anxiety when needed and imovane for the night."'[41] Finally, Elisabeth also clearly distances herself from the elderly by condescendingly referring to them as a group without individual qualities: '"I really love old people", Elisabeth says. "They are so cute, aren't they?"'[42] To conclude, Strandberg's geriatric Gothic deals with the horrors of old age on several levels. By transferring the classic possession plot to a nursing home, Strandberg manages to include not only a severe critique of contemporary Swedish society and the privatisation of welfare services, but he also highlights an aspect of identity often regarded as less relevant or less interesting and thus subordinated to such categories as gender, sexuality, class and ethnicity: age.

This chapter has demonstrated how the novels of Lindqvist and Strandberg explore the problems of the Swedish welfare state in different ways, questioning its status by portraying its shortcomings, traumas and fears. In *Hanteringen av odöda* and *Rörelsen*, Lindqvist explicitly addresses Swedish politics by referring to or quoting iconic leaders of the past associated with the welfare state, and *Rörelsen* deals with the tragic death of Olof Palme, still an unresolved case, and describes the political climate at the time of the murder. *Hanteringen av odöda* in many ways illustrates the incapacity of the state to take care of its weakest members, in this case the undead, and the residential Million Programme area where the undead are kept becomes a nightmare version of a *folkhem* in ruins. The uncanny effect of the story is made stronger by the connection between the awakening of the dead and climate change, reflecting the ecological anxiety of the welfare state. Strandberg's *Hemmet* can be regarded as the logical next step of the exploration by its depiction of the consequences of welfare profiteering in the form of a haunted nursing home. The story also effectively mixes supernatural horror and social critique with the universal fear of old age and of losing control over oneself on the one hand, and the anxiety over having to take the decision to put a loved one in an institution on the other.

Notes

1. N. Wennö, 'Låt fulskräcken komma in', *Dagens Nyheter* (14 June 2009), www.dn.se/kultur-noje/film-tv/lat-fulskracken-komma-in. Accessed 4 January 2019.
2. J. Ajvide Lindqvist, *Handling the Undead*, trans. E. Segerberg (New York: Thomas Dunne Books/St. Martin's Press, 2011), p. 116.
3. For a study of the image of the *folkhem* in Swedish crime fiction on film and television, see D. Brodén, *Folkhemmets skuggbilder: En kulturanalytisk genrestudie av svensk kriminalfiktion i film och TV* (Stockholm: Ekholm & Tegebjer, 2008). See also M. Demker, Y. Leffler and O. Sigurdsson (eds), *Culture, Health and Religion. Sweden Unparadised* (New York: Palgrave Macmillan, 2014), pp. 1–17, for a general introduction to the Swedish welfare state at the millennium.
4. 'Det måste en gång bli så att klassamhället Sverige avlöses av folkhemmet Sverige', quote, www.svenskatal.se/1928011-per-albin-hansson-folkhemstalet/. Accessed 4 January 2019. My translation.
5. M. Arnstad, 'Hem ljuva folkhem', *Språktidningen*, January 2016, p. 4, http://spraktidningen.se/artiklar/2015/12/hem-ljuva-folkhem. Accessed 4 January 2019. My translation. On *folkhem* ideology, see also S. Hadenius, *Modern svensk politisk historia: Konflikt och samförstånd* (Stockholm: Hjalmarsson & Högberg: 2003); Y. Hirdman, *Att lägga livet tillrätta: Studier i svensk folkhemspolitik* (Stockholm: Carlssons: 1989); R. Qvarsell et al. (eds), *I framtidens tjänst: Ur folkhemmets idéhistoria* (Stockholm: Gidlund, 1986).
6. J. A. Lindqvist, *Let the Right One In*, trans. E. Segerberg (London: Quercus, 2009), p. 2.

7 Lindqvist, *Let the Right One In*, p. 144f.
8 Gregersdotter regards the zombie as a metaphor in the welfare discourse and she also focuses on the motifs of pain and grief. K. Gregersdotter, 'The Scandinavian Zombie and the Welfare State: A Reading of John Ajvide Lindqvist's *Handling the Undead*', in J. Fernandez-Goldborough (ed.), *Making Sense of Pain: Critical and Interdisciplinary Perspectives* (Oxfordshire: Inter-Disciplinary Press, 2010), pp. 211–18.
9 S. Wijkmark, 'Ecology, Telepathy, Melancholia in John Ajvide Lindqvist's *Handling the Undead*', *Edda. Nordisk tidskrift for litteraturforskning*, 104:2 (2017), pp. 145–60. DOI: 10.18261/issn.1500-1989-2017-02-05. The analysis of *Hanteringen av odöda* in this chapter is a brief summary of the results of this article.
10 Al Gore's documentary *An Inconvenient Truth* was released in 2006.
11 Lindqvist, *Handling the Undead*, p. 2.
12 Lindqvist, *Handling the Undead*, p. 7.
13 Lindqvist, *Handling the Undead*, 'Prologue', no pagination.
14 Lindqvist, *Handling the Undead*, p. 240.
15 'När jag skrev "Hanteringen av odöda", där det skapas ett interneringsläger för zombier, undrade många om det var en kritik av hur samhället behandlar avvikande. Men romanen handlar om hur människor hanterar zombier, inget annat. Jag hade ingen avsikt att skriva någon allegorisk berättelse. Samtidigt förstår jag ju att bilderna som jag håller fast vid förmodligen har flera betydelseplan, det är väl anledningen till att jag inte kan sluta tänka på dem.' Interview by Jacob Lundström, 'John Ajvide Lindqvist: Jag hade zombieskräck sommaren efter min pappas död', *Dagens Nyheter* (29 September 2018), www.dn.se/kultur-noje/john-ajvide-lindqvist-jag-hade-zombieskrack-sommaren-efter-min-pappas-dod/. Accessed 3 January 2019. My translation.
16 Lindqvist, *Handling the Undead*, p. 1.
17 'Lyssna på rörelsen'. J. A. Lindqvist, *Rörelsen. Den andra platsen* (Stockholm: Ordfront, 2015), p. 7. All translations of quotations from the novel are mine.
18 'Varför? Varför?' Lindqvist, *Rörelsen*, p. 274.
19 'Rummets utseende och dess placering djupast och längst in kunde skapa en känsla av klaustrofobi när jag stod i badkaret med de klena duschstrålarna sipprande över kroppen. Jag tror att det berodde på bergväggarna. Även om jag inte kunde se dem så kunde jag *förnimma* dem omkring mig, deras ålderdomlighet och tyngd'. Lindqvist, *Rörelsen*, p. 16.
20 'Jag hade fått mitt första röstkort… och jag tänkte använda det för att rösta på sossarna. Dels hade jag väl ett vagt vänsterengagemang hemifrån, och dels kändes alternativen frånstötande. Något lurigt med de borgerliga nunorna, medan Palme alltid var Palme'. Lindqvist, *Rörelsen*, p. 12.
21 'Palmebusters. En parafras på Ghostbusterssloggan där man inuti det röda stopptecknet istället för ett spöke kunde se en långnäst Olof Palme med ondskefullt utseende'. Lindqvist, *Rörelsen*, p. 171.
22 'Snart blir det Sovjet av hela skiten, vet du. Spetsnazförband på gatorna och ubåtar i Östersjön och Palme sitter där och flinar och gnuggar händerna medan pengarna åker in i löntagarfonderna och försvinner till Moskva. Fy fan… Om någon fimpade det där aset skulle jag fan dansa på hans grav."' Lindqvist, *Rörelsen*, pp. 31–2.
23 'Det var gym och solarier och Susanne Lanefelt som studsade runt i pastellfärger och man skulle sluta sig inom sitt bruna, slimmade skinn och förverkliga sina

möjligheter. Satsa på dig själv! Yuppies hade börjat flasha sina Rolexar kring Stureplan och kreditmarknaden hade avreglerats så att man kunde låna tills man stupade. Lämpligt nog accelererade omvandlingen av hyresrätter till bostadsrätter så att det fanns något att köpa för de lånade pengarna.' Lindqvist, *Rörelsen*, pp. 212–13.

24 'Sofia var engagerad i SSU i Sundbyberg. En kväll… var hon på ett möte som skulle handla om… Socialdemokratins vägval inför framtiden. Hon var rätt upprymd när hon kom hem, både föredraget och den efterföljande diskussionen hade varit spännande. Det hade i korthet handlat om de urvattnade löntagarfonderna kontra Meidners ursprungliga vision, om de möjligheter som fanns i ett kollektivt ägande, det gemensamma ansvaret som leder till större samhörighet mellan människor och i förlängningen lycka. En underbar chans som höll på att gå till spillo. "Men", frågade jag, "kan människor egentligen vara tillsammans?"' Lindqvist, *Rörelsen*, p. 120.

25 '… kunder'. M. Strandberg, *Hemmet* (Stockholm: Norstedts, 2017), p. 17. All translations of quotations from the novel are mine.

26 On representations of old age in the horror film, see C. J. Miller & A. B. Van Riper (eds), *Elder Horror: Essays on Film's Frightening Images of Aging* (Jefferson, North Carolina: McFarland & Company Inc., 2019).

27 '… åttiotalsutgåvorna av Stephen King och Dean R. Koontz står kvar'. Strandberg, *Hemmet*, p. 123.

28 'Dom råkar inte ha byggt hemmet på en gammal indiansk begravningsplats eller nåt sånt?' Strandberg, *Hemmet*, p. 257. Both in *The Shining* (1977) and *Pet Semetery* (1983) the occult is related to a location built on ancient Indian burial ground.

29 'Det brukar skämtas om Exorcisten-scener här i personalrummet när de fått se ovanligt tvära humörsvängningar och personlighetsförändringar, plötsligt uppdykande låtsaskompisar, kaskadspyor.' Strandberg, *Hemmet*, p. 285. Friedkin's film is based on the novel with the same name by William Peter Blatty from 1971. However, it is fair to say that it is the film that has received most attention, and to assume that it is the film rather than the novel that is referred to in *Hemmet*.

30 C. Clover, *Men, Women and Chain Saws. Gender in the Modern Horror Film* (Princeton: Princeton University Press, 2015), p. 67. Also, from her 1992 perspective, Clover pointed out regarding the genre of the occult (in late twentieth-century film) that it is very 'vast and untidy', but can be defined to include those works 'that have as their central concern human responses to ghostly or satanic doings', p. 65.

31 In *The Fountain of Age*, Betty Friedan addresses the problem of old age and describes denial of the aging process as the 'age mystique' and the elderly as segregated from society. Nursing homes are for her similar to 'concentration camps' from which one 'will never return'. B. Friedan, *The Fountain of Age* (New York: Simon and Schuster, 1993), p. 41.

32 'Ett nytt hem i hemmet.' Strandberg, *Hemmet*, p. 10.

33 S. Freud, 'The Uncanny' (1919), *The Standard Edition of the Complete Psychological Works of Sigmund Freud. Vol. 17 (1917–1919); An infantile Neurosis and Other Works*, trans. L. Strachey (London: Hogarth Press, 1955), pp. 217–56.

34 See Freud, 'The Uncanny', p. 226.

35 'Nina har sett demensblicken otaliga gånger genom åren. Tomheten i ögonen. Men hon har aldrig sett den hos någon som stått henne så nära som Monika. Det är något helt annat. Det är nästan outhärdligt.' Strandberg, *Hemmet*, p. 63.

36 'Han vill inte vara beroende av den svenska äldrevården när han inte klarar sig själv längre.' Strandberg, *Hemmet*, p. 184.
37 'Plastmattan i entréhallen är grön, spräcklig för att fläckar och märken ska synas så lite som möjligt.' Strandberg, *Hemmet*, p. 9.
38 'Lägenheterna är små och det finns inte många sätt att möblera dem på. De har badrum, men inga kök. Inga plattor som kan glömmas påslagna. Fönstren går inte att öppna mer än på glänt. Du kan låsa dörren inifrån om du vill, men personalen har nycklar så att de alltid kan ta sig in. På avdelning B och C, som vetter mot skogen, har lägenheterna balkonger. De är inklädda med hönsnät, för att du inte ska kunna ta dig ut den vägen... De nya ägarna försöker få personalen att kalla er som bor här för kunder, trots att ni sällan själva valt att flytta hit.' Strandberg, *Hemmet*, pp. 9–10.
39 'När dina anhöriga får erbjudandet om en plats på Tallskuggan har de högst en vecka på sig att tacka ja eller nej. Det måste gå undan för att hemmet inte ska förlora pengar på tomma lägenheter.' Strandberg, *Hemmet*, p. 10.
40 '... avklippta, effektiva. Tonlösa. Känslolösa. Och varför skulle de vara något annat? Monika Edlund är bara ännu ett namn för henne. Efter det här mötet kommer hon inte ens att vara det. Hon kommer att vara D6, kort och gott.' Strandberg, *Hemmet*, p. 16.
41 '"Inga konstigheter när det kommer till medicinering", fortsätter Elisabeth. "Trombyl, atorvastatin, metroprolol, ramipril och brilique. Haldol vid behov och imovane till natten."' Strandberg, *Hemmet*, p. 17.
42 '"Jag älskar verkligen gamla människor", säger Elisabeth. Dom är så härliga, visst är dom?."' Strandberg, *Hemmet*, p. 41.

4

Yvonne Leffler

Nordic Gothic crime: places and spaces in Johan Theorin's Öland quartet series

Since the turn of the millennium, there has been a boom of a certain kind of Nordic crime story that international scholars call 'Nordic Noir', sometimes also known as 'Scandinavian Noir' or 'Scandi Noir'. These crime stories are narrated from the viewpoint of the investigating detective and are often set in a bleak urban landscape in combination with a desolate wintry countryside, as in Stieg Larsson's *Millennium* trilogy (2005–2007). The first part, *Män som hatar kvinnor* (2005; *The Girl with the Dragon Tattoo*, 2008), is located both in the Swedish capital Stockholm and in a freezing cold northern Sweden. There are also Nordic crime stories situated in a small community known as an idyllic rural holiday area that during the police procedure is transformed into an ominous place, as in Henning Mankell's series about the Swedish police detective Kurt Wallander's work in and around the coastal holiday town of Ystad. Whatever the setting, the investigation of the crime exposes a morally complex society and a tension between the apparently calm social surface and the dark drives beneath and behind the murder, drives such as misogyny and racism. Due to its popularity, Nordic Noir has been extended to the production of film and television, including internationally successful TV series, such as the Danish *Forbrydelsen* (2007–2012; *The Killing*) and the Danish-Swedish *Broen/Bron* (2011–2018; *The Bridge*). While *Forbrydelsen* has resulted in an American adaptation, *The Killing* (2011–2014), *Broen/Bron* has given rise to one French-British and one American adaptation, titled *The Tunnel* (2013–2018) and *The Bridge* (2013–2014) respectively. The TV productions often feature a female protagonist worn down by conflicting cares and thus far from heroic. Her endeavours – both professionally and in her private life – strengthen the social criticism and the exposure of the dark secrets and hidden hatreds in the Nordic welfare states. Thus, they contradict the established notion of social justice and equality in the Nordic societies.

In the past decade or so, a Gothic subgenre to Nordic Noir has emerged. Here the police procedure is complicated by seemingly supernatural happenings; the initially realistic depiction of the crime investigation is replaced by Gothic tropes, uncanny characters and a mythological world lurking beneath or beyond modern society. The references to Mark Frost and David Lynch's 1990 TV series, *Twin Peaks*, are notable. Still, the Nordic writers and production teams have formed a specific Nordic version of what could be called 'Gothic crime', a domestication of Gothic styles and devices within the realistic settings and modes of writing of modern crime. For example, Icelandic Yrsa Sigurðardóttir incorporates ghostly elements connected to the specific Nordic landscape in her plots. In *Auðnin* (2008; *The Day is Dark*, 2011) the legendary and evil Inuit spirit Tupilak haunts the detective team during their investigation of a murder at a remote and desolate research station in Greenland. In *Þóra Guðmundsdóttir* (2010; *Ashes to Dust*, 2010) the devastating volcanic eruption in Iceland in 1973, which buried an entire village in lava and ashes, influences the investigation. Also, in some TV series, the local place, and in particular untamed nature, is the very source or prerequisite of the crimes taking place. This kind of series often opens with the female protagonist leaving her everyday life in the city for a new job in a distant area on the outskirts of modern civilisation. Anders Engström and Henrik Björn's Swedish TV drama *Jordskott* (2015) and Johan Kindblom and Thomas Tivemark's *Ängelby* (2015) are both set in fictitious communities in Swedish forests and the two female protagonists' mystical experiences contest the customary image of today's Nordic society. As in some of these TV productions, the story revolves around the mystery of a missing person, a child in *Jordskott* and a young boy's body in *Ängelby*. In both cases, the disappearance is inextricably entangled with the conflicts between uncanny elements wishing to protect the forest and the local community at large. The investigation is increasingly inhibited by the interventions of presumed supernatural powers and, in *Jordskott*, even nature beings known from Nordic mythology. When the mystery is to some extent solved, the actual existence of supernatural phenomena and creatures is confirmed rather than negated.

One of the most internationally recognised and awarded novelists of this kind of Gothic crime is Swedish Johan Theorin, with his quartet of novels set on the Swedish island of Öland in the Baltic sea: *Skumtimmen* (2007; *Echoes of the Dead*, 2008), *Nattfåk* (2008; *The Darkest Room*, 2009) *Blodläge* (2010; *The Quarry*, 2011) and *Rörgast* (2013; *The Voices Beyond*, 2015). In each novel, the detective work is obstructed by seemingly supernatural happenings linked to the geographical and meteorological peculiarities of the island, its history and popular beliefs. Thus, Theorin's stories are clearly situated within a Nordic tradition where the crime and the monstrous are connected to the Nordic location, as well as to some ancient and uncivilised 'Other' to be found outside modern urban society.

Theorin's novels are also interesting because they revive a tradition in Scandinavian crime fiction going back to the first Nordic crime stories from the 1820s and 1830s. Contrary to the social realist tradition of the late twentieth century and the crime fiction of renowned writers such as Maj Sjöwall and Per Wahlöö, the distinguishing feature of early crime fiction is a mix of a whodunit-plot with supernatural occurrences and an uncanny atmosphere.[1] The stories are set in remote locations outside urban areas, either in a rural village or the countryside. Two early examples are Danish Steen Steensen Blicher's *Præsten i Vejlbye* (1829: *The Rector of Vejlbye*, 1909) and Norwegian Mauritz Christopher Hansen's *Mordet på Maskinbygger Roolfsen* (1839; *The Murder of Engine Maker Roolfsen*). Although the two crime mysteries are complicated by eerie circumstances, everything is given a natural explanation at the end; what at first seems to be caused by supernatural powers, turns out to be part of the criminals' plotting and staged crime dramas. More distinctly Gothic are Swedish Carl Jonas Love Almqvist's *Skällnora kvarn* (1838; *Skällnora Mill*) and Finnish-Swedish Zacharias Topelius' 'En natt och en morgon' (1843; 'A Night and a Morning'). Both stories are structured as a journey from the everyday world into a nightmarish desolate domain where the inhabitants' strange behaviour is in line with norms unfamiliar to the investigating detective. In both stories, the detective finds himself in a situation where the distinction between reality and imagination dissolves because of mystifying subplots, distorted viewpoints and unreliable narrators. Although the detective investigates the entangled circumstances behind the suspected murder, he is not in control, nor does he arrive at a satisfying solution. At the end of Almqvist's *Skällnora kvarn*, the amateur detective is even more unsure than he was at the beginning about what really happened and whether a murder was ever committed.

Also in Theorin's quartet of novels, the local landscape and its particular mythology plays an active part in the crime investigation. The characters' connections to the history of the island and old popular beliefs associated with certain places constantly obstruct and complicate the police work. In this way, Theorin expands the dialogue between Gothic conventions and realism that shaped the very first Gothic story, Horace Walpole's *The Castle of Otranto* (1764). According to Walpole's preface to the second edition, the novel was intended as 'an attempt to blend the two kinds of romance, the ancient and the modern', through which he wanted to combine the 'imagination and improbability' of the former romance with the latter's fidelity to nature, that is, to both observe the rules of probability and nature and still leave 'the powers of fancy at liberty to expatiate through the boundless realms of invention'.[2] Noting that Theorin employs the same blend of Gothic and realistic narration, this chapter will examine how Gothic elements are used in his crime stories set on Öland. I will demonstrate how the modern crime investigation is combined with the depiction of a haunted Gothic space, where old conceptions of supernatural powers and hidden crimes activate repressed memories of a dark past. Thus, special attention is paid to the representation of setting as a central aspect of the crime and subsequent investigation. The plot revolves, I argue, around a complex relationship between location, time and focalisation, and forms a multifaceted web that the detective must unravel in order to solve the mystery. The focus on the local place, its uniqueness as well as its imagined history, makes Theorin's crime novels what could be termed 'place-focused stories', or 'topofocal stories', in which setting plays a vital role.[3] However, and contrary to most Nordic Gothic, it is not primarily untamed nature, the Nordic wilderness, that generates horror. Theorin's crime stories demonstrate another use of setting and the characteristic landscape on the island of Öland. Therefore, human geographer Yi-Fu Tuan's distinction between place and space is used as a point of departure to explore the specific Gothic setting in these novels.[4] It is thus possible to make a more precise distinction between local place and Gothic space than is normally done in studies on Gothic setting, where place and space are often used in a more general sense or to explore different national Gothic traditions.[5]

The detective and the settings

Johan Theorin's four crime novels are closely knit together. Each story portrays one of the four seasons on Öland in the Baltic Sea and the

Swedish titles consist of local words referring to something characteristic of the regional climate or folk memories. The Swedish title of the first novel is *Skumtimmen*, which means 'the twilight hour', and it refers to that time of the day, especially in autumn, when it is getting dark and in the past frightening ghost stories were told. The second novel is set in midwinter and its Swedish title is *Nattfåk*, which is a specific kind of feared snowstorm on Öland, a 'blizzard' in the English translation. The third novel takes place in the spring and the Swedish title *Blodläge*, 'blood layer', refers to a reddish layer in the local chalk stone that is also, according to popular belief, said to be the remains a violent prehistoric battle between two kinds of mythological creature: trolls and elves. In the last novel, it is summer and the Swedish title, *Rörgast*, consist of the word '*rör*', which is a Bronze Age burial site, and '*gast*', which is a lingering vindictive kind of ghost. Thus, all the Swedish titles contain local, archaic and ominous words for something that is both uncanny and connected with local customs and myths.

The setting of the novels is the northern part of the island, north of the town Borgholm, which the characters regularly pass or visit. The Öland Bridge, between the island and the mainland of Sweden is frequently mentioned, as well as the closest town on the mainland, Kalmar. However, most of the places on the island are given fictitious names, such as Marnäs and Stenvik. Still, all the locations are easy to track on a map and, according to the author, the places in the novels are inspired by specific sites on the island. On his Swedish website, Theorin introduces his Öland quartet and informs his readers about the circumstances behind his choice of setting and how it is related to actual places.[6] In the English translation of the second novel, *The Darkest Room*, a map of the island is included on the first page to introduce the geographical location and the most important sites to non-Scandinavian readers, as the main characters often return to the same villages, cottages, quarries and boathouses in the novels.[7] Frequently, the same place reappears at different times and with different functions and significance in the novels.

In contrast to most contemporary crime novels, the protagonist in Theorin's stories is not an investigating police officer but an 80-year-old amateur detective, Gerlof Davidsson, a former skipper, who is suffering from rheumatism. Thus, the crime mysteries are never solved through professional police work, but by the workings of an old brain in an ailing body confined to a chair at the nursing home or a seat in the garden of Gerlof's summer cottage. Gerlof's advantage is that he has lived all his life on the island and is familiar with local history, social hierarchy and lifestyle. He is also good at forecasting and understanding weather and wind directions, which helps him in his detective work. In particular, he is well acquainted with local legends and myths. Although he is not superstitious, he keeps an open mind to popular belief and the workings of the human imagination. He answers when he is asked by the dead woman's husband in *Nattfåk* if he believes in ghosts: 'I neither believe nor don't believe.'[8] Because of his age, experience and open-mindedness he knows how to console those who claim that they have experienced something paranormal, and he understands how it may affect their behaviour, as for example in the last novel *Rörgast*, when a twelve-year-old boy believes he has visited a ghost ship and that he is hunted by a malicious ghost.

Most of the crime scenes are set close to Gerlof's summer cottage at Marnäs and some of the killers and victims are his old friends and neighbours or related to their families. For example, the first novel's plot revolves around his cottage and boathouse. It is to this place that his daughter Julia returns when she and Gerlof reopen the case of her six-year-old son's mysterious disappearance twenty years ago. It was at the cottage that the boy was last seen and it is at the nearby quarry that Gerlof's old friend and neighbour Ernst Jansson is killed at the beginning of the novel. Gerlof's cottage also plays an important part in the third and fourth novel when Gerlof decides to leave the nursing home to live in his own house during the summer. The nearby quarry, where the murder is committed in the first novel, is also of central importance in the third novel when the murder victim's nephew moves into the deceased man's cottage. Thus, what in one novel is the place of a murder is in another novel the protagonist's family home. In that way, the history of certain places is repeated and expanded on in each novel. The setting becomes a literary landscape of references that reminds the reader of what happened in the former novels.

The places are also associated with certain historical events and popular legends. On the first page of the second novel, *Nattfåk*, for example, a quotation from a Swedish folktale from the nineteenth century is included to anticipate the murder and the ghostly events around the site of the crime:

> The dead gather every winter to celebrate Christmas. But on one occasion they were disturbed by an old spinster. Her clock had stopped, so she got up too early and went to church in the middle of the night on Christmas Eve. There was the murmur of voices as if there were a service going on, and the church was full of people. Suddenly the old woman caught sight of her fiancé from the days of her

youth. He had drowned many years ago, but there he was, sitting in a pew among the others.⁹

What is told in the old folktale will be repeated in the present time of narration in the novel. In this novel, as well as in the other three, what occurred at a certain time in the past is described retrospectively in separate chapters, adding layers of important information about the location. *Nattfåk* is set at the lighthouses at Eel Point, and the accidents and tragic deaths that took place there in the past are retold in flashbacks and in separate chapters. Thus, the location is repeatedly charged with ill-omened meaning leading up to the climax of the plot. Accordingly, what once happened in the past seems to happen again and is thus integrated into the present time of narration.

Not only the place but also the characters are linked to the history of the island. As indicated, the protagonists frequently return to houses where older generations have lived. As the protagonists settle and take over a house, including remaining equipment, the history of the place and its inhabitants is recalled and activated, as for example when a young family moves into the lighthouse-keeper's manor house at the two lighthouses at Eel Point in *Nattfåk*, or when Ernst Jansson's nephew takes over his murdered uncle's cottage in *Blodläge*. Sometimes the history of a certain place is told by an elderly local person who has lived at the site or on the island all his life. The amateur detective, Gerlof Davidsson, is one of these local elderly narrators, but his function is also to encourage other inhabitants to enlighten him or the investigating police officer. Because of the connection between the history of the place and the murder, the motives for the committed crime often form part of a repetitive pattern. The present crime is connected to past transgressions, and thereby the wrongdoings in the past both complicate and motivate the present actions.

Especially when the killings are not classified as murders to begin with but as accidental deaths, the connection to the history of and life on the island is of vital importance. In these cases, the investigating police officers are unable to discover and interpret the traces indicating a planned crime, while Gerlof immediately suspects that a murder has been committed because he is familiar with the place and the way in which it influences a person's actions. He is therefore able to reconstruct the victim's last minutes in life. In the first novel, *Skumtimmen*, it is only Gerlof who suspects that his friend, stonemason Ernst Jansson, has not slipped by accident but was pushed down into the quarry because he had discovered something about what happened twenty years ago, at the time of the disappearance of Gerlof's grandson Jens. Thus, the present murder is immediately connected with something that happened in the past. In this novel, the reader is led to believe that Gerlof's grandson and Ernst Jansson were murdered by Nils Kant, who killed several people many years ago and thus had to escape from the island. Although Kant is supposed to be long dead and buried, a rumour argues that is was not his body that was interred in the local churchyard. Instead, he is said to be alive and to have returned to the island in disguise, which means that he might be guilty of other crimes. Whether this is true or not will not be revealed until the close of the novel. Consequently, the disappearance of Jens twenty years before the death of Ernst is from the very beginning connected to the mystery of Kant, his escape from and possible return to the island.

Only the third novel, *Blodläge*, differs somewhat from the aforementioned pattern. The first crime, burning down a house, does not take place on the island but on the mainland. The investigating officer also immediately recognises it as an act of arson. Gerlof therefore plays a less prominent role as detective in this novel. Nevertheless, it is he who in the end reveals previously undiscovered clues because he is able to interpret old photos and predict the action of a visitor who he suspects to be the killer. He also eventually stops the criminal from committing his last murder, since Gerlof happens to be familiar with the intended place of the crime; he knows the secrets and peculiarities of the place and can calculate its effects on the intended victim's as well as the killer's likely behaviour in the location, the old quarry.

Familiar place contra Gothic space

In recent studies, Gothic locations and geographies have been approached through national literary traditions with a focus on local traditions and literary settings, rather than as spatial tropes.[10] Although Theorin's place-focused crime stories can be seen as part of a specific Nordic tradition, they also present a different spatial model; they are not set in the Nordic wilderness and the landscape is not depicted as obscure and labyrinthine woodlands. Instead, the location is an open landscape of meadows, forest groves and moorland with windmills. Still, it is possible to make a distinction between what Yi-Fu Tuan calls 'place and space' from the perspective of human environmental experience, where 'place' refers to a location filled with social meaning, and 'space' is an abstract concept and a location void of social connections.[11] While place is security, enclosure and stability, according to Tuan, space represents movement, freedom and threat.[12]

In Theorin's novels, the crime sites are local places created by human endeavours and experience and are therefore of social significance, especially to the detective Gerlof. But close to the crime site, there is always a space void of human recognition and significance. This empty space is in one sense what Tuan calls 'mythical space', that is, the ambiguous space of defective knowledge, but unlike Tuan's mythical space, it is not necessarily surrounding the familiar and empirically known place, nor is it mainly a component of a person's worldview or lack of perception.[13] Instead, in Theorin's novels it is sometimes located outside or beyond the actual place of crime and sometimes at the very heart of it as a hidden space, a secret sealed-up room. In both cases, it represents horror vacui and is the very source of terror.

In the first two novels, the murders are committed in hostile locations beyond populated places and in desolate areas close to the protagonists' homes. In *Skumtimmen*, Gerlof's grandson Jens is believed to either have drowned or have been killed on the moorland outside the garden, an environment none of the protagonists is familiar with. When the boy leaves the secure garden, the unfamiliar space on the other side of the wall is depicted from the boy's viewpoint:

> The world on the other side was huge, with no boundaries, but it was also grey and blurred. The fog that had drifted in over the island that afternoon prevented the boy from seeing much of what lay outside the garden, but at the bottom of the wall he could see the yellowish-brown grass of a small meadow. Further away he could just make out low, gnarled juniper bushes and moss-covered stones sticking up out of the earth. The ground was just as flat as in the garden behind him, but everything looked much wilder on the other side; strange, enticing.[14]

When Jens leaves the safe place of the garden, he enters the vast moorland associated with the memory of the legendary villain Kant, who once made the moorland his realm. According to rumours, it was on The Great Alvaret moor that Kant spent most of his time, committed at least two murders and left his assumed treasure. It was also on the moor that he escaped, never to be seen again, after he shot a police officer. Because of Kant's evil doings in the past, the moorland is still haunted by his spirit. When Gerlof resumes his investigation, he is convinced that his young grandson did not drown but was killed on the moor. However, who the murderer is remains a mystery to the very end of the novel.

Also in the second novel, *Nattfåk*, the crime is committed at the most hazardous spot on the coast of Öland at Eel Point, close to the two lighthouses and their manor house once built as '[s]ome kind of sacrificial offering' to counteract all shipwrecks and 'bad luck' connected to the spot.[15] The place still remains an ominous site where the northern lighthouse flashes only to anticipate the coming death of an inhabitant at Eel Point. Because of Gerlof's experience at sea, he is the only one who instantly suspects that a murder has been committed when the mother of the family who just bought the house, Katrine Westin, is found dead by the shore next to the lighthouses. Hence, Katrine's death is also linked to previous killings at the lighthouses, not only wrecked ships but tragic and sudden deaths among the inhabitants of the lodge. The previous accidents and murders that haunt the place seem to be emanating from another space, a secret room inside the barn. It is this hidden and sealed-up prayer room for the dead that Katrine finds just before her death. It is also this hidden room that her mourning husband Joakim discovers when he tries to reconstruct her last days in life. Just as Katrine did before her death, her husband must recognise and believe in the ghost stories linked to the place and accept his dead wife's ghostly presence in the house before the secret memorial room is exposed to him and he can accept his loss.

Similarly, in the last two novels, the disclosure of the mystery and the climax of the plot are linked to a concealed space close to or within a familiar location. In the third novel, the actual crime, the arson, takes place on the mainland, but although it is not committed on the island, it is aimed at a person connected to Öland, the brother of Gerlof's deceased friend, the stonemason Ernst Jansson. Therefore, it also affects Ernst's nephew Per Mörner, who at the beginning of the novel moves into his uncle's cottage at the same time as he is struggling with his painful family situation, a seriously ill daughter, a trying ex-wife and a troublesome father. In the parallel plot, a young woman, Vendela, and her controlling husband settle in their new summerhouse at the site of her childhood, the quarry. While she is reminded of her upbringing, other crimes are exposed, among them the burning of her father's farm when she was a child. Vendela's as well as Per's arrival at the quarry stirs up past wrongdoings and triggers evil deeds in the present connected with the area around the quarry. These activities seem to be linked to popular belief about the place and its mythological significance. Vendela returns to resume her interaction with the elves of popular belief at a nearby rock – 'the elf stone' – which she believes to be a passageway between the world of humans and the realm of elves, or what Vendela calls 'The Kingdom of the elves'.[16] At the same time as she initiates her offering to the elves, Gerlof starts to read his deceased wife's diary and learns about her relationship with a visitor whom she called '*bytingen*', the local Swedish word for 'changeling', used in folktales for a troll's child left by its troll mother in place of a human child. In both cases, the mythological creatures seem to inhabit an unknown but nearby space beyond the human dwellings at the quarry. Although the first crime, the initial arson, is solved and the circumstances surrounding Gerlof's wife's visitor are clarified, the possible interaction between Vendela and the elves is never given a satisfactory explanation. However, Vendela reaches a sceptical understanding of what she has experienced when she is eventually reunited with her husband Max: 'She no longer believed in the power of the elves. And yet, in their own way, the elves seemed to have granted her wish when it came to Max's heart.'[17]

In the last novel, *Rörgast*, supernatural activities are again part of the crime plot. Most of these are described from a boy's point of view, first by Gerlof as a young teenager in the introductory flashback set in the summer of 1930 and then by the twelve-year-old Jonas Kloss in 1999, the year of the crime story in the novel. In the flashback, Gerlof recollects when as a fourteen-year-old boy he was working as a gravedigger and, together with several other people, heard a knocking sound from the grave of Jonas Kloss' great grandfather, Edvard Kloss. In the present time of the narration, Jonas tries one night to save himself from a sinking rubber boat by climbing on board an anchored cargo ship. On board the ship, he sees zombielike seamen and an axeman. When he escapes the ship and ends up at Gerlof's cottage, he is convinced that he has been on board a ghost ship, especially as there are no traces of the ship the next morning. To Jonas, his experience is connected to a nearby Bronze Age burial site, an uncanny haunted place that appears to be of crucial importance to the mystery of the lost cargo ship and the return of a ghostly killer. A hidden room under the burial site is literally the point of departure for the final catastrophe that hits the Kloss family.

However, in this novel the terror is not, as much as in the former novels, located to a place and its secret space, but more distinctly to the past. Even more than in the other three novels, the distinction between the present and the past is blurred in *Rörgast*. At the very core of the story is Gerlof's uncanny experience at the graveyard when he was a boy. The dead man that was heard knocking in his coffin is the ancestor of young Jonas' family who now owns and runs the tourist-accommodation establishment that seems to be the source and target of organised crime. Yet, the motives of an avenging homecomer actually originate in what took place in the graveyard in 1930. Told in several inserted flashbacks is the story of an abused victim who becomes a relentless pursuer after prolonged exposure to evil. Thus, a chain of events is exposed and what takes place in the present appears to originate in the secrets of the past.

The past haunting the present

As demonstrated above, Theorin's four crime stories set on the island of Öland are founded on supernatural occurrences connected to local sites, popular beliefs and Swedish folk tales. The murder soon appears to be linked to old popular beliefs that lurk below the surface of familiar everyday life in the present time of narration. The disappearance of Gerlof's grandson Jens in *Skumtimmen* first appears to be the doing of the evil spirit of the legendary villain Nils Kant, who according to folk memories is haunting the moorlands of The Great Alvar. The death of Katrine in *Nattfåk* gives the impression of being part of the history of the ill-omened, seemingly cursed, place of the twin lighthouses at Eel Point and the presumed return of its former but now dead inhabitants. What happens in the present at the quarry at Stenvik in *Blodläge* initially seems to be linked to the local folktales about elves and trolls; at first the homecoming Vendela appears to be able to influence her surroundings by offerings to the elves. In *Rörgast*, the present-day crime is linked to two boys' supernatural experiences occuring seventy years apart: the first took place at the churchyard of Marnäs in 1930 and the second at sea outside Gerlof's holiday cottage at Stenvik in 1999.

In addition to affecting the reader emotionally, the uncanny elements highlight certain aspects of the past and the workings of the human mind. The supernatural features direct the reader to note details and relationships that would otherwise have been ignored or deemed of little relevance to the crime plot. For example, in *Blodläge* Vendela's gifts to the elves make the reader pay attention to whether her wishes come true and perhaps also search for a natural or psychological explanation when they do. In *Nattfåk*, the depiction of a Christmas present that widower Joakim buys and leaves in the sealed-up room for his killed wife makes the reader pay special attention to the pale-green fabric, which Joakim later finds close to his wife's grave and which makes him feel 'a sudden icy chill down his back'.[18] In this way, the narration directs the reader to consider the existence of phenomena not acknowledged and recognised by modern science and ideology, and also to take into account to what extent a person's belief in them might influence his or her perception and behaviour, as well as produce both fear and desire that may direct that person's future actions. In some cases, the supernatural elements highlight moral aspects of life and death, as for example in *Nattfåk* when Joakim discovers the hidden part of the barn, the prayer room for the dead and the objects left in it. His relationship to death and a possible afterlife changes. When he enters the hidden room, he also enters into another dimension of reality or supernatural order. During Christmas, when he visits the room to leave a Christmas gift for his dead wife, a green tunic, he not only notices but also accepts the presence of his dead wife Katrine:

> Out of the corner of his eye he saw that a shadow with a pale face had stopped beside his bench, and was standing there motionless.
> 'Katrine?' whispered Joakim, without daring to turn his head.
> The shadow slowly sat down beside him on the bench.
> 'Katrine,' he whispered again.
> Tentatively he groped in the darkness and his fingers brushed against another hand. It was stiff and ice-cold when he took hold of it.
> 'I'm here now,' he whispered.
> There was no reply. The figure bent its head, as if in prayer.[19]

Joakim's ghostly experiences in the sealed-up room also makes him re-evaluate his bond to both his dead sister and his wife, and his reconciliation also results in the revelation of important information about their lives and deaths. In the end, his unearthly experiences in the memorial room for the dead save him and his children from being robbed and burnt to death.

However, the supernatural manifestations of an older order may also encourage the reader to imagine the darkest possible outcome, as for example in *Skumtimmen* when Julia, the mother of the missing boy, enters the deserted house that once belonged to the villain Nils Kant's mother. In the house, Julia immediately feels a cold presence of something waiting for her. By the dark window, she discerns an old woman who immediately rises from her chair and moves towards her. Although Julia tries to escape, she feels the woman's hatred as a hard shove against her back. Before she falls downstairs and loses her consciousness, she hears in her mind the old woman's words: 'He deceived me!'[20] What these ominous words refer to, neither Julia nor the reader discovers until the very end of the novel. Nevertheless, they create an uncanny connection between Julia and Nils Kant's mother and thereby also between their sons, the six-year-old Jens and the callous murderer Nils Kant.

Theorin's use of Gothic elements stresses that humans are part of a specific geographically and socially defined location and its history. They are bound to the history of a certain place rather than just confined to their individual life cycle; as individuals, they are linked to a chain of events in history and their topographical and cultural origin. Hence, the focus is not so much on the investigation of the crime that is committed in the present time of narration, as on its historical background and local context. Gerlof's detective work highlights the history of the island and its local customs, and what takes place in the present is incorporated in a complex network of events. Certain parts of the novels, such as the subplot about the burglar Henrik and his mystical experiences in *Nattfåk* or the one about Vendela's offerings to the elves in *Blodläge*, are at first not linked to the crime that has been committed or its investigation. However, the Gothic elements of the subplots are always and instantly connected to a place and its nearby or hidden Gothic space of both previous transgressions and coming evil, that is, the final crimes in the novels. Thereby, the supernatural occurrences provide the investigators – and Gerlof in particular – with important information. It is also because of these warnings that it is often possible for Gerlof to prevent the last intended crime.

The subplots also influence the investigation of the main crime, a suspected or confirmed murder, in other ways. Besides the murderer, there are several other criminals in action, such as the burglars in *Nattfåk* and the thief Lisa in *Rörgast*. The novels also portray villains who might not commit legally defined crimes, but who still act unscrupulously, such as Vendela's bullying husband Max in *Blodläge* and the treasure hunter Anders Hagman in *Skumtimmen*. The main crime in the present time of narration is also influenced by crimes committed in the past, such as Nils Kant's killings in *Skumtimmen* and Vendela's father's insurance fraud in *Blodläge*. Many of the wrongdoings both in the past and the present time of narration are linked to the background of the victims and the murderers. They also create an eerie connection between past and present actions that questions rather than restores any imagined continuity between past and present and the concept of a linear temporality. The supernatural manifestations in particular confirm another order, not a linear history of events but a timeless or eternal cyclic order, and occasionally a reversed causality where the present influences the past, as well as the other way around. Thus, the interplay between past and present not only displaces and confronts contemporary social concerns and a realistic mode of representation, but also challenges Gothic conventions as such.

As in most Gothic stories, there is in Theorin's novels a haunting past, but the true evil is not primarily located in the past but in the present. The events in the present are linked to deeds in the past but in comparison to what once happened, the present crimes far exceed the previous wrongdoings in terms of transgressive cruelty and devious planning. The spectral returns of past scenes of violence and tragedy are thus there mainly to enhance the atmosphere of terror, often by highlighting the unreliable mode of focalisation and by targeting the metaphorical or psychological aspects of the representation. They are also there to throw the detective off track from the crime investigation in the present time of narration; the reported supernatural occurrences direct Gerlof – and the reader – to find clues that might be of importance for the general background of the crime but not for finding the murderer. In *Skumtimmen*, for example, the present-time narration is frequently punctuated by flashbacks connected to the story of Nils Kant, thereby directing the reader's attention to the rumour of his return to the island, while the men guilty of the disappearance of the boy Jens and the death of the stonemason Ernst are kept out of sight. When the present murderer and his accomplices are finally exposed, their motives and action appear even more malevolent and devious than any crime ever committed by the disowned offender in the past, that is, Nils Kant. By using the story about Nils Kant as a terrifying background, the unscrupulous planning and merciless crimes of the present-time murderer are magnified.

In that way, the flashbacks are there to anticipate more hideous terrors in the present time of narration as a consequence of a modern lifestyle on Öland, that is, mainly capitalist exploitation and commercial interests. As most Gothic stories, Theorin's novels take their bearings from the modern conditions of change; they demonstrate how modernity, today's industrial and urban society and its economic and technological procedures shape both individual humans and monsters at the same time. In the end, the real threat to the protagonists and the society of Öland is not the individual killers but certain aspects of modernity, and in particular the exploitation of the island by the tourist industry. The true criminals are all capitalist usurpers, such as the leading members of the Kloss family, who run a thriving tourist-accommodation establishment in *Rörgast*, and the hotel and restaurant owner Gunnar Ljung, who has made a fortune by stealing land from poor people to sell at a high price in *Skumtimmen*. These capitalists and businesspeople are selling out the island and its local attractions to wealthy tourists from the mainland, especially from the Swedish capital of Stockholm. Even the minor villains operating on the island in the present time of narration arrive from the mainland to exploit the assets of the island. In *Nattfåk*, two callous burglars from the mainland have a hold on a local craftsman, Henrik, as an accomplice, in order to identify holiday homes worth breaking into; and in *Rörgast*, the thief who specialises in robbing drunken tourists is a visiting musician and disc jockey from the mainland. The master criminals are, however, always local businesspeople and entrepreneurs who have turned their back on the local inhabitants and their traditional way of life. Thus, the main threat is, to some extent, the bridge connecting the idyll of Öland to the mainland and an urban way of life that represents commercial excess.

Modernity and transgression

Johan Theorin's realistic depiction of a modern crime investigation in combination with metaphorical images of supernatural elements, creates narratives that enact an uncanny return of the repressed and the revival of outmoded superstition and supernatural causes. As with most Gothic, his Öland quartet series explores the return of the past. At the beginning, the evil haunting the present seems to be located in a nowadays forgotten or unfamiliar space beyond or within historically or socially significant local places. However, during the crime investigation, the true terror and evil appear to be located not in the past but in the present. Compared to the present murders, the wrongdoings in the past appear as unfortunate coincidences or acts of God rather than as planned acts of evil by a cunning malicious mind. The exposure of certain aspects of the past of Öland places the reader in what resembles an anthropological or ethnographical position in relation to the actions depicted. On the one hand, the stories are set in a familiar location on Öland, an emblem of sunny summer holidays to most Swedes. On the other hand, the crimes committed unravel activities in the past and peculiarities in the local landscape and society that turn the reader into an observer of a *terra incognita* of human behaviour and an alien realm of myth and seemingly supernatural forces. Although the aim of the crime investigation is to detect and demystify, the unravelling of hidden secrets and motives also result in mystification and a move from the known to the unknown, in a way that exposes incomprehensible forces in nature and in human beings, both in the past and the present.

According to Fred Botting, Gothic writing is characterised by excess and transgression; for example, an excess of obscurity that shadows the progress of rationality and modernity with disturbing counter-narratives, as well as an excessive display of the horrors of transgression in order to assert certain social and moral values.[21] In Theorin's novels, the transgressive acts are always related to time, the return of the repressed past in the present, as well as the reverse: the exaggeration of present transgression against the background of past misbehaviour. Unlike most Nordic Gothic of today, Theorin's stories do not highlight the same kind of environmental issues as, for example, Sigurðardóttir's Icelandic crime stories and the Swedish TV drama *Jordskott*,[22] nor do they address postcolonial issues, as do these stories and many contemporary Nordic horror films, such as the Norwegian films *Thale* and *Troll Hunter*.[23] Instead, the novels are set in an open rural landscape and the fear-provoking threat is not an avenging nature, its colonised native population or its nature beings. Instead, the true terror is the transgression of modern commercial greed. Thus, Theorin's novels represent that kind of Gothic story that some Marxist Gothic scholars, such as David Punter, would claim centre on issues of social anxiety connected with class and capitalism. [24] Theorin's Öland novels stress the tyranny of today's free tourist enterprise and the ways in which obsessive avarice turn people into offenders. His true monsters are thus always people with commercial interests belonging to the native population and therefore working from a stable position within the local community.

As most Gothic, Theorin's novels are what William Patrick Day calls – drawing on Northrop Frye's seminal work *The Secular Scripture* – 'a fable of identity fragmented and destroyed beyond repair, a fable of the impossibility of identity'.[25] However, in the end, it is not one of the criminals but the detective Gerlof who illustrates what Day names 'the theme of descent'.[26] Eighty-year-old Gerlof is the protagonist who progressively moves from a higher to a lower world, from the natural world of today to the underworld of the past, not in search of a lost identity, but losing identity as his crime investigation makes him confront the gloomier aspects of his society and his private life. He is not only growing older with a decaying and ailing body, but during his detective work in the four novels he also loses his oldest and best friends. When he is trying to prevent the final catastrophe in the last novel, *Rörgast*, he does it by sacrificing his bosom friend, his companion and former mate John Hagman, who has been a dear friend since he started to sail as a young skipper on his cargo boat. Like for most Gothic heroes, there is no real ascent from the underworld for Gerlof. Not even death is offered as an escape for him. Instead – on the last pages of the final novel – he must return to life and thereby he eventually becomes an embodiment of torment and bereavement.

Thus, Theorin's Gothic crime novels defy any simple resolution. His novels can be claimed to combine fidelity to nature with mystery and imagination, the way that Walpole proposed in his preface to the second edition of *The Castle of Otranto* in 1764. Theorin's novels question rather than restore any imagined division between life and death, past and present, nature and culture, reason and passion in order to examine the limitations of reason and today's rational and secular world view. His criminals are to some extent examples of Gothic characters that shadow the progress of enlightenment with counter-narratives that expose the dark side of modernity, something many scholars have seen as the main theme of Gothic.[27] The superstitious and mythological past of Öland lingers forcefully in the present, and when the crime is eventually solved some of the supernatural aspects of the events are never rationally explained; they leave a sense of uncertainty and irresolution about what influenced what. As the murdered woman's husband Joakim tells Gerlof: 'Before we came here, I didn't believe the dead could come back… but now I don't know what to be believe. A number of remarkable things have happened here.'[28] At the end of *Skummtimmen*, the reader, just like Joakim, is left with a feeling that uncanny and paranormal forces are embedded in the natural world of today, as well as in the modern human mind. That kind of nagging ambiguity is the very essence of Johan Theorin's Gothic crime novels.

Notes

1 For an investigation of Gothic elements in early Nordic crime stories, see Y. Leffler, 'Early Crime Fiction in Nordic Literature', in M. Ascari and S. Knight (eds), *From the Sublime to City Crime* (Monaco: Liber Faber, 2015), pp. 161–82.

2 H. Walpole, *The Castle of Otranto: A Gothic Story*, ed. with intro. by W. S. Lewis and notes by J. W. Reed, Jr. (Oxford, New York: Oxford University Press, 1984), pp. 7–8.

3 For a topofocal definition applied on fantasy, see S. Ekman, *Writing Worlds, Reading Landscapes: An Exploration of Setting in Fantasy*, diss. (Lund University: Centre for language and literature, 2010), p. 12.

4 Y.-F. Tuan, *Space and Place: The Perspective of Experience* (London: Edward Arnold, 1977); Y.-F. Tuan, 'Space and Place: Humanistic Perspective', in S. Gale and G. Olsson (eds), *Philosophy in Geography* (Dolrecht: cop, 1979), pp. 387–427. Although Tuan uses the same distinction in *Landscape of Fear*, here he writes: '"Landscape of fear" refers both to psychological states and to actual tangible environments.' *Landscapes of Fear* (Oxford: Basil Blackwell, 1979), p. 6.

5 Space and place are often used without a clear distinction to cover different aspects of setting, as in the anthology by L. Phillips and A. Witchard (eds), *London Gothic:*

Place, Space and the Gothic Imagination (London and New York: Continuum Literary Studies, 2010). Gothic topography is used to explore location in relation to national and geographical traditions, as in P. M. Mehtonen and M. Savolainen (eds), *Gothic Topographies: Language, Nation Building and 'Race'* (Farnham and Burlington: Ashgate, 2013); and in 'Part II: Gothic Locations', in C. Spooner and E. McEvoy (eds), *The Routledge Companion to the Gothic* (London and New York; Routledge, 2007), pp. 49–124. A distinction between heterotopic or disciplinary place and Gothic space is made by C. D. Edelson, *Siting Horror: Place and Space in American Gothic Fiction*, diss. (University of California Riverside, 2007). Different categories of space are explored in A. H. von der Lippe (ed.), *Dark Cartographies: Exploring Gothic Spaces* (Oxford: Inter-Disciplinary Press, 2013).
6   *Johan Theorin.* johantheorin.com. Accessed 21 October 2018.
7   J. Theorin, *The Darkest Room*, trans. M. Delargy (London: Doubleday, 2009), p. 5.
8   Theorin, *The Darkest Room*, p. 254.
9   Theorin, *The Darkest Room*, p. 6.
10 See, in particular, Mehtonen and Savolainen (eds), *Gothic Topographies*; 'Part II: Gothic Locations', in C. Spooner and E. McEvoy (eds), *The Routledge Companion to Gothic*, pp. 51–123.
11 Tuan, *Space and Place*, pp. 3–18; Tuan, 'Space and Place: Humanistic Perspective', pp. 387–427.
12 Tuan, *Space and Place*, p. 6.
13 About mythical space, see Tuan, *Space and Place*, pp. 86–7.
14 J. Theorin, *Echoes from the Dead*, trans. M. Delargy (London: Doubleday, 2008), pp. 7–8.
15 Theorin, *The Darkest Room*, p. 10.
16 J. Theorin, *The Quarry*, trans. M. Delargy (London: Doubleday, 2011), pp. 104, 109 *et passim*.
17 Theorin, *The Quarry*, p. 403.
18 Theorin, *The Darkest Room*, p. 184.
19 Theorin, *The Darkest Room*, p. 343.
20 Theorin, *Echoes from the Dead*, p. 227.
21 F. Botting, *Gothic* (London and New York: Routledge, 1996), pp. 1–23.
22 About environmental themes in *Jordskott*, see H. Mäntymäki, *Epistemologies of (Un)sustainability in Swedish Crime Series Jordskott* (Green Letters: Studies in Ecocriticism, 2017) www.tandfonline.com/doi/full/10.1080/14688417.2017.1415159.
23 See J. Höglund, 'Revenge of the Trolls. Norwegian (Post) Colonial Gothic', *Edda*, 104:2, 2017, pp. 115–29; www.idunn.no/edda/2017/02/revenge_of_the_trolls.
24 D. Punter, *The Literature of Terror. A History of Gothic Fiction from 1765 to the Present Day* (London: Longman, 1980).
25 W. P. Day, *In the Circles of Fear and Desire: A Study of Gothic Fantasy* (Chicago and London: The University of Chicago Press, 1985), p. 6.
26 Day, *In the Circles of Fear and Desire*, p. 6.
27 Botting, *Gothic*, p. 23.
28 Theorin, *The Darkest Room*, p. 234.

5

Maria Holmgren Troy

'The Chosen Ones': Sara B. Elfgren and Mats Strandberg's teenage witch trilogy

The first novel in Mats Strandberg and Sara B. Elfgren's Engelsfors trilogy, *Cirkeln* (2011), was eagerly awaited and received a great deal of attention in the Swedish press. Indeed, one newspaper article with the heading '"Cirkeln" – en svensk "Twilight"?' ('"The Circle" – a Swedish "Twilight"?') informs the public about the novel already being an international success before it was released: the month before it hit the Swedish market the translation rights had been sold to publishers in Great Britain, Germany, Denmark and Norway, and a Swedish film version was already underway.[1] Four years later, the entire trilogy – *Cirkeln* (2011), *Eld* (2012) and *Nyckeln* (2013) – was available in English translation as *The Circle* (2012), *Fire* (2013) and *The Key* (2015), among a number of translations into other languages. Together with Danish Lene Kaaberbøl's novels in the *Vildheks* (*Wildwitch*) series for younger readers,[2] *Cirkeln* can be seen as part of a twenty-first century Nordic Gothic trend focusing on young witches in a Nordic setting. For young adult and older readers, the Engelsfors trilogy is arguably the prime example of this trend.[3]

The newspaper article mentioned above frames *Cirkeln* and the whole projected trilogy in terms of recent American and British fantasy book series that have also been adapted into films: J. K. Rowling's books about Harry Potter (1997–2007), Stephenie Meyer's Twilight novels (2005–2008) and Suzanne Collins's Hunger Games trilogy (2008–2010). However, rather than mentioning any of these, Strandberg is quoted as stressing the love that he and Elfgren share for the American TV series *Buffy the Vampire Slayer* (1997–2003), *My So-Called Life* (1994–1995) and *Twin Peaks* (1990–1991), as well as the Swedish movie *Fucking Åmål*

(1998; *Show Me Love*, 1999).[4] Regarding interest from 20th Century Fox, among others, in the rights to an American remake, Strandberg suggests that it is probably 'thanks to Stieg Larsson and John Ajvide Lindqvist that Sweden is so interesting abroad at the moment'.[5] Larsson's Millennium trilogy (2005–2007), the epitome of Nordic Noir, spawned both Swedish and American film adaptations, as did Lindqvist's celebrated vampire novel *Låt den rätte komma in* (2004; *Let the Right One In*, 2007). Film adaptations of a popular novel or series of novels obviously represent one kind of circulation of Gothic across media and national boundaries.

This chapter, however, primarily examines Gothic aspects of the Engelsfors trilogy with an emphasis on the Nordic setting and the employment of a collective protagonist. The different aspects under scrutiny are the use of focalisation, the Gothic plot, the place of witchcraft, the school as a place of evil, doppelgängers and divided selves, and having and sharing power. In addition, although authors may not always be the most reliable sources regarding their own works, I follow the lead of Strandberg's comments and relate the trilogy to TV series and films from the 1990s, in particular to *Buffy the Vampire Slayer*. That Elfgren and Strandberg should name a number of TV series and films from the 1990s as the main inspiration for the trilogy makes eminent sense: they were teenagers during that decade. The English-language editions of the first novel actually carry the authors' dedication 'to our teenage selves'. So, answering the question of whether the Engelsfors trilogy is a Swedish *Twilight* (or *Harry Potter* or *Hunger Games*),[6] I believe, is less relevant than comparing it to *Buffy*. Albeit not the main focus of this chapter, this comparison will help pinpoint some of the similarities and differences in Nordic and American varieties of Gothic which focus on teenagers and young adults.

Elfgren has actually called the trilogy 'kitchen-sink fantasy',[7] emphasising the particular genre hybridity that it shares with Lindqvist's vampire novel: a combination of dark social realism and supernatural elements. The merging in Scandinavian fiction of social realism with Gothic fantasy (or the paranormal), Olu Jenzen suggests, 'provides the latter with a possibility to retain strong mimetic qualities, yet interrogate realism's ideological gesture.'[8] She explains that the 'genre of social realism, or realism in its critical form, has at its heart the idea of recording life on the social margins, foregrounding authenticity as a politicised mode'; it developed in the Scandinavian countries in the early twentieth century 'in tandem with the tradition of working-class literature' and was related to 'the development of the Scandinavian modern welfare state'.[9] This welfare state and 'its legacy' are scrutinised in *Låt den rätte komma in* and the Engelsfors trilogy, which 'express a sentiment of disillusion with the "Swedish Model"', which is linked in these novels to the idea of homogeneity and the policing of differences.[10] As Maria Nilson points out, *Cirkeln* repeatedly returns to what it means to break the conventions of normality in a small Swedish town.[11] What is 'normal' here – like in *Fucking Åmål*, set in an even smaller Swedish town, and *My So-Called Life*, set in a fictional Pittsburgh suburb – has to do with issues of class, age, gender, sex and sexual orientation, as well as peer pressure and the expectations of parents, teachers and other adult figures.

Although the focus in this chapter is on the novels, similar to the Buffyverse, the World of Engelsfors is a transmedial storyworld; to date it consists of *The World of Engelsfors* website, the comic book *Berättelser från Engelsfors* (2013; *Tales from Engelsfors*) with eight tie-in stories, the Swedish film adaptation of *Cirkeln* (2015), fan fiction and fan art.[12] Like *Buffy*, the Engelsfors trilogy is set in a small town where the senior high or upper-secondary school ('*gymnasiet*' in Swedish) is the natural setting for the teenage protagonists and also serves as the Gothic focal point of evil. In both *Buffy* and the Engelsfors trilogy, the school year is used as a structural device or frame: one season or novel more or less encompasses one school year. Moreover, the teenage protagonists are repeatedly faced with the task of saving the world in addition to maturing and working out their relationships to each other and to other people. However, there are also significant differences, some of which have to do with the sustained focus on a group of teenage witches in the Swedish novels, while others are related to the specific Swedish historical, cultural and social settings.

'Female and multiple': focalisation in the Engelsfors trilogy

David Punter proposes that 'on the whole, witches are female and multiple',[13] and I would argue that the Engelsfors trilogy gives ample support for that proposition in a particularly Nordic context; although internally fraught, the main character of this trilogy is a collective: the Circle or the Chosen Ones. The trilogy does not focus on an individual protagonist, or even on a young protagonist surrounded by friends and helpers, which is the case in recent Gothic crossover productions such as *Buffy* and *Harry Potter*, which tellingly feature the name of the singular

Chosen One in their titles. Shifting focalisation is employed throughout the trilogy and this narrative technique is highly effective since it emphasises that the witch protagonists are multiple, as well as giving the reader access to very different points of view and the dreams, desires and fears of the characters that form the Circle.

At the beginning of *Cirkeln*, the seven protagonists who constitute the Circle are introduced: Elias, Minoo, Vanessa, Anna-Karin, Rebecka, Linnéa and Ida. The narration in *Cirkeln* is focalised through the first five, and primarily through Minoo, Vanessa and Anna-Karin. Elias is killed at school in the first chapter and less than one third into the novel Rebecka is killed by being pushed off the roof of the school. In both cases, it looks like suicide, but since their deaths are focalised through Elias and Rebecka, the reader knows that is not the case. The focalisation in the second novel, *Eld*, alternates between all of the surviving Chosen Ones. This also means that we learn more about Elias, since he was Linnéa's best friend and the reader now has access to her point of view, including her memories. Linnéa, the alienated Goth girl who lives on her own in an apartment provided by the social services,[14] and Ida, the popular leader at school and a bourgeoise bully, are the most antagonistic members of the Circle. The events in this novel take place from the end of the summer to Easter the next year; that is, it does not cover the entire second school year. Ida is killed at the end of this novel, further reducing the number of surviving Chosen Ones.

The last novel, *Nyckeln*, begins with a section entitled 'The Borderland', and these sections recur throughout the novel. Most of these sections are focalised through Ida, who first encounters Matilda (a witch who was burned in the 1600s) in a realm between the living and the dead, and later Elias, who also serves as a focaliser, as does Rebecka late in the novel. Time and space work differently in this realm; Ida, who is frantically running through the Borderland, is sometimes thrown back in history and to other regions of the world where she observes the fate of earlier Chosen Ones. Sometimes she also glimpses current activities and overhears conversations in which she tries in vain to participate as she temporarily arrives at different places related to the other Chosen Ones in her circle. These sections – which are interspersed between the numbered sections that are focalised through the four living Chosen Ones and sometimes Anna-Karin's familiar, a fox – also work to fast-forward parts of the story set in the present, which begins where *Eld* ended and ends on graduation day in early summer the following year.

Plotting the trilogy: major Gothic storylines and events

On a night when the moon appears to be blood red, the six teenage girls are mysteriously drawn to Kärrgruvan, a dilapidated fairground with a dance pavilion. The amnesiac school caretaker, Nicolaus, is there, looking for the Chosen One who is supposed to lead the fight against evil and prevent the apocalypse and whom he is ready to guide. He is shocked when he realises that there are six Chosen Ones instead of one. The six form an unlikely circle with little or nothing in common, but they have to try to cooperate in order to survive and carry out their mission. After Rebecka's death they are informed by the school's principal, Adriana Lopez, a witch working for the Council (an organisation that regulates the use of magic) that they are witches important in the struggle against the demons that want to destroy the world. All of them, apart from Minoo, have magic powers that belong to one of six elements (air, earth, fire, water, metal and wood), powers that have already manifested themselves in Vanessa's invisibility, Anna-Karin's power to control others, Rebecka's pyro- and telekinetic powers, Ida's ability to serve as a medium and Linnéa's ability to read minds. While struggling with their own problems at home and at school, with their loves and animosities and with each other, they are training in secret with Nicolaus to refine and strengthen their magic powers. They are also meeting with the principal – who has introduced them to the *Book of Patterns* through which entities called the guardians are supposed to communicate with them.

Towards the end of *Cirkeln*, the five Chosen Ones discover that Max, a young maths teacher with whom Minoo is in love and who loves her, is the demons' Blessed One and the murderer; by killing them, he has managed to appropriate the powers of Elias (shape-shifting) and Rebecka. Minoo's relationship with Max is a variation on what Christine Jarvis describes as 'the horror story centred on the schoolgirl with the dangerous boyfriend'.[15] The battle against Max involves all of the Chosen Ones and takes place in school, which is repeatedly singled out as a place of evil. Minoo manages to overpower him as she discovers her own magical powers, which like his take the form of black smoke. This novel ends with the five of them visiting Elias' and Rebecka's graves on the last day of school before the summer vacation.

Eld is characterised by an increase of Gothic motifs, but also by a greater focus on realistic relationships with and between parents. At the beginning Nicolaus' familiar, a scruffy one-eyed cat, leads Linnéa to Nicolaus' grave. After the Chosen Ones have dug it up Nicolaus recovers his memory; he is more than 400 years old and the father of Matilda, who was burned alive at the stake in the 1600s and who communicates with the Chosen Ones through dreams and through Ida in her capacity as a medium. The school, as well as the rest of Engelsfors, is increasingly caught up in a positive-attitude self-help movement called Positive Engelsfors, initiated by Elias' parents. The Chosen Ones worry about the sect-like character of this movement and at the movement's Spring Revel there is an attempt at mass human sacrifice, which they manage to prevent but not without another great loss: Ida dies while saving everybody else. The novel ends with Ida's funeral seen through her own eyes.

Nyckeln is very much concerned with power, both magical power and the power of different kinds of love. In this novel, the supernatural activity in Engelsfors increases exponentially and reaches a crescendo. Olivia, who is the demons' Blessed One and behind the murders and attempted human sacrifice in *Eld*, returns to Engelsfors stronger than ever before, but she is stopped by Vanessa. Walter Hjorth, the chair of the Council and a very powerful witch, gathers an alternative circle of witches that he believes will be able to become the Key to close the portal and stop the apocalypse instead of the Chosen Ones. He recruits Minoo, whose magical powers are unique, and she starts to train with Walter's circle.

While Minoo is occupied with the alternative circle, the rest of the Chosen Ones together with Nicolaus and three other friends, two of whom are witches with newly discovered powers, search through tunnels and caves under Engelsfors and finally find the portal, which like Hellmouth in *Buffy* is located directly under the school. Portents, one for each element, signal that the portal will open soon and the demons will enter and cause the apocalypse unless the Chosen Ones or Walter's circle manages to close it. It ultimately becomes clear that only the Chosen Ones can close the portal and that the guardians have misled and lied to them as well as to Walter to serve their own purposes. In order to close the portal, the living Chosen Ones must join the dead in the Borderland to complete the Circle and become the Key. After closing the portal – time being different in the Borderland – saying goodbye to Elias, Ida and Rebecka before they pass on means that Vanessa, Linnéa, Anna-Karin and Minoo are missing from October until graduation day in June in Engelsfors. They return to an Engelsfors where elemental magic is even stronger than before, but where the magic of the demons and guardians is gone. The Council is still a power to reckon with and

Adriana is organising the resistance, which may include, in addition to many witches, the now entirely non-magical Minoo, who is told that she has other powers.

The place of witchcraft

Comparing the geographical setting of the Engelsfors trilogy with that of *Buffy* highlights the particularity of the kind of Nordic Gothic that Elfgren calls 'kitchen-sink fantasy', a mixture of social realism and Gothic that comments relentlessly on social issues as it exposes the Gothic aspects of school and family life. The fictive town Engelsfors – which is loosely modelled on Fagersta, where Strandberg grew up,[16] and located in relation to actual Swedish towns mentioned in the trilogy such as Västerås, Örebro and Borlänge – is very different to the fictive demon-infested but otherwise bourgeois setting of Sunnydale, which is supposed to be located north of Los Angeles and is reminiscent of Santa Barbara.[17] Something that they have in common, though, in addition to a more hellish than usual high school, are their ironic designations. Although certainly sunny during the daytime, as the focal point of evil and darkness, Sunnydale belies the paradisiacal connotations of its name; it is far from what can be expected of a sunny dale in California. The name Engelsfors consists of the words 'angels' (*ängels*) and 'rapids' (*fors*), but angels are both literally and metaphorically absent in this town threatened by demons, where human bullies of different ages often have the upper hand. As Minoo sums it up at the beginning of the trilogy: 'Pretty name, shitty town'.[18]

Located in the middle of Sweden, in an area called Bergslagen (the Swedish 'rust belt'), Engelsfors is a small town characterised by post-industrial gloom and decline: 'Out in the middle of nowhere, surrounded by deep forests where people often lose their way and disappear. Thirteen thousand inhabitants and high unemployment. The steel works closed down twenty-five years ago.'[19] The caves and tunnels explored by the Chosen Ones in *Nyckeln* are remnants from centuries of mining and iron works, as are names such as '*Dammsjön*' (the dam lake) and '*Kärrgruvan*' (the bog mine). In contemporary Engelsfors, the only industry mentioned is Ida's father's sawmill, which burns down after her death and is not rebuilt;[20] Ida's family instead chooses to leave Engelsfors. Recent attempts at boosting service industries are shown as failures: the old manor house has been converted into a hotel, but failed to attract tourists, much to insular Engelsforsers' unconcealed glee, and the city mall is more or less abandoned. It opened six years ago, but '[n]ow there is nothing there but shuttered shops and Sture & Co., hangout of choice for all the local drunks. The entire building sits in constant gloom because no one can be bothered to replace the light bulbs in the ceiling'.[21] It is in this gloomy mall, Mona Moonbeam sets up her shop, the Crystal Cave, in which she tells people's fortunes and sells new age paraphernalia, and where the Chosen Ones can purchase ectoplasm and sometimes try to procure the help of this older, eccentric witch. Mona Moonbeam represents the figure of 'the witch as chancer, [as] probable charlatan'.[22] Similar to Anya, the ex-vengeance demon in *Buffy* who is employed by Buffy's Watcher Giles when he opens his magic shop, Mona has a well-developed business sense and embraces capitalism. This overly tanned, chain-smoking middle-aged witch, with a 1980s' taste in fashion is, however, far from the physically youthful and attractive Anya.

Although situated in a province called Västmanland, Engelsfors is relatively close to Dalarna, one of the provinces in Sweden where the persecution of witches raged most intensely between 1668 and 1676.[23] There are resonances with historical witch hunts in the trilogy that for obvious reasons are missing in *Buffy*'s California, located far from Salem. The trilogy alludes to the Swedish historical witch hunts and trials through the fate of Nicolaus' daughter Matilda, who was the Chosen One in Engelsfors in the 1600s but gave up her elemental magic powers instead of trying to close the portal. Despite her firm conviction that a future Chosen One would be able to take her place and defeat the demons once and for all, the Council regarded this relinquishing of magic powers as a betrayal. As Nicolaus tells the Chosen Ones, 'In those days, witch-hunting was at its height in this country. It goes without saying that no real witches were affected. That is, except those who the Council wanted to dispose of', which included Matilda. He goes on to tell them that in Sweden, 'the practice was to behead convicted witches first and to burn the body afterwards. But Matilda was marched straight to the pyre and tied to the stake...'.[24] While she is burned alive, her mother, Nicolaus' wife, throws herself on the pyre and burns to death with her.

Another particularly Nordic Gothic aspect is the forest, which comes across as a living and, in *Eld*, dying entity with its own sinister agency. 'Every single child in Engelsfors learns that "you should stick to the forest paths"'.[25] Maps and compasses do not work in this 'forest that seems somehow larger when you are in it than when you look at it from the outside' and '[s]everal people disappeared without a trace during Anna-Karin's childhood'. For Anna-Karin, who has lived on a farm and had to go by bus to school in Engelsfors where she has been relentlessly bullied, the forest felt like a safe place until the abnormally hot summer at the beginning of *Eld* when she notices the absence of birdsong and the buzzing of insects and for 'the first time feels the typical Engelsfors response to the forest: a sense of unease'.[26] A dead tree that resembles a human being suddenly appears to the hot, thirsty and slightly dizzy Anna-Karin who thinks, 'Obviously, that's ridiculous. Trees don't sneak up on you. Let alone dead trees', but she leaves the path and finds other dead trees: 'It is not only the drought that is killing the forest, she realizes, without knowing how she knows. The forest is dying for another reason.'[27]

'School is a place of evil'[28]

School has become an increasingly common Gothic setting in Swedish young adult and crossover fiction since the publication of *Cirkeln* in 2011. Two examples are Elfgren's 2017 novel *Norra Latin*, a ghost story that carries the name of an upper-secondary school in Stockholm as its title, and Magnus Nordin's *Djävulens märke* (2018; *The Devil's Sign*) about a rowdy secondary-school class and a demonic supply teacher.

The Engelsfors trilogy obviously follows the example set by *Buffy* in making literal what many teenagers experience: 'High school is hell'.[29] Joss Whedon, creator of the TV series, explains its popularity with 'the central myth of high school as horrific'. In *Buffy*, as Whedon puts it, '[t]he humiliation, the alienation, the confusion of high school is taken to such great proportions that it becomes demonic'.[30] In her article 'School is Hell: Gendered Fears in Teenage Horror', Jarvis argues that the school setting is 'so integral to the fears' in horror stories aimed at teenagers 'that its significance often goes unnoticed'.[31] She suggests that schools in this kind of fiction, of which *Buffy* is her prime example, often have traits that resonate with those of the Gothic mansion: 'dark echoing corridors, secret rooms and, especially, underworlds – mysterious basements or tunnels undermining the superficially secure institutions'.[32] I would add that the school as a Gothic setting has these aspects in common with the hospital in productions such as Lars von Trier's Danish TV series *Riget* (*Kingdom*, 1994, 1997) and Stephen King's American adaptation, *Kingdom Hospital* (2004), which I discuss in Chapter 8.

Schools and hospitals in the Nordic countries are generally public institutions that are part of the tax-funded welfare system; accordingly, the school in Engelsfors is run by the local municipal government.[33] There is no choice of school in the area, which adds to the claustrophobic, oppressive atmosphere in the sense that it is impossible for students who are considered different in one way or another to put some distance between themselves and their persecutors and to find a more congenial context when they move on from secondary to upper-secondary school. Schools, as Jarvis notes, 'are mini-societies, not mini-families', which means that the schoolgirl in the teen Gothic narrative does not have a given 'role' – 'the bride, daughter or dependent relative of the gothic novel' – or place, but instead must negotiate one for herself with all of the tensions, anxieties and fears that such sexualised and gendered negotiations in this 'wider community' and terrifying setting entail.[34] At the beginning of *Cirkeln*, while taking the bus to school, 'which is oddly distant from the town centre', Vanessa muses on it being like 'a prison, isolated from the rest of civilisation'.[35] Profoundly alienated from her schoolmates, Minoo, who diverges from the norm in Engelsfors by being a brilliant and committed student, thinks that '[c]oming to school is like being deported to an alien planet – every day'.[36] On the night of the blood-red moon at Kärrgruvan, when Ida serves as a medium for the first time, the Chosen Ones are informed by Matilda that school 'is a place of evil', [37] which is not news to most of them. The day after, there is a crack right through the middle of the schoolyard: 'It's not very wide, but it winds from the soccer field to the dead trees'.[38] This crack is an early physical sign that indicates that the forces of evil are stirring beneath.

As is repeatedly demonstrated in *Buffy*, where the high school is located directly on top of Hellmouth, school in contemporary horror stories 'is also the place where the control schools should exert breaks down... Forces of chaos break through the very fabric of the school building, demonstrating the ultimate inability of the adult world and its rules to protect young people'.[39] It is in the school that the battle against Max takes place; the school is also the site of Positive Engelsfors' Spring Revel and the attempted mass human sacrifice. In *Nyckeln*, school is the site of the portents tied to the different signs announcing the impending apocalypse; indeed, the portent connected to the air element actually means that the school temporarily disappears: 'All [Elias] can see is a large, dark triangle in the snow. As if a giant has removed the entire building'.[40] Another and particularly disgusting portent is when the food in the school cafeteria turns into maggots:

> When [Ida] looks around, the maggots are everywhere. They well up over the edges of the hot food containers. Crawl across the tables.
> At one of the tables, someone is throwing up noisily. Several more follow suit. Others spit out porridgy mouthfuls of chewed food and maggots.
> The large room is filling with a stench, a heavy smell of rotting. Of *death*.[41]

This portent, which is related to the element of wood, is witnessed by the deceased Ida in one of the Borderland sections, whereas both she and Elias, who also dwells in the Borderland, see the school disappearing and reappearing.[42]

The earth-element portent, causing everybody in school to say aloud everything that they think, reveals not only the students' vacuous, sexual and body-obsessed thoughts, wishes and phobias, but also lays bare the teachers' unsavoury and violent thoughts. Jarvis suggests that teachers in Gothic teen stories 'are rarely shown as human beings with whom the young people can have a relationship'. Moreover, '[t]hey are often revealed as dangerous'.[43] This is certainly the case in Engelsfors, where teachers are ineffectual and/or hurtful. Linnéa, who can read minds, is especially bothered by the lewd male art teacher's thoughts about his teenage female students. The principal Adriana Lopez is at first suspected to be the demon who has murdered Elias and Rebecka. Although Adriana believes in the Chosen Ones and would like to protect them, she fails to do so and is severely punished by the Council for siding with them. Jarvis emphasises that the depiction of teachers in Gothic teen fiction is 'strongly suggestive of confusion and disillusionment towards adults, indicative of the painful nature of maturing and recognising that those who care for you and have power over you are flawed',[44] and the Engelsfors trilogy is no exception in this regard. As a good student from a well-to-do home, Minoo is the character who experiences this most strongly and painfully. For example, her first love, the maths teacher Max, murders Elias and Rebecka and tries to kill the rest of the Chosen Ones; and the powerful witch Walter Hjorth, whom she fully trusts and respects, is exposed in the end as lethally manipulative, self-serving and hungry for unlimited power.

Doppelgängers and divided selves

The Engelsfors trilogy, with its focus on maturing teenagers and Gothic, has a double investment in identity issues such as ambiguous or fragmented selves and transgressions of the boundaries between 'I' and 'non-I'. Similar concerns are also brought to the fore in *Buffy*: for instance, in the Season 3 episode 'Doppelgangland', in which Willow, with whom Minoo shares many traits, encounters an evil but also much more self-assured vampire version of herself, and in the Season 4 episode 'Who Are You', when the antagonistic vampire slayers Buffy and Faith switch bodies. In *Cirkeln*, the Chosen Ones must confront the notion of the 'doppelgänger', an important Gothic trope,[45] when trying to find Rebecca's murderer; while in *Eld*, the body-switch motif is employed and developed.

The already complex and at times fragmented existence of being on the verge of adulthood is thus further complicated by the Chosen Ones' ontological status as witches fighting evil. In *Cirkeln*, Vanessa experiences acutely that she has multiple, contradictory selves:

> There are far too many Vanessas now, and she no longer knows which is the real one. The Vanessa she is when she's with Michelle and Evelina is different, for example, from the Vanessa who's trying to save the world. And then there's the Vanessa she has to be when she's with Wille [her boyfriend], and the Vanessa who's trying not to be too much of a burden on Sirpa [Wille's mother], plus the Vanessa who wants to leave school with at least a pass grade in her final exams... She's lost her way among all her different personas.[46]

Michelle and Evelina are Vanessa's best friends with whom she shared everything before discovering that she is a witch. They are party girls, which makes Vanessa a somewhat unlikely Gothic heroine: she is sexy, enjoys sex and is not afraid of dressing and acting provocatively. In other words, based on her appearance and demeanour she is the kind of girl who is traditionally killed first in horror movies. Vanessa, being a horror film aficionado, sometimes also reads situations in her own life in terms of horror conventions. Her life in narrow-minded Engelsfors is about to become even more complicated after she and Linnéa become a seemingly incongruous loving couple. The bisexuality thus constitutes yet another doubling in the trilogy.

The question about doppelgängers can be linked to Jarvis' suggestion that the focus in teen horror of suspecting that the 'husband' is a monster or murderer shifts to the 'boyfriend'.[47] This issue arises after Rebecka's boyfriend Gustaf not only appears to be the one who killed Rebecka – as seen in a vision that Anna-Karin and Ida share – but also later seems to have been in two different places at the same time: Vanessa spies on him at Rebecka's grave while he kisses Minoo in another location. Anna-Karin, Ida and Minoo agree that there is something wrong with the Gustaf that they saw in the vision through Rebecka's eyes and the one Minoo encountered. Ever the good student, much like Willow in *Buffy*, Minoo does research to find an answer and presents her findings to the others: '*Doppelgänger* is German, meaning literally 'double walker'... There are Norse myths about *vardøgern*, a kind of ghost-like premonitory apparition of a person who hasn't been there yet. In the far north of

Finland it's called an *etiänen*. All the mythologies agree that the appearance of a doppelganger is a bad omen. If you see your own doppelganger it's usually a sign that you're going to die.'[48] She argues that 'a kind of sister phenomenon known as *bilocation* [that] appears throughout the world', and that involves the creation of a double, may be more relevant to solving 'the mystery of Gustaf and his doppelganger'.[49] The idea of Gustaf being the murderer is compounded by him being not only the most popular and attractive but also the kindest male student: he speaks up against bullies, Ida has had a secret unrequited crush on him for years and he has become Minoo's friend after Rebecka's death. But as Linnéa callously puts it: 'If Gustaf is such a thoroughly nice guy, like you say, he'd never be able to murder someone. Why not create a double to do your dirty work for you?'[50] A truth serum later reveals that Gustaf is not the murderer. It is instead Max who has used his shapeshifting powers to assume Gustaf's shape when he murdered Rebecka and kissed Minoo. Max is attracted to Minoo because she reminds him of Alice, a girlfriend whom he murdered to become the demons' Blessed One. Alice looked like a woman (Proserpine, the Empress of the Underworld) in a pre-Raphaelite painting: 'Speaking of doppelgangers,' Anna-Karin says to Minoo, 'the woman in the paining is a total carbon copy of you', which has eluded Minoo since, while disparaging her own appearance, she thinks that the woman in the painting is beautiful.[51] In this entangled Gothic web of doubles and assumed identities it is Max and Minoo's relationship that realises the idea of the boyfriend as monster and murderer.

The transgression of a unified self is further explored in *Eld* where the Chosen Ones switch bodies with each other in order to evade being caught lying at the Council's trial at which Anna-Karin is charged with having knowingly broken the Council's laws regulating the use of magic. Besides temporarily removing the Chosen Ones' magical powers, the body-switch trope is used to great effect and serves a number of significant purposes. Malin Alkestrand argues that it 'represents a unique version of [this] motif as it includes five characters that are all focalisers during the body switch' and that it is 'portrayed as a learning process that becomes central to the characters' identity development and ability to cooperate in the fight against evil'. As she puts it, through 'living a different girl's life for three days, they learn not only about the life, habits and struggles of the person whose body they reside in but also about their own strengths and weaknesses, and their privileges or lack thereof'.[52] Thus, not only does the body switch defamiliarise the protagonists' own bodies to themselves; it also effectively highlights the importance of social differences and the existence or lack of nurturing home environments, which is not always linked to social class in the trilogy. What makes the body switch in *Eld* unusual, in addition to the focalisation through five characters, I would argue, is that the exchange is not one to one: Minoo's mind is in Linnéa's body, Linnéa's in Vanessa's body, Vanessa's in Anna-Karin's body, Anna-Karin's in Ida's body and Ida's in Minoo's body.[53] By temporarily giving up their magical power in this 'musical-chair' switch, the five teenage witches in the Circle share the social, bodily and emotional power of their home environments and themselves. This sharing leads to greater empathy with and understanding of each other and to character development, which means that once they regain their own bodies and magical powers they are stronger and more cooperative. It makes the Circle a more coherent and powerful collective protagonist.

Power: having it, sharing it

Power of different kinds is obviously central to the Engelsfors trilogy, since on the whole '[t]he witch is a figure of power, however used or abused'.[54] As Punter observes, 'the witch occupies this liminal space where many things might be possible, many things are forbidden, and forbidden, transgressive knowledge is the ambition, the hope of circumventing the world of the normal and the everyday'.[55] The magical powers of witches in the Engelsfors trilogy are used and abused in various ways and the Chosen Ones have to deal with ethical aspects of having supernatural strength and power over, as well as clandestine insights into others' thoughts, memories and behaviour. Like Willow in *Buffy*, members of the Circle become addicted to magic and give in to the temptation of using magic for personal reasons and gain.

Here the American horror movie *The Craft* (1996) is also a significant source of inspiration.[56] *The Craft* was released in Sweden, Denmark and Norway in 1996 under a title that translates into 'the vicious circle' or 'the circle of evil': *Den onda cirkeln*; *Den onde cirkel*; and *Den onde sirkel*. Like the Engelsfors trilogy, it focuses on a group of high-school witches representing different elements and needing to join in order to fully realise their magical powers. However, as the Nordic film titles indicate, unlike the Circle in the Engelsfors trilogy, these girls, three of whom are misfits and outsiders at school, do not practise magic in order to stop the apocalypse and save humanity; they use it for personal gain and in order to get revenge. *The Craft* ends with a spectacular magical showdown between the lower-class Goth girl Nancy Downs, who has become extremely powerful and evil, and the bourgeois protagonist and new addition to the Wicca circle of four, Sarah Bailey. Sarah is victorious in the end and the only one in the Circle who retains her magical powers.

The way that Anna-Karin uses her magical powers to begin with resembles how the high-school witches in *The Craft* use magic to gain popularity and to get even with students who have bullied, slighted or slandered them. She makes Erik, the bully, pee in his pants in front of everybody in the schoolyard; she makes herself popular in school and takes over Ida's best friends; and she makes Jari, with whom she is in love, become attracted to her. At home, she changes her constantly depressed, passive and negative mother into a nurturing, positive parent. Her life is finally endurable and even gratifying, which means that it is near impossible for her to stop using magic to improve her everyday reality when the Chosen Ones are informed about the Council's laws. When Nicolaus and the other Chosen Ones try to convince her to stop in order not to put herself and them at risk, Anna-Karin realises that she is addicted to using magic: 'In year nine an ex-junkie had talked to the class. He'd said that when he'd tried the drug for the first time it had felt like coming home. Now Anna-Karin knows what he'd meant. Her power makes her feel intoxicated, high.'[57] Later, at a party, Vanessa and Linnéa point out that using magic to make Jari want to have sex with her is unethical and amounts to rape and although she is angry and argues with them she finally stops enchanting him that night.[58] At the end of *Cirkeln*, Anna-Karin muses on how hard it is to stop herself from using magic when the hatred born of being abused over the years still bubbles up inside her, but she resists for the sake of the other Chosen Ones.[59]

Minoo also at times uses her magical powers like an addict uses drugs. She can shut out the world and shut off her emotions by spending time in the black smoke that is an emanation of her powers. In *Nyckeln*, under the tutelage of Walter, Minoo learns to both release and control her already considerable powers. Walter is a perfect example of English historian Lord Acton's often quoted observation that 'Power tends to corrupt, and absolute power corrupts absolutely', and he finally imprisons her in the manor house. Here, being separated from the other Chosen Ones, Minoo, who has developed into the most powerful witch in the world, is in danger of being corrupted as well as misled. She does, however, manage to destroy Walter and appropriate his powers when it is time to close the portal and stop the apocalypse, which must be done by the joint effort of all members of the Circle, dead and alive.

In *Buffy*, Willow also struggles with a severe addiction to using magic and even magically interferes with her lover Tara's memories to mend their relationship, which is torn apart because of this addiction. When Tara is murdered, Willow turns in anger and despair to the darkest kind of magic and becomes Dark Willow, who not only flays Tara's murderer alive but comes close to single-handedly bringing on the apocalypse. Nevertheless, it is also Willow who helps stop the apocalypse at the end of the last season of *Buffy* by using magic to turn all potential slayers into actual slayers. Philip E. Wegner reads this move as a 'truly revolutionary... overturning' of an old 'patriarchal order' that has 'regulated the power of the slayers by determining that only a single Chosen One [can] exist at any one time'. He suggests that 'the climactic scene' of the potential slayers all over the globe 'coming to consciousness of their own agency represents one of the truly utopian moments of recent television history'.[60] It is indeed a powerful illustration of awakening girl power and it means that the series ends with a number of Chosen Ones instead of one single Chosen One. But this is the end of the series and these are slayers, not witches.

The Engelsfors trilogy begins and ends with the Chosen Ones, plural. The protagonists as collective or the collective as protagonist is built into the very structure of the novels through the focalisation, which shifts between the seven characters that form the Circle. Due to the expert use of this shifting focalisation, the strong forward movement in the trilogy is very much character-driven. Moreover, in terms of 'monstrous kinships', as Wegner calls the consensual new family constellations that he sees replacing 'blood kin' in *Buffy*,[61] although dysfunctional at first, the Circle is one of those constellations: 'Just as siblings don't choose each other, the Chosen Ones haven't either. And, like siblings, they have to live with each other.'[62] At the end of the trilogy, after they have returned from the Borderland, Anna-Karin introduces Minoo, Vanessa and Linnéa to her grandfather who recognises them as her 'second family'.[63] Despite their differences, and helped by the body switch in *Eld* and their interactions in the Borderland in *Nyckeln*, the Chosen Ones have developed into a functional and loving group of 'siblings' by the end of the trilogy.

The Swedish Engelsfors trilogy employs and adapts a number of Gothic themes and motifs that have been used earlier in, for example, American films and TV series: the school as a place of evil, doppelgängers and divided selves and the witch's attraction to dark magic. Nevertheless, in addition to the sustained focus on the collective as a protagonist, what makes this trilogy a distinctively Nordic Gothic production – with a gloomy atmosphere that it shares with Nordic Noir – is the way in which the geographical and social setting is used to ground the Gothic elements in particular historical contexts, past and present.

Notes

1. H. Fahl, '"Cirkeln" – en svensk "Twilight"?', *Dagens Nyheter* (31 March 2011), www.dn.se/dn-bok/cirkeln-en-svensk-twilight/. Accessed 3 February 2018.
2. The six novels of Kaaberbøl's series about the wild witch are *Ildprøven* (2011; *Wildfire*, 2016), *Viridians blod* (2011; *Oblivion*, 2016), *Kimæras hævn* (2011; *Life Stealer*, 2016), *Blodsungen* (2012; *Bloodling* 2016), *Fjendeblod* (2013; *Enemy Blood*) and *Genkommeren* (2014; *The One Who Returns*).
3. In *Teen Noir*, Maria Nilson discusses the first two volumes of the trilogy among other teenage novels in a chapter that deals with powerlessness and frustration in the everyday life of teenagers who are exposed and vulnerable but also chosen. M. Nilson, *Teen Noir: Om mörkret i modern ungdomslitteratur* (Lund: BTJ förlag, 2013). Nilson's discussion of the novels in the trilogy is one of very few outside news media and B.A. theses. A notable exception is Malin Alkestrand's Ph.D. dissertation, which examines the Engelsfors trilogy in the context of teaching fundamental values in school. M. Alkestrand, *Magiska möjligheter*: Harry Potter, Artemis Fowl *och* Cirkeln *i skolans värdegrundsarbete* (Göteborg: Makadam förlag, 2016). See also Alkestrand's article in English on an aspect of *Eld*, 'Walking in Someone Else's Shoes: The Body Switch in the Engelsfors Trilogy', *Barnboken* 40 (2017), pp. 1–19.
4. Fahl, '"Cirkeln" – en svensk "Twilight"?'.
5. Fahl, '"Cirkeln" – en svensk "Twilight"?'. 'Vi har nog Stieg Larsson och John Ajvide Lindkvist att tacka för att Sverige är så intressant utomlands just nu.' My translation.
6. When asked about their favourite novels, the fantasy series that both Strandberg and Elfgren mention is Philip Pullman's *His Dark Materials* trilogy (1995–2000). Elfgren also lists Lev Grossman's *Magicians* trilogy (2009–2014). Neither of them brings up *Harry Potter*, *Twilight* or *The Hunger Games*. World of Engelsfors, 'FAQ', www.worldofengelsfors.com/frequently-asked-questions/. Accessed 10 December 2017.
7. My translation. In Swedish the word is '*köksbänksfantasy*'. See, for instance, J. Jägerfeld, 'De har nyckeln till tonårens magi', *Modern Psykologi* 1 (2015). Although it certainly shares some traits with the British kitchen-sink realism of the 1950s and 1960s to which the expression alludes, the angry young men have been replaced by angry young women in the trilogy. Olu Jenzen calls Lindqvist's *Let the Right One In* and Elfgren and Strandberg's *The Circle* 'paranormal social realism' in a chapter on 'Social Realism and the Paranormal in Scandinavian Fiction', in *The Ashgate Research Companion to Paranormal Fiction* (Farnham: Ashgate, 2013).
8. Jenzen, 'Social Realism and the Paranormal in Scandinavian Fiction', p. 232.
9. Jenzen, 'Social Realism and the Paranormal in Scandinavian Fiction', p. 231.

10 Jenzen, 'Social Realism and the Paranormal in Scandinavian Fiction', p. 233.
11 Nilson, *Teen Noir*, p. 124.
12 T. Haglund, 'Fankulturen förlänger fantasins universum', *Svenska Dagbladet* (22 February 2015, part 3), pp. 6–7.
13 D. Punter, 'Figuring the Witch', in A. Jackson (ed.), *New Directions in Children's Gothic: Debatable Lands* (New York: Routledge, 2017), p. 73.
14 'Traditionally, the Goth girl as viewed in the media is attractive, quirky, intelligent and sensitive but troubled, and adopts black clothing in order to express her sense of difference from her immediate community', C. Spooner, *Post-Millennial Gothic* (London: Bloomsbury, 2017), p. 99. Linnéa fits this bill. An earlier example of the Goth girl as witch is the character Nancy Downs in *The Craft* (1996).
15 Jarvis points out that 'Buffy's relationship with the vampire, Angel, epitomises the horror story centred on the schoolgirl with the dangerous boyfriend... He fascinates and attracts her, but ultimately, once she has been to bed with him, literally threatens to devour her, reverting to his vampiric habits.' C. Jarvis, 'School is Hell: Gendered Fears in Teenage Horror', *Educational Studies* 27:3 (2001), p. 262. DOI 10.1007/s10583-007-9058-0.
16 H. Fahl, 'En ort som gjord för mörk magi', *Dagens Nyheter* (23 April 2012), www.dn.se/dn-bok/en-ort-som-gjord-for-mork-magi/. Accessed 3 February 2018.
17 Engelsfors is also very different from other fictive and real towns and cities infested with vampires or witches on the Californian coast in American popular culture, such as fictive Santa Carla (recognisably Santa Cruz) in *Lost Boys* (1987) and Los Angeles in *The Craft* (1996), *Angel* (1999–2004) and *Moonlight* (2007–2008).
18 S. B. Elfgren and M. Strandberg, *The Circle*, trans. P. Carlsson (London: Hammer, 2012), p. 17. '*Fagersta*' translates into 'beautiful town' ('*fager*' means beautiful and '*sta*' is short for '*stad*' which means 'town').
19 Elfgren and Strandberg, *The Circle*, p. 17.
20 This may be a possible nod to *Twin Peaks*, where the sawmill burns down at the end of the first season.
21 Elfgren and Strandberg, *The Circle*, p. 148.
22 Punter, 'Figuring the Witch', p. 74.
23 '[I]n 1676, the witch trials came to an end after almost ten years of turmoil involving thousands of people as witnesses and suspects and with more than 300 executions', B. Ankarloo, 'Witch Trials in Northern Europe 1450–1700', in B. Ankarloo, S. Clark and W. Monter (eds), *Witchcraft and Magic in Europe: The Period of the Witch Trials* (London: Athlone Press, 2002), p. 90.
24 S. B. Elfgren and M. Strandberg, *Fire*, trans. A. Paterson (London: Hammer, 2013), pp. 108, 109.
25 Elfgren and Strandberg, *Fire*, p. 20.
26 Elfgren and Strandberg, *Fire*, p. 21.
27 Elfgren and Strandberg, *Fire*, p. 22.
28 That 'school is a place of evil' in Engelsfors is repeated in *Cirkeln*, and in most cases verbatim. See Elfgren and Strandberg, *The Circle*, pp. 110, 193, 489, 521, 559.
29 Sara Magee refers to what she calls Joss Whedon's aphorism 'High school is hell' in her article 'High School is Hell: The TV Legacy of *Beverly Hills, 90210*, and *Buffy the Vampire Slayer*', *Journal of Popular Culture*, 47:4 (2014), p. 885.
30 Whedon quoted in Magee, 'High School is Hell', pp. 885–6.

31 Jarvis, 'School is Hell', p. 257.
32 Jarvis, 'School is Hell', p. 260.
33 Elfgren and Strandberg, *Fire*, p. 283.
34 Jarvis, 'School is Hell', p. 260.
35 Elfgren and Strandberg, *The Circle*, p. 25.
36 Elfgren and Strandberg, *The Circle*, p. 28.
37 Elfgren and Strandberg, *The Circle*, p. 110.
38 Elfgren and Strandberg, *The Circle*, p. 130. '*Skolgård*' in the Swedish original has been translated into 'playground' ('*lekplats*' in Swedish) here, but to me 'schoolyard' seems like a more direct and appropriate translation for the grounds directly outside an upper secondary school.
39 Jarvis, 'School is Hell', p. 258.
40 S. B. Elfgren and M. Strandberg, *The Key*, trans. A. Paterson (London: Hammer, 2015), p. 671.
41 Elfgren and Strandberg, *The Key*, p. 489.
42 Elfgren and Strandberg, *The Key*, pp. 671–72.
43 Jarvis, 'School is Hell', p. 264.
44 Jarvis, 'School is Hell', p. 266.
45 For a discussion of doubles and divided selves in nineteenth-century Gothic literature, see R. Jackson, *Fantasy: The Literature of Subversion* (London: Methuen, 1981), pp. 108–9, 113–16.
46 Elfgren and Strandberg, *The Circle*, pp. 506–7.
47 'The focus on demons with sexual connotations (vampires, phallic serpents in the basement) and on boys who might just be murderers or demons, conveys the intensity of some girls' fears about and fascination with sexual threats within the school.' Jarvis, 'School is Hell', pp. 261, 266.
48 Elfgren and Strandberg, *The Circle*, p. 413.
49 Elfgren and Strandberg, *The Circle*, pp. 413, 444.
50 Elfgren and Strandberg, *The Circle*, p. 414.
51 Elfgren and Strandberg, *The Circle*, p. 521.
52 Alkestrand, 'Walking in Someone Else's Shoes', p. 3.
53 Elfgren and Strandberg, *Fire*, p. 473.
54 Punter, 'Figuring the Witch', p. 77.
55 Punter, 'Figuring the Witch', p. 68.
56 *World of Engelsfors*, 'FAQ', www.worldofengelsfors.com/frequently-asked-questions/. Accessed 10 December 2017.
57 Elfgren and Strandberg, *The Circle*, pp. 193–6.
58 Elfgren and Strandberg, *The Circle*, p. 384.
59 Elfgren and Strandberg, *The Circle*, p. 587.
60 P. E. Wegner, *Life between Two Deaths, 1989–2001: U.S. Culture in the Long Nineties* (Durham: Duke University Press, 2009), p. 215.
61 Wegner, *Life between Two Deaths, 1989–2001*, pp. 198, 205–7.
62 Elfgren and Strandberg, *The Circle*, pp. 587–8.
63 Elfgren and Strandberg, *The Key*, p. 819.

6

Sofia Wijkmark

Nordic troll Gothic

The Gothic has always told stories about ambiguous creatures from various folkloric traditions. In recent years, in particular the vampire and the zombie have enjoyed a global revival as sources not only of horror, but also of delight: they can either represent the threat of complete human extinction or be portrayed as individuals with whom the reader or viewer can identify or even love and admire. In contemporary Nordic Gothic the use of Nordic folklore is a common feature, and this chapter focuses on what might be regarded as a current trend: troll fiction.

According to Nordic folklore and mythology, the troll is a creature of the wilderness, and questions of environmental destruction and human aggression against nature are certainly present in one way or another in all of the examples examined in this chapter. Consequently, the concept of 'ecogothic' will be a necessary starting point for the discussion. Ecogothic can be understood as a way of exploring the environment from a non-anthropocentric point of view, re-examining the representations of nature in Gothic fiction and its non-human and monstrous characters as embodying questions of identity, species and ecology. Of course, for humans, adapting the point of view of the Other, the non-human, is an impossible pursuit. Ecogothic rather has to do with 'exposing the monstrous human gaze', as David Del Principe puts it.[1] Yet fiction can give us a chance to envision what it could be like to see the world from the beetle's perspective, think like a cyborg or feel the thirst for blood like a vampire. The question of species is often on the agenda in contemporary troll fiction, and the writings of Donna Haraway on the subject are definitely important to keep in mind.[2] However, as I have argued elsewhere, I consider Timothy Morton's theory of dark ecology to be specifically relevant to the discourse on ecogothic, primarily for emphasising the uncanny as important to the understanding of literature and other art forms from an ecological point of view, and even to ecological thinking in general.[3]

Dark ecology is described as a form of aesthetics based on uncertainty and melancholy, and as an expression of the horrific and ugly aspects of ecology that, according to Morton, are essential to ecological awareness. Of particular interest is his discussion of the concept of 'Nature' and his definition of what ecological thinking should be about. His premise is that we must move away from the 'ghost of "Nature"', Nature with a capital N, an 'ideal image' of something that is remote or located in the past and separated from humankind.[4] Instead, it is essential to acknowledge all lifeforms – humans, animals, plants and others – as connected to each other and to the surrounding environment. Morton argues for what he calls 'an upgraded version of animism':

> When we think the ecological thought, we encounter all kinds of beings that are not strictly "natural." This isn't surprising either, since what we call "nature" is a "denatured," unnatural, uncanny sequence of mutations and catastrophic events: just read Darwin. The ecological view to come isn't a picture of some bounded object or "restrictive economy," a closed system. It is a vast, sprawling mesh of interconnection without a definite centre or edge. It is radical intimacy, coexistence with other beings, sentient and otherwise— and how can we so clearly tell the difference? The ecological thought fans out into questions concerning cyborgs, artificial intelligence, and the irreducible uncertainty over what counts as a person. Being a person means never being sure that you're one. In an age of ecology without Nature, we would treat many more beings as people while deconstructing our ideas about what counts as people. Think Blade Runner or Frankenstein: the ethics of the ecological thought is to regard beings as people even when they aren't people. Ancient animisms treat beings as people, without a concept of Nature.[5]

Contemporary Nordic troll Gothic certainly deals with the issues outlined above. It explores how humans are connected to other lifeforms and to the surrounding environment, and whether a troll could count as a person. Species and other categories are closely scrutinised. Further, Nordic troll Gothic frequently contrasts different versions of nature, especially highlighting the ugly, uncanny and chaotic, as opposed to the well-organised, enclosed and comfortable.

Changelings and shapeshifters

Trolls inhabit children's fiction, both historically and in the present, and not only in the Nordic countries. In recent Nordic Gothic, however, the troll is also established as a character in adult fiction. An important precursor is Selma Lagerlöf's short story 'Bortbytingen' (1908; 'The Changeling', 1923), a cautionary tale featuring a troll as one of the protagonists.[6] On a journey through a deep forest, a farmer and his wife drop their child on the ground when the horses are frightened by a troll woman hiding by the path with her child. Mesmerised by the beauty of the human infant, the troll woman rapidly decides to switch the children, and the farmer and his wife are left with a changeling. This causes a matrimonial conflict. The wife refuses to leave the changeling behind, because she cannot bear to see a harmless child of any species suffer. The farmer, on the other hand, finds the changeling so repulsive that he tries to get rid of him by any means possible, even through violence and attempted murder. When the farm burns to the ground, and it is understood that the changeling is probably responsible, the woman risks her own life to save him from the flames. This is the turning point for the farmer; he leaves his wife and home and returns to the forest where he miraculously finds their son. Simultaneously, at home the wife discovers that the changeling has disappeared. Her sacrifice of the one thing that is most precious to her – the love of her husband – has made the trolls powerless, forcing them to let the human child go. Furthermore, they have treated him the same way that she treated the changeling, which means that she has saved her son's life. The farmer learns his lesson and the story ends with the reunion of the human family. 'Bortbytingen' was written for the Swedish women's magazine *Idun*, and from a conventional human point of view the moral of the story is that, like the farmer's wife, women need to stand up for what they know to be right in matrimonial conflict. Nevertheless, a reading focusing solely on the conflict of the human family neglects important aspects.

'Bortbytingen' has an eeriness and ambiguity that can be described as Gothic. The troll child has monstrous features such as sharp fangs and claws, but when the woman finds him on the ground, she seems unable to distinguish him from her own offspring; and as he grows older, he acts self-destructively and aggressively, but she is still strangely attached to him. Similarly, the human child reacts with curiosity and joy when looking into the monstrous face of the troll woman. The Gothic theme of doubling is strengthened when it is revealed that the human boy has lived a parallel life in the forest with the trolls, a horrific insight for the father who nearly caused his death by trying to kill the changeling. By shifting focus to the non-human, a darker and more complicated aspect of the story becomes obvious. The ending is apparently happy, and the farmer family is indeed reunited. However, something is missing: the reader never learns what happens to the changeling. He just disappears.[7] Even more significant is the fact that the narrative is never focalised through the changeling, despite the fact that he is present in more scenes than any other character.

This strategy of maintaining a distance, keeping the point of view outside the consciousness of the troll, also dominates in contemporary Nordic Gothic. However, Kerstin Ekman's novel *Rövarna i Skuleskogen* (1988; *The Forest of Hours*, 1998) is narrated mainly from the point of view of the troll-protagonist Skord, and may also be regarded as something as unique as a paraphrase of Virginia Woolf's *Orlando*; the troll moves through epochs and changes gender in the same way as Orlando.[8] The story begins in the Middle Ages, in the fourteenth century, and ends 500 years later. During this period, Skord evolves from a creature with a very primitive intellect to becoming almost human. Initially, the troll brain is described as incapable of holding on to thoughts and memories. However, it has the capacity to discern the specifics of humankind – for example, that they prefer 'a particular appearance' that does not involve the uncanny intermingling of the familiar and the strange: 'They wanted to look like one another, and not like rotting tree stumps or twisting branches or foxes or mossy stones. Looking like these things frightened them.'[9] To a troll, the interconnectedness with everything that belongs to the forest is a given, and Skord moves unhindered between species and other categories. His name can be understood as a fusion of the Swedish words '*skog*' (forest) and '*ord*' (word), denoting his in-betweenness: troll/nature and human/culture. To the human characters Skord's appearance is animal-like, but he can easily blend in with humans by putting on clothes and having a haircut and his androgynous looks help him to appear both male and female. His shapeshifting also has supernatural qualities: he can use the body of a mammal or bird when needed and communicates telepathically with animals.

During his life, Skord does everything from living as a robber in the Skule forest or as a cross-dressing prostitute in the town of Uppsala, to experimenting with alchemy and medicine. Most of the time he gives the impression of being harmless, but when he – possibly by supernatural means – sets fire to a farm as revenge for the mistreatment of a human beggar child who becomes his friend, his personality is revealed to have a dangerous and unpredictable side. *Rövarna i Skuleskogen* has primarily been interpreted with a focus on the human: through the centuries Skord lives with humans and learns to speak their language, and his development can of course be regarded as becoming human. However, Ekman's troll narrative can also be regarded as an attempt to approach something non-human. The psyche and intellect of the troll are radically different from those of humans, and Skord has difficulties understanding the human order of things. *Rövarna i Skuleskogen* can hardly be described as a Gothic novel, but rather the Gothic is one of many genres and forms that this multifaceted and complex narrative encompasses. It contains several classical Gothic themes and motifs such as the supernatural, the uncanny, the double, alchemy and robbers, as well as episodes with a distinct Gothic atmosphere or a setting described in terms of medieval horror.

Ekman's novel may also in many ways be regarded as a contemplation on the forest, a topic that has engaged the author for decades. As she demonstrates in her essay *Herrarna i Skogen* (2007; *The Masters in the Forest*), for humans the depth of the forest has often been synonymous with horror, and throughout history it has represented something impenetrable and dangerous that humans have tried to conquer.[10] The Skule forest is the main setting of the novel and from the point of view of the human characters it is a demonic and dangerous place. Human primeval fear of the forest is experienced by Magister Ragvaldus, a scholar past his prime who, for better or worse, mentors Skord for a period. Assaulted by robbers and left naked and alone on the ground, the forest transforms before him:

> The air grew cooler. The insects emerged. The forest was silent. A high wind moved through treetops and droned like the sea. He wanted to pray, but found no words – only visions. He wanted to reach out with his hand and break a twig off a wayfaring tree to have something to use as protection against the midges. But he dared not touch anything. He kept stumbling on.
> The forest did nothing. It sent neither bear nor wolf to him. It allowed the brambling to go on whistling and the water of the streams to go on rustling between the stones. The Magister was left to sink deeply into his pain and his visions.
> For as long as he had lived, he had been aware that he would die. His soul would then be liberated from its shell and leave it behind somewhere, on the ground or in a bed. Whatever happened to his body, whether eaten by the ants or the worms which feed on corpses, would be immaterial to his soul. But what was happening now frightened him. So many of them wanted to eat him already. He was swelling up with their bites. They were wanting to get into his body and dissolve it while he still lived.
> All forest things were impure and dissolute. They wanted to merge with one another. Fluids seeped and penetrated, tissues ruptured and roots worked their way through the torn fibres. The ground wanted him to lay down on it. If he did,

his body would dissolve while he was alive. His soul would disintegrate, and when he had liquefied and been transformed beyond recognition, there would be nothing left to rise upwards.[11]

The forest seems to possess a malign agency and the disturbing threat of dissolution of both body and mind, the intrusion of death and decay into that which is still alive and breathing, as well as the threat of insanity resulting in the dissolution or fragmentation of identity, is a perfect illustration of the uncanny.

Understood as a parallel to Skord's experience of humankind and its society, this scene also clearly demonstrates the opposition between the human and the troll in the novel. Ekman's troll becomes a bearer of ecological reflection and a critique of civilisation, a characteristic that it shares with the trolls of post-millennial Nordic Gothic. Human houses are among Skord's greatest fears and he imagines them with 'jaws of stone' and 'sharp claws'.[12] Nevertheless, he eventually spends a night in a cottage. Confused and struck by claustrophobia, he experiences how things uncannily 'change their shapes' before his eyes: 'He hears a faint noise and sees one of the black cauldrons come to life and move across the hearth. Terrified, he observes it fold its legs underneath its belly and settle down.' He notices that the only door is locked, compared to a fox's lair which has always at least two ways out, and senses '[t]oo many smells, too many things. He thinks: it would be a mad fox who collected everything he could find and drag it into his lair… The man sleeping in his bed must be mad.'[13]

'It looks at me like a puppy-dog, but there are live coals in its orange eyes'[14]

At the turn of the millennium, Charlotte Weize's Danish short story 'Skifting' (1996, 'Changeling'), Johanna Sinisalo's Finnish novel *Ennen päivänlaskua ei voi* (2000; *Not Before Sundown*, 2003), John Ajvide Lindqvist's Swedish short story 'Gräns' (2006; 'Border', 2012, adapted to film by Ali Abassi in 2018), the Norwegian films *Trolljegeren* (André Øvredal, 2010, *Trollhunter*) and *Thale* (Alexander Nordaas, 2012), Swedish director Henrik Björn's TV series *Jordskott* (2015), and Stefan Spjut's Swedish novels *Stallo* (2012) and *Stalpi* (2017) all deal with the troll as a transgressive character.[15] These stories show great variation in their depiction of the appearance and properties of trolls. Some trolls can blend in with humans without difficulty, and live together or alongside humans without revealing their true nature – this is the case in 'Skifting', 'Gräns' and *Jordskott*. In Spjut's novels, as well as in 'Gräns' and *Jordskott* the trolls rob humans of their children in accordance with the traditional myth of the changeling. The trolls of *Trolljegeren* are giant, grotesque and violent creatures with a primitive intellect and a taste for human flesh. The troll of Sinisalo's novel, on the other hand, is sexually attractive to humans. However, this is not because of his appearance: he looks like a small animal with a silky black fur and sharp claws. Instead, his juniper-like smell makes him irresistible since he exudes a strong dose of pheromones.

A common feature, however, is that the trolls are described as a dying species on the verge of extinction, which has been exploited, excluded or imprisoned by humans. In *Trollhunter* they live in reservations, hidden by the government, and in 'Gräns', one of the rare stories focalised by the troll, they have been forced to adapt to human society by '[h]uman beings who didn't believe in trolls'. However, as the troll protagonist Tina observes, 'if they found any, they locked them up in mental institutions, operated to remove their tails, sterilised them and forced them to learn the language of human beings. Tried to forget they even existed. Until we come and take your children.'[16] In *Jordskott*, the mining company of the small town of Silverhöjd where the series takes place uses every means available in their exploitation of the forest. The trolls have been the victims of what can best be described as a genocide and their habitat has been destroyed. As Johan Höglund has pointed out in his postcolonial analysis of *Trolljegeren* and *Thale*, the horror of some of these stories from a human perspective resides in what can be regarded as the 'revenge of the trolls'.[17] Stealing human children or, as in the case of *Trolljegeren*, hunting humans as prey, can be understood as a reaction to either the humans' maltreatment of the subaltern troll or to their exploitation of the environment.

In Sinisalo's *Ennen päivänlaskua ei voi* Haraway's concept of companion species could certainly be regarded as being put to the test. The troll is portrayed as a strange combination of pet, lover and monster, as is indicated in the quote from the novel used in the subheading. *Ennen päivänlaskua ei voi* tells the story of Mikael, a photographer in Tampere who finds a young troll in his backyard and decides to take him home. Soon the intoxicating pheromones exuded by the troll make it difficult for Mikael to resist the urge to approach him sexually, even though he is technically only a cub. The troll in turn acts jealously when Mikael returns home with the smell of another man on his body, hurting and then ultimately killing one of Mikael's lovers. However, an element of at least a potential future revenge is present in *Ennen päivänlaskua ei voi* as well: at the end of the novel it becomes apparent that the trolls have started to mobilise to be able to defend themselves, or maybe to carry out some sort of armed attack. The open ending depicts Mikael following the troll into the deep forest, possibly to join the troll community. In the forest, they are welcomed by what seems to be the alpha-male troll with a gun in his hands and it is understood that the trolls are the ones who have stolen weapons from arms depots, not the Russian mafia as Mikael assumed when he watched the TV news report on the incident.

Similar to Selma Lagerlöf's changeling, Sinisalo's troll is only perceived through the human gaze, even though he is one of the protagonists. The novel is divided into short chapters, each either narrated in the first person by one of the five main human characters, or consisting of excerpts from other texts, both fake and authentic. The excerpts are derived from the various newspapers, websites, folkloristic, literary, historical, scientific and other sources that Mikael turns to in a desperate search for knowledge on the behaviour and eating habits of trolls – for instance, he learns from Lagerlöf's 'Bortbytingen' that trolls eat disgusting things such as frogs and mice. Andrew Nestingen analyses the novel's formal structure in detail and concludes that the number of chapters narrated by a character reflects his or her importance to the story. Significantly Nestingen does not comment on the troll as a character or on his lack of a voice. Instead, he argues that the excerpt chapters 'form a heterogenous construction of the troll' and thus the troll ends up a mere textual device, a formal entity comprised of quotes, rather than a character in its own right. Nestingen regards the new troll mythology created from bits and pieces of folklore and fiction as part of Sinisalo's project to 'promote heterogeneity' and to criticise 'the national disclosure tradition' of Finnish literature in a time of change – the dissolution of the Soviet Union, Finland gaining EU membership, globalisation and neoliberalism.[18] Nestingen also points to the fact that the novel undermines categories 'enforc[ing] identities', such as 'human and animal, nation and Other, straight and gay', and he understands this strategy as compelling 'the reader to reconstruct a more heterogeneous worldview'.[19] Previous research has primarily discussed Sinisalo's novel as queer literature because of its depiction of gay relationships, or as fantasy fiction.[20] I argue, however, that the novel's sometimes very dark atmosphere, its focus on species and on the different connections between monstrosity and ecology that gradually unfold, both in the story itself and in the numerous excerpts from other text sources, also qualify it as ecogothic.

Sinisalo's version of the troll is complex and ambiguous. In the fictional universe of the novel trolls are discovered to exist in the early twentieth century and are categorised as mammals. However, the notion of the troll as an animal is continually challenged. Several excerpts discuss the question of species, some for instance indicating that trolls are very closely related to humans and others speculating on convergent evolution. Environmentalism is also a recurrent topic in the discussion and trolls are described as an endangered species that '[d]isappeared completely from Central Europe along with deforestation.'[21] On the TV news scientists comment on the possibility that in the present, climate change and environmental destruction have affected the trolls. Normally very shy creatures that hibernate during winter, trolls are now being sighted unusually often: 'In the rural commune of Jyväskylä, as many as three sightings of trolls are alleged to have taken place during the last week. That equals the whole count during the last forty years.'[22] This is explained rationally by a biologist as the result of the warmer climate making the trolls less cautious, since they have to search for food during the off-season. Another expert tries to explain the behaviour as due to pollution: 'poisoning of the environment may cause exceptional behaviour in animals... trolls which have eaten bird's eggs may have their systems saturated with tetrachloride dibenzonic-p-dioxin.'[23] Accordingly, from this point of view trolls can be regarded as vulnerable and victimised. A different angle is presented in the '*Finnish Evening News*', giving voice to people who have had close encounters with trolls and portraying them as a threat. The argument and vocabulary are recognisable from the ongoing wolf debate in Nordic countries: 'How long will it have to be before we realize a full-grown troll is a wild beast two meters tall and that a little child is just a snack for it?... They ought to bring bounty money back. Of course they're all going on about nature preservation now, but I'd like to see that green gage's face if some wolf or bugaboo snapped up his own brat on the way to school.'[24] The excerpts from folkloristic texts support this perception of the trolls as dangerous, describing them as degenerate and even demonic creatures, 'agents of the dark powers' or 'servants of Satan.'[25]

Ennen päivänlaskua ei voi is mainly set in an urban environment, but Sinisalo's troll is closely associated with the forest. As opposed to 'the fake woods adjoining cities' and 'the so-called nature reserves' – Nature with a capital N organised by humans – the forest of the trolls is perceived by Mikael as 'gloomy and tangled, it cascades violently upwards from its mossy floor to the sky, as if the earth were thrusting it out of its breast and bursting with effort. It's full of struggle. Species fight against species, a creeper's suffocating a tree'.[26] In this human vision of the forest as uncanny, hostile and chaotic, the highly intertextual *Ennen päivänlaskua ei voi* certainly bears the mark of its precursor *Rövarna i Skuleskogen*. In the description of the relationship between Mikael and the troll, whom he names Pessi after a tale by the Finnish author Yrjö Kokko, the metonymical aspect of the troll is also highlighted. During an erotically charged moment, Mikael thinks of Pessi as a personification of the forest: 'I stretch my hand out and slide it around his sweet, narrow, smooth burning-hot waist. Pessi's ears tremble. I have a massive erection, as if part of my stomach and thighs were rock-hard aching flesh. I've locked him in here: I've tried to capture part of the forest, and now the forest has captured me.'[27] The scene indicates the Gothic dimension of their relationship where fear, taboo and desire gradually become intermingled and further hints at the human not being the one in control.

Indeed, towards the end of the story Pessi is no longer portrayed as the rather cute animal that he initially appeared to be, but as 'a shred of night torn from the landscape and smuggled inside... a sliver of tempestuous darkness, a black angel, a nature spirit'.[28] When trolls are suddenly sighted on the streets of Tampere by one of Mikael's lovers, Dr. Spiderman, the Gothic atmosphere of the novel becomes palpable: 'My eyes drag the dim street, and suddenly my thoughts and memories seem to be merging into a double exposure out there: a black shadow. An almost invisible black shadow – two black shadows, absolutely soundless, economically fluent as flowing water; two pieces of darkness are dissolving in the dusk around the streetside refuse bins. And I can't be at all sure: did I really see what I think I saw?'[29] Fog, twilight, dark shadows in the alley, ambiguous visual impressions – the scene contains all the standard attributes of a Gothic city. The ambiguity is related to the uncanny presence of the trolls in human territory. The mission of the trolls is not clear to him, but the underlying cause is easier to figure out: 'Large-scale forest industry, pollution and the diminution of game have cornered them. Global warming'. Dr. Spiderman, who is a veterinarian, thus draws the same conclusions as the biologist on the TV news. But his analysis is not as neutral, since he has witnessed the rage of Pessi and seen the slayed body of Mikael's lover: 'They're on their way back... They're eating our leftovers, they're even stealing a little, and sleeping in our abandoned buildings and barns, as in the tales. They're pushing out their own territory into ours, little by little, so we'll not even notice until they're already in our midst. I hope they'll be satisfied with that.'[30] Mikael discovers that Pessi can create images – for instance, he paints the wall of the apartment with the blood of one of Mikael's lovers – but he never really communicates with language or signs. However, at the end of the novel, some sort of communication takes place for the first time. Significantly, this is when the alpha-male meets them in the forest, and the message is clear: 'It waves the gun barrel with a movement that's idiotically well known from the movies and yet chillingly strange when performed by – An animal. An animal? But the signal's clear. We're on our way now, and I'm a prisoner.'[31]

Sinisalo's troll character thus definitely challenges the notion of categories, being described as both cute and monstrous, human-like and animal-like, lover and pet, victim and perpetrator. The end also indicates a possible power shift from human to troll. However, the human and the troll are clearly separated in Sinisalo's story. In Stefan Spjut's novel *Stallo* and its sequel *Stalpi* the relationship between humans and trolls is portrayed as complex and intermingled on a deeper and different level. Spjut's extensive exploration of the secret lives of trolls is examined in the following section, where the focus is primarily on *Stallo*, since the troll mythology is established and, for natural reasons, more elaborately described in the first novel.

When species mate

Spjut's novels engage in the question of what happens when species meet – and mate. At the core of his mythology is the close kinship between troll and human, despite the obvious monstrosity of the troll. Trolls and humans can breed, hence pointing towards humanity's affinity with the trolls and, at the same time, towards humans' own strangeness and monstrosity. The trolls of *Stallo* also have different ways of communicating with humans, and for the humans this communication can be a truly horrific experience. The story is mainly set in the northern part of Sweden, Norrland, and more specifically in the regions of Lappland, Norrbotten and Västerbotten, during the winter of 2004. The protagonist Gudrun lives in the town of Kiruna and runs the souvenir shop Gunnar Myrén AB. The shop is named after her deceased father, a renowned nature photographer whose books are still bought by the tourists, and who by accident once happened to capture a strange naked creature on camera, riding on the back of a bear – a troll.[32]

In *Stallo*, the documentation of trolls is central to the plot. Gudrun's daughter Susso has dedicated her life to the search for other creatures of the kind that her grandfather stumbled upon. Through her cryptozoology homepage she is contacted by an elderly woman who has spotted a small man with a strange appearance and yellow animal-like eyes. Susso manages to capture him on wildlife camera, and shortly thereafter the elderly woman's grandson disappears without a trace. When engaging in the search for the child, Susso traces two families housing trolls on their desolate farms and, as it turns out at the end, some of the humans are actually human-troll hybrids. The novel begins with a prologue set in the 1970s, describing the disappearance of a boy named Magnus in the south of Norrland. The boy had never been found and his mother, who herself was a suspect in the case, insisted that a ten-foot tall troll came out of the woods and took her child. This disappearance in the past has a connection to the present: Magnus turns out to be the one who has abducted the elderly woman's grandson. His mother had told the truth about the giant; Magnus was abducted and has been raised by one of the families that houses trolls. Now they need a new child because, according to the mythology of the novel, trolls need to have children playing around them, otherwise they become unruly and dangerous. The plot of *Stallo* revolves around the intimate relationship between humans and trolls at the old farm where Magnus lives, and it is described how he is eventually forced to repeat the crime of kidnapping a child, switching roles from victim to perpetrator. As the story develops, Susso kills a troll in self-defence and the sequel *Stalpi* engages very literally with the theme of revenging trolls. Susso is kidnapped, brutally beaten and abused by a clan of sinister trolls, humans and hybrids that regard her as their worst enemy. However, as with humans there are different kinds of troll. They can also act as helpers to some humans, and at the end of *Stalpi*, Susso is finally rescued with the help of both a troll and a hybrid.

Nicholas Royle has described the uncanny as 'a crisis of the natural, touching upon everything that one might have thought was "part of nature": one's own nature, human nature, the nature of reality and the world'.[33] In *Stallo* and *Stalpi*, Spjut deals with all this and the north of Sweden becomes the site of the uncanny.[34] From a human perspective, the trolls of *Stallo* and *Stalpi* are horrifying, but they can also be uncannily irresistible. Their physical appearance is described as a repulsive mixture between human and animal, with a monstrous face, wrinkled, pale skin and crooked legs. They come in all sizes and are capable of shapeshifting.

Each troll can transform itself into a specific mammal according to size: the smaller ones into different kinds of mice and the giants into bears. Some of the small trolls can be used as bait for kidnappings; they are not only cute in their animal form and thus irresistible to children, but they also possess the ability to calm humans down. The giants, on the other hand, are described as very dangerous, due to the combination of extreme physical strength and a proneness to violence. The common denominator of all trolls, however, is that most of the time they are completely unfathomable and unpredictable. The people who live with trolls spend much time and effort trying to foresee what consequences one act or another will hold for them.

What Susso's grandfather Gunnar Myrén was able to capture on camera is an in-between creature that challenges our systems of classification: 'It looks like a monkey, but of course it most definitely is not a monkey. It is not an animal. And it is not a human being. It is something else. Something in between.'[35] Susso's mother Gudrun describes the figure in the photograph as 'something extraordinary and elusive… something that will not allow itself to be categorized. A hybrid that has not been given a scientific description or a habitat'.[36] The trolls of *Stallo* are indeed transgressive creatures. Not only are they able to cross the demarcations between species by becoming animals, but they can also breed with humans. Furthermore, the trolls are capable of telepathy, hence can also transgress or dissolve the boundaries of the individual's psyche. In this respect they are comparable to Ekman's troll Skord, but the psychic powers of the trolls of *Stallo* are a bit more sophisticated: they can read the human mind and erase memories, and they can transmit their feelings and needs to humans or put them under their spell, sometimes with fatal consequences.

What if?

The existence of telepathy explains why the humans harbour trolls and do everything they can to satisfy and protect them, even abducting children and killing. Here, Spjut uses the myth of '*bergtagning*' ('to take into the mountain'), a kind of enchantment during which people under the influence of trolls disappear in the woods and are spirited away into the mountain where the trolls live in rock shelters. If they ever return home, they do so with distorted minds. In studies on folklore, this myth has been understood as explaining different personality disorders or mental illnesses, something that Spjut relates to in his novels.[37] However, the uncanny and sometimes incomprehensible behaviour accompanying mental illness is here reversely taken as a proof for the existence of trolls. Their telepathic power is a blunt tool, as is demonstrated for instance in *Stallo*, when they cause memory loss in a couple of snooping policemen visiting the old farm. Börje, Magnus' stepfather, explains to him how it works:

> [']When he scrapes the details of the event out of them, other things come too. And the memory of it will sit inside them like an old nightmare. They will never be themselves again, believe me. In many cases it ends in suicide.'
> 'Because no one believes them?'
> Börje shook his head.
> 'It's more like a burn. They'll feel the pain but have no memory of the fire. They won't know what they've experienced, but it will hurt and they will suffer a personality change, as the newspapers say. Start to drink. Slap the wife about. And then it ends with a gun in the mouth. Either that or they kill themselves driving.'[38]

The erasing of memories will come with irreparable damage, but it disguises itself as mental illness.[39] In *Stalpi*, one of the protagonists is a man who suffers from brain damage and amnesia caused by the psychic powers of the trolls. He loses his job and his family due to his irrational and aggressive behaviour and the episodes focalised by him convey a nightmarish existence where '[e]verything seemed familiar but yet strange to him', which is the very definition of the uncanny.[40]

Spjut bases his fictional universe partly on the Sámi myth of the Stallo people (or 'Stalo', as it is sometimes spelled), and the novel skilfully blurs distinctions between fiction and reality by referring to authentic archaeological and ethnological findings and conclusions related to Sámi mythology. The Stallo people are mythological creatures, but due to nondescript ancient remains in the Sámi region, the so-called '*stalotomter*' ('Stalo settings'), researchers have been speculating on the possibility of a reality behind the myth. For instance, in his article 'Staloproblemet i samisk historia' (1983; 'The Stalo Issue in Saami History', 1983), the ethnographer Rolf Kjellström claims that:

> The majority of scholars want to see a historical background to the Stalo figure. One has guessed that it has to do with either Vikings or "adventurers" of one kind or the other... in general it seems as if certain details in the description of Stalo lack a counterpart in the Saami and their culture. I therefore share the opinion that there is a historical kernel and that the stalo traditions can not only be made-up or borrowed but at least partially must reflect historical contacts with another people.[41]

Spjut integrates these theories in *Stallo* by having Susso reflect on them: 'many archaeologists were convinced there was some kind of underlying truth to the myths of Stallo. Ancient settlements and trapping pits that could not be linked to the nomadic Sámi culture had been excavated in various places in northern Scandinavia.' She thinks of the Stallo people as 'oscillating between myth and scientific knowledge in a way that interested her'.[42] Fiction and reality also become intertwined when John Bauer (1882–1918) appears as a character in the novel.[43] Bauer is one of Sweden's most famous artists, known primarily for his paintings and drawings of trolls and other fairy-tale creatures. In Spjut's story, he meets the Stallo people during a journey to the north of Sweden that he undertook in real life to do research for his illustrations to the book *Lappland. Det stora svenska framtidslandet* (1907; *Lappland. The Great Swedish Land of the Future*). One of them, a squirrel in his animal shape, decides to follow Bauer to the south, moving in with him, and later appears as a helper to Susso, thus playing an important role in the story.

If trolls exist alongside humans, the question is why there is no evidence of their existence. This problem is obviously very important to Spjut, and the question is at the core of the detailed realism that enhances the uncanniness of the fictional universe of *Stallo* and *Stalpi*. The ability of the trolls to manipulate human consciousness and to erase memories, in addition to their shapeshifting, provides one answer. An important detail is also that the trolls are described as always transforming into their animal shapes when they die, thus explaining why no troll skeletons have ever been found. The archaeological and ethnological references and the presence of John Bauer add to the speculative touch of the novel.[44] What if there is a reality behind the Sámi stories, and what if John Bauer actually had real models when creating his many famous paintings of trolls?

Limes Norrlandicus

Spjut repeatedly directs readers' attention towards the arbitrariness of different kinds of limits and constructions, not only when it comes to lifeforms and individuals but also in relation to the setting and the environment. To begin with, the wilderness of northern Sweden is related to the idea of Nature as ideal and a construction. The protagonist Gudrun makes a living off this construction, just as her father the photographer Gunnar Myrén did, selling it to tourists in her souvenir shop. 'I make a living from the landscape,' she states, '[m]y business is the exotic, shimmering image of Lapland.'[45] Gudrun sells not only her father's photo books in her shop, but also a mixture of handicrafts and bric-a-brac, such as 'sweatshirts with prints of wolf heads, the northern lights, reindeer herds and magic inscriptions'.[46] The landscape portrayed in the novel, however, is the opposite of the idealised postcard version of Nature with a capital N that can be visited for recreation or for a safe adventure, and that is printed onto the shop's sweatshirts, pins and fridge magnets. Boring small-town life or Gothic nightmare in desolate old houses are what readers get, and instead of the midnight sun and northern lights, there is a compact darkness, snow in all shapes and forms, and a chilling cold that makes noses drip and fingers turn stiff. The only thing in the shop that seems to have some kind of counterpart in the fictional reality is, ironically, the troll. However, the cute and friendly trolls of Rolf Lindberg's famous picture books, also available 'pictured on napkins and paper cups and plates' are radically different from the Stallo people.[47]

The prologue of *Stallo* is quite different from the rest of the novel, especially in its depiction of the environment, but it is of no less importance. As mentioned earlier, it consists of a flashback to the 1970s and describes the disappearance of the boy Magnus. More specifically, it depicts how Magnus and his mother spend the days before the kidnapping in an isolated cabin in the woods, a classic location of Gothic horror. The cabin is located in the national park of Färnebofjärden, an interesting place from a regional and biological point of view that also has implications for the interpretation of the novel. The southern point of Norrland is located in the region but, more importantly, it is crossed by *Limes Norrlandicus*, the biological border zone separating northern and southern Sweden. On the official home page of Sweden's national parks, Färnebofjärden is described as a region where 'the strange meeting between the plant and animal species of southern and northern Sweden takes place'.[48] A strange meeting of species is indeed what *Stallo* is all about.

The prologue offers a framework for the analysis of the rest of the novel: it has to do with borders and boundaries, but also with their dissolution. The scenery comprises dense vegetation and a multitude of lifeforms. The cabin is located at the end of the road, deep in the forest, and summer is at its height. Insects make whizzing, cheeping and snapping noises, animals are sniffing around, the branches of fir trees tingle on the skin and high grass writhers around one's legs. The forest appears to have agency. Magnus is exploring the surroundings in detail with extreme curiosity, and from his point of view as a child he observes the relationship between the human and the non-human even before the trolls enter the stage. The upgraded animism that Morton calls for seems to come to him naturally. The distinction between lifeforms or species is not sharp, neither is the one between the living and the lifeless. An uprooted tree can suddenly turn into a 'man who will not move out of the way'.[49] During an excursion on his own, leaving the deceptively safe backyard, he experiences a dissolution of his own boundaries, significantly crossing a bridge:

> Holding onto the rail he walks across the bridge. His mother's lips mouth a warning inside him, but he is already on his way into the sea of grass on the other side. It is so tall that he disappears in it. When the wind blows the leaves bend and brush against each other. They become waves that whisper. He can be just like an animal in the grass. A shrew, perhaps. Nothing is visible apart from strips of green slicing against each other. Holding his hands in front of him he uses them to part the rustling reeds. This is what it is like for the shrew. Exactly like this.[50]

In the mind of the child, human, animal and plant merge and there is no conflict between fantasy and reality; both can exist simultaneously and create a world of pleasure and excitement. At the same time, this world can be frightening and dangerous. From the beginning there is already a sense of the underlying threat of something unknown lurking in the shadows of the forest. As Magnus hears strange noises and spots something from the corner of his eye, he is hit by the primeval horror of the forest, rooted deep in humanity. Soon it is revealed that his fear is justified. Unnaturally bold wild animals approach the cabin, and shortly thereafter he is abducted.[51]

'Who will survive and what will be left of them?'

The vast wilderness of Norrland is without doubt a residence of the uncanny in *Stallo*, but the novel's primary Gothic location is the home, represented first and foremost by the old, isolated farm where the kidnapped/kidnapper Magnus lives with his stepparents Börje and Ejvor, his stepsister Signe and a bunch of trolls. Magnus has always thought of Börje and Ejvor as a couple, but it turns out that they are siblings, implying the Gothic theme of incest. The desolate and dramatic location of the farm and its function as a site of horror is emphasised throughout the novel. A cottage on the property where the trolls are kept is the epicentre of fear and darkness. It is described as ancient and decayed, and when covered in snow it almost seems to dissolve, fusing with its surroundings. The inside, however, is even more horrific. It reeks of rotten meat and excrement and is very untidy. At the beginning of the story Ejvor is killed by the trolls while cleaning the cottage, and her body is left to decompose where it was found since the trolls might want to save the corpse to eat. The cottage also has a huge, dark cellar described as labyrinthine and seemingly immeasurable.

The old desolate farmhouse is a classic Gothic convention, but it has also become one of the most typical locations of the modern horror film; the farm of *Stallo* has more in common with the dirty and decaying 'terrible places' associated with the latter.[52] Filled with equal amounts of trash and body parts, these houses have come to represent the distorted mind of the killer or sometimes an entire family of killers. It is also obvious that Spjut uses horror film aesthetics to enhance the monstrosity of the trolls.[53] In one of the more nightmarish scenes in *Stallo*, a wolverine shapeshifter appears wearing an owl's head as a mask over its face, mimicking the trophy or fetish aspect of the serial killer repeated in many films. In *Stalpi* this is taken a step further as a wolf shapeshifter wears a mask made of a human face, reminiscent of the notorious character Leatherface from *The Texas Chainsaw Massacre* (1974).

The tribute to Tobe Hooper's cult classic, from which the quote in the subheading to this section is borrowed, has multiple implications.[54] The horror films of the 1970s and 1980s provoked contradictory reactions and interpretations and were branded as video violence or video nasties – *The Texas Chainsaw Massacre* is one of those films that has become a synonym for film violence.[55] For example, Carol Clover's seminal study *Men, Women and Chain Saws* (1992) references it in the title and the first edition also has a close-up screenshot of Leatherface on the cover. The allusion to *The Texas Chainsaw Massacre*, and to the graphic violence of the medium of horror film in general, intensifies the ambiguity already present in the novels and the uncanny, transgressive character of the trolls. The troll clan can be regarded as a version of the deviant 'terrible' family typical of the genre – 'murderous, incestuous, cannibalistic' – and the regional setting of Norrland becomes a Swedish version of the American white trash, hillbilly or redneck backwoods often used as a setting.[56] Especially in *Stalpi*, Norrland develops into a hostile, marginal region of Otherness, and the effect is equal parts comedy and horror. The troll clan has settled in a small, isolated village and the setting has a very typical backwoods horror atmosphere, with shabby cars parked in the high grass around decayed houses fenced with tarpaulin. The inhabitants are described as deranged and violent outcasts with the stereotypical attributes of jailbirds. The scenes that are acted out in this specific setting are often characterised by a bizarre and grotesque humour mixed with horror. However, this marginalised existence must be put in relation to the fact that the trolls appear to be a dying species, and then perhaps the laughter gets stuck in one's throat. They live in scattered groups, and do not procreate at the same pace as they are dying because of their slow life cycle. If thinking in terms of ecology, the outcast otherness of the trolls and hybrids of the clan can thus be regarded as an ugly and uncanny representation of the extinction of species.

As has been demonstrated in this chapter, late twentieth and twenty-first century troll fiction can often be understood in terms of ecogothic and dark ecology, and the stories use the character of the troll to explore limits and question categories. In *Stallo* and *Stalpi*, as well as in the other stories examined in the chapter, nature, and especially the forest, is the dark and chaotic site of the uncanny and it can even sometimes be depicted as having an agency of its own, contributing to the dissolution of boundaries. Spjut's novels takes it to the extreme, as his human characters experience a radical and uncanny intimacy with the non-human: strange creatures infiltrate their psyches and their DNA and it becomes impossible to draw a line between Self and Other.

Notes

1 D. Del Principe, 'Introduction: The EcoGothic in the Long Nineteenth Century', *Gothic Studies*, 16:1 (2014), p. 1. See also A. Smith & W. Hughes (eds), *Ecogothic* (Manchester: Manchester University Press, 2013); S. Wijkmark, 'Fördömelse från trädkronorna! Ekogotik och mörk ekologi', *Aiolos* 56:1 (2017), pp. 133–8.
2 D. Haraway, *The Companion Species Manifesto: Dogs, People and Signinficant Otherness* (Chicago: Prickly Paradigm, 2003); *When Species Meet* (Minneapolis: University of Minnesota Press, 2008).
3 See also S. Wijkmark, 'Ecology, Telepathy and Melancholia in John Ajvide Lindqvist's *Handling the Undead*', *Edda. Nordisk tidskrift for litteraturforskning*, 104:2 (2017), pp. 145–60. DOI: 10.18261/issn.1500-1989-2017-02-05. The concept is described both in Morton's *Ecology Without Nature: Rethinking Environmental Aesthetics* (Cambridge: Harvard University Press, 2007), and in *The Ecological Thought* (Cambridge: Harvard University Press, 2010). In *Dark Ecology: For a Logic of Future Coexistence* (New York: Columbia University Press, 2016), Morton explores it further.
4 Morton, *The Ecological Thought*, p. 5.
5 Morton, *The Ecological Thought*, p. 8.
6 For a comparative analysis of Lagerlöf's 'Bortbytingen' and John Ajvide Lindqvists 'Gräns', see S. Wijkmark, 'Trollen i Selma Lagerlöfs "Bortbytingen" och John Ajvide

Lindqvists "Gräns"', in M. Karlsson and L. Vinge (eds), *Spår och speglingar* (Hedemora: Gidlunds, 2011), pp. 344–61. See also U-B. Lagerroth, 'The Troll in Man – A Lagerlöf Motif', in *Scandinavian Studies* 1 (1968), pp. 51–60.

7   See L. Jakobson, 'På de avvisade trollens sida', *Svenska Dagbladet* (13 August 2006), www.svd.se/pa-de-avvisade-trollens-sida. Accessed 27 March 2019.

8   See R. Wright, 'Androgyny in Kerstin Ekman's *Rövarna i Skuleskogen* and Virginia Woolf's *Orlando*', in H. Kress (ed.) *Litteratur og kjønn i Norden* (Reykjavik: Háskólaútgáfan, 1996), pp. 676–8.

9   K. Ekman, *The Forest of Hours*, trans. A. Paterson (London: Chatto & Windus: 1996), p. 12.

10 Ekman, *Herrarna i skogen*, 2007. See also Chapter 2. For a discussion on Ekman's *Herrarna i skogen* as ecogothic, see S. Wijkmark, 'Fördömelse från trädkronorna!', p. 136. As Ekman herself has pointed out, *Herrarna i skogen* has many obvious parallels to *Rövarna i Skuleskogen*. Ekman describes in an interview that she got the idea of this book in the 1970s and that she thought that a lot of the material that she collected through the years would be integrated in *Rövarna i Skuleskogen*. S. Lenas, 'Damen i skogen', *Dagens Nyheter* (18 March, 2007) www.dn.se/dn-bok/damen-i-skogen/. Accessed 18 January 2019.

11 Ekman, *The Forest of Hours*, p. 89.

12 Ekman, *The Forest of Hours*, p. 17.

13 Ekman, *The Forest of Hours*, pp. 39–40.

14 J. Sinisalo, *Not Before Sundown*, trans. Herbert Lomas (London and Chester Springs: Peter Owen, 2003), p. 34.

15 See also S. Wijkmark, 'Trollen i Selma Lagerlöfs "Bortbytingen" och John Ajvide Lindqvists "Gräns"', in M. Karlsson and L. Vinge (eds), *Spår och speglingar* (Hedemora: Gidlunds, 2011), pp. 344–61; 'Stefan Spjuts Stallo som ekogotisk norrlandsskildring', in P. Degerman, A. Johansson & A. Öhman (eds) *Norrlandslitteratur: Ekokritiska perspektiv* (Makadam: Göteborg, 2018), pp. 196–212.

16 J. A. Lindqvist, *Let the Old Dreams Die and Other Stories*, trans. M. Delargy (London: Quercus, 2012), p. 68.

17 J. Höglund, 'Revenge of the Trolls: Norwegian (Post) Colonial Gothic', *Edda. Nordisk tidskrift for litteraturforskning*, 104:2 (2017), pp. 115–29. DOI: 10.18261/issn.1500–1989–2017–02–05.

18 A. Nestingen, *Crime and Fantasy in Scandinavia: Fiction, Film and Social Change* (Seattle and London: University of Washington Press, 2008), pp. 159, 167.

19 Nestingen, *Crime and Fantasy in Scandinavia*, p. 189.

20 Nestingen describes it as a fantasy novel. However, his focus in the analysis on monsters, narrative indeterminacy and fragmentation has a clear relevance for my argument. For a queer perspective, see R. Adkins, *The 'Monstrous Other' Speaks. Postsubjectivity and the Queering of the Normal* (Oregon: UMI Dissertations Publishing, diss., 2010); A. Lönngren, 'Trolls! Folklore, Literature and Othering in the Nordic Countries', in A. Lönngren, D. Heede, H. Grönstrand and A. Heith (eds) *Rethinking National Literatures and the Literary Canon in Scandinavia* (Newcastle Upon Tyne: Cambridge Scholars Publishing, 2015), pp. 205–30.

21 Sinisalo, *Not Before Sundown*, p. 97.

22 Sinisalo, *Not Before Sundown*, p. 96.

23 Sinisalo, *Not Before Sundown*, p. 97.

24 Sinisalo, *Not Before Sundown*, p. 57.
25 Sinisalo, *Not Before Sundown*, p. 32.
26 Sinisalo, *Not Before Sundown*, p. 233.
27 Sinisalo, *Not Before Sundown*, p. 114.
28 Sinisalo, *Not Before Sundown*, p. 176.
29 Sinisalo, *Not Before Sundown*, p. 188.
30 Sinisalo, *Not Before Sundown*, pp. 226–7.
31 Sinisalo, *Not Before Sundown*, p. 231.
32 The following analysis of *Stallo* is a shorter, but also partially developed version of an article previously published in Swedish, S. Wijkmark, 'Stefan Spjuts Stallo som ekogotisk norrlandsskildring', pp. 196–212.
33 N. Royle, *The Uncanny* (Manchester: Manchester University Press, 2003), p. 1.
34 See also Wijkmark, 'Stefan Spjuts Stallo som ekogotisk norrlandsskildring', p. 199.
35 Spjut, *Stallo*, trans. S. Beard (London: Faber & Faber, 2015), p. 78.
36 Spjut, *Stallo*, p. 79.
37 See for example E. Schön, *Troll och människa. Gammal svensk folktro* (Stockholm: Natur och Kultur: 1999), p. 119f.
38 Spjut, *Stallo*, p. 249f.
39 See also Wijkmark, 'Stefan Spjuts Stallo som ekogotisk norrlandsskildring', p. 203.
40 'Allt tycktes honom bekant men ändå främmande'. Spjut, *Stalpi* (Stockholm: Bonniers, 2017), p. 71. All translations of quotations from this novel are mine.
41 'Flertalet forskare vill i stalofiguren se en historisk bakgrund. Man har då gissat på att det rör sig om antingen vikingar eller om "äventyrare" av något slag... generellt verkar det som om vissa detaljer i beskrivningen av Stalo saknar motsvarigheter hos samerna och deras kultur. Jag delar därför uppfattningen att det i stalotraditionerna finns en historisk kärna och att traditionerna inte enbart kan vara uppdiktade eller utgöra lånestoff utan måste åtminstone delvis reflektera historiska kontakter med ett annat folk.' R. Kjellström, 'Staloproblemet i samisk historia', in Jørn Sandnes (ed.), *Folk og resurser i nord. Foredrag fra Trondheimssymposiet om midt- og nordskandinavisk kultur 1982*, p. 216. My translation. See also E. Manker, *Fångstgropar och stallotomter. Kulturlämningar från lapsk forntid* (Stockholm: Geber, 1960).
42 Spjut, *Stallo*, p. 114. See also S. Wijkmark, 'Stefan Spjuts *Stallo* som ekogotisk Norrlandsskildring', pp. 203–4.
43 See also Wijkmark, 'Stefan Spjuts Stallo som ekogotisk norrlandsskildring', p. 204.
44 See also Wijkmark, 'Stefan Spjuts Stallo som ekogotisk norrlandsskildring', p. 205.
45 Spjut, *Stallo*, p. 73.
46 Spjut, *Stallo*, p. 74.
47 Spjut, *Stallo*, p. 74. See also Wijkmark, 'Stefan Spjuts Stallo som ekogotisk norrlandsskildring', p. 207.
48 'där det märkliga mötet mellan syd- och nordsvenska växt- och djurarter äger rum'. Sveriges nationalparker. www.sverigesnationalparker.se/park/farnebofjardensnationalpark. Accessed 19 January 2019. My translation. See also Wijkmark, 'Stefan Spjuts Stallo som ekogotisk norrlandsskildring', p. 208.
49 Spjut, *Stallo*, p. 12.
50 Spjut, *Stallo*, p. 10.
51 See also Wijkmark, 'Stefan Spjuts Stallo som ekogotisk norrlandsskildring', pp. 208–9.

52　C. Clover, *Men, Women and Chain Saws. Gender in the Modern Horror Film* (Princeton: Princeton University Press, 2015), p. 30.

53　Clover, *Men, Women and Chain Saws*, p. 30f. As Berenice Murphy has pointed out, both the cabin in the woods and the old isolated farm are typical locations more specifically of the backwoods horror. See B. Murphy, *The Rural Gothic in American Popular Culture. Backwoods Horror and Terror in the Wilderness* (Houndmills, Basingstoke, Hampshire: Palgrave Macmillan, 2013).

54　The phrase appears on the famous original poster.

55　Clover, *Men, Women and Chain Saws*, p. 22. For a discussion of the debate on video violence in Sweden, see M. Ullén (ed.), *Våldsamma fantasier: Studier i fiktionsvåldets funktion och attraktion* (Karlstad: Kulturvetenskapliga skriftserien 2, 2014); S. Wijkmark, 'John Ajvide Lindqvist's Little Star. Gothic Horror and the Remediation of Video Nasties', *Gothic Studies*, 20:1 (2018), pp. 77–94.

56　Clover, *Men, Women and Chain Saws*, p. 30.

Johan Höglund

Indigenous hauntings: Nordic Gothic and colonialism

Since the late 1970s, Gothic has typically been understood as a genre launching a furtive yet often strongly subversive critique of Enlightenment and modernity. Gothic helped identify and interrogate the various ills that this era's faith in rationality and turn towards liberal capitalism produced. One of the gravest such ills was colonialism, a project that generated tremendous wealth in Europe and North America, but also incomprehensible suffering through slavery, genocide, poverty and war in the Global South.[1] Observing how crucial colonialism was to the Enlightenment project, Andrew Smith and William Hughes, in *Empire and the Gothic* (2002), identify a common agenda among postcolonial and Gothic scholars: 'historical examination of the Gothic and accounts of postcolonialism indicate the presence of a shared interest in challenging post-enlightenment notions of rationality'.[2] Indeed, the relationship between Gothic, colonialism and imperialism has been one of the more important concerns of Gothic Studies since the late 1980s.[3] As Tabish Khair observes in *The Gothic, Postcolonialism and Otherness* (2009), Gothic, more than any other literary genre, is a 'writing of Otherness' capable of producing a certain and often hostile understanding of the non-European subject whether this figure was encountered in the colonies or in the streets of European metropoles.[4] At the same time, as Rebecca Duncan shows in *South African Gothic* (2018), Gothic has also often been used to interrogate past and present colonial discourses and practices.[5]

The Nordic region, as well as Gothic produced within the region, is largely absent from most studies that discuss the connection between

Gothic and colonialism, despite the fact that this part of the world is constantly depicted in Gothic writing as an uncanny yet explorable space that has much in common with the Global South. In particular, the northernmost parts of the Nordic region, known as the Arctic or sub-Arctic, loomed large in the imagination of European nineteenth-century explorers and many Gothic writers mine it for content. Mary Shelley's *Frankenstein* (1818) is told entirely from a ship frozen into the ice of the Arctic, and one of Conan Doyle's first published short stories was 'The Captain of the Pole-Star' (1883), based on his own experiences as a surgeon on a ship that headed to the Arctic from Scotland in 1880.[6] The connection between the Arctic and Gothic horror has lived on far beyond the nineteenth century. In the Swedish-American drive-in horror movie *Rymdinvasion i Lappland* (1959, *Terror in the Midnight Sun*), space invaders and a gigantic King-Kong-like monster haunt the icy wastes of northern Sweden. John Carpenter's classic Gothic body-horror movie *The Thing* (1982), and its 2011 'prequel' using the same title, take place in the Arctic, in neighbouring American and Norwegian research stations. Similarly, Nicholas Feuz's French novel *Horrora Borealis* (2018) also imagines the very far north of Scandinavia as a site of horror.[7]

There is also a wealth of Gothic produced within the Nordic region that explores the Arctic or sub-Arctic as spaces of dark and monstrous Otherness. The northernmost region of Sweden is the location of Stefan Spjut's internationally well-received Gothic horror novels *Stallo* (2012) and *Stalpi* (2017), discussed in more detail in Chapter 6. Mikael Niemi's Gothic crime novel *Koka Björn* (2017) also locates horror to the far north, as does the Swedish-French co-production *Idjabeaivváš* (2016, *Midnight Sun*). The fact that the Sámi, the indigenous population, still inhabit the northern reaches of Norway, Sweden, Finland and Russia is central and informs these narratives in different ways, as this chapter will discuss in detail.

Because the Arctic and sub-Arctic in Greenland, Sweden, Norway and Finland have long been, and remain, the home of indigenous populations that still contest Nordic colonialism, it is not surprising that Nordic Gothic set in this region brings up colonial issues. However, Nordic Gothic that considers colonialism also takes place in very different locations. John Ajvide Lindqvist's short story 'Gräns' (2006; 'Border', 2012) is set in Kappelskär, a port located an hour north of Stockholm, a location that becomes the site of an intersectional, and overtly post-normative and postcolonial Gothic story. Similarly, Peter Høeg's *Frøken Smillas fornemmelse for sne* (1992; *Miss Smilla's Feeling for Snow*, 1993), discussed below, clearly investigates postcolonial themes, but locates them mostly to the urban spaces of the Danish capital Copenhagen.

In addition to the body of international and Nordic Gothic texts that take place in recognisably Nordic geographies, there is some Gothic that occurs in, or connects to, Nordic colonialism practised in the Global South. As described below, several Nordic nations had overseas colonies in Asia, Africa, North America and the Caribbean, and these colonial endeavours also left a mark on Nordic culture. As Elisabeth Oxfeldt has observed in *Nordic Orientalism: Paris and the Cosmopolitan Imagination 1800–1900* (2005),[8] Norwegian and Danish artists contributed during the nineteenth century to what Edward Said has influentially termed 'Orientalism'. Nordic Gothic writers also produced texts in this tradition. Karen Blixen, writing under the pseudonym Isak Dinesen, moves in and out of an Orientalised Global South in her popular *Seven Gothic Tales* (1934). In this and other Gothic texts, Africa, the Middle East, the Caribbean and Asia typically appear as exotic and desirable spaces inhabited by the European Other.

Here, as mentioned above, Nordic Gothic often performed the same work as British or French Gothic, in that its 'language of otherness becomes conflated with images of *colonial* otherness'.[9] This type of Gothic is often referred to, using a term coined from Patrick Brantlinger's expression, as 'Imperial Gothic', and it typically relies on Orientalist xenophobic plots that revolve around invasions by a non-European, non-normative Other who threatens the stability of the society and the categories made possible by, and sustaining, imperialism.[10] There are such Nordic Gothic texts, as will be discussed below. However, as in international Gothic, there are also a significant number of Nordic Gothic texts that are conscious of the discourse of Orientalism, and that seek to counter its influence by contributing to the decolonisation of literature, film and of actual colonial spaces. These texts can usefully be described as Nordic postcolonial Gothic as they seek to undo the very categories on which Imperial Gothic rests.

This chapter first reviews some of the emergent scholarship that exists on Nordic colonialism. The chapter then surveys a number of Gothic texts that debate a variety of postcolonial concerns tied to the history and people of the Nordic Region. Of particular interest to the chapter is how Nordic Gothic participates in both the dismantling and the reinvigoration of colonial discourses. As the chapter illustrates, a complex ideological landscape becomes available to audiences in many Gothic texts produced across the Nordic region. While discussing a number of texts from this perspective, including *Frøken Smillas fornemmelse for sne* (1992; *Miss Smilla's Feeling for Snow*, 1993), Kim Leine's *Profeterna i Evighetsfjorden* (2012; *The Prophets of Eternal Fjord*, 2015) and Stefan Spjut's *Stallo* (2012), the chapter gives particular attention to the Swedish/French TV series *Idjabeaivváš*, set in the region often called Sápmi today, and inhabited by the indigenous Sámi. As the chapter shows, *Idjabeaivváš* is a good example of Nordic (post)colonial gothic in that it makes extensive use of Gothic effect to discuss the relationship between the Sámi and the Swedish state. Featuring a number of Sámi actors and activists, *Idjabeaivváš* caused considerable controversy, illustrating not only the centrality of colonialism in any understanding of the Nordic region, but also the difficulties that arise when using Gothic to interrogate colonialism.

The Nordic colonial and postcolonial Gothic

The lack of attention to Nordic Gothic in general, and to Nordic Gothic that discusses colonialism in particular, should be attributed not only to the general reluctance by scholarship to look beyond Anglophone Gothic, but also to the often held belief that the Nordic countries remained outside the nineteenth-century colonial project. However, a number of recent studies have observed that the Nordic nations were in fact active participants in various colonial projects inside and outside the nation's borders. As argued by Keskinen et al in *Complying with Colonialism: Gender, Race and Ethnicity in the Nordic Region* (2009):

> [N]orth-European countries have taken, and continue to take, part in (post) colonial processes. The lure of an enterprise as powerful and authoritative as the Western civilising project, attracts even those who never belonged to its centre or were its main agents. Nations, groups and individual subjects are drawn by the promise of power to adopt the discourses, imaginaries and material benefits connected to this project. The Nordic countries see themselves as part of the Western world, drawing their value systems from the Enlightenment, and showing themselves to be willing to defend these values sometimes even more forcefully than the former colonial centres.[11]

In recent years, a growing number of texts have explored the ways in which the Nordic nations took part in various of colonial ventures, and enthusiastically contributed to the creation of both the ideological and the material structures that made the pan-European colonial project possible.[12] This interdisciplinary research observes how the Nordic nations pursued their own colonial agendas by invading and occupying land in the Caribbean, Africa, Asia and South America, by participating in the slave trade, and by settling territory inhabited by the indigenous Sámi and the Greenland Inuits. In addition, it studies how the influx of Middle Eastern culture into the Nordic region, brought on by large number of war refugees from the region, needs to be understood as part of a postcolonial/neocolonial geopolitics. Finally, it considers how Nordic film, literature, music and art negotiates this long and complex imperial history.

Although all colonialism can be concisely defined, in the words of Ania Loomba, as 'the conquest and control of other people's land and goods', it is common to differentiate between different types of colonial project.[13] The most common type of colonisation that the major European empires engaged in was overseas colonialism, where European explorers, missionaries, military, traders, teachers and other agents of empire travelled across the Atlantic, the Pacific or simply the Mediterranean to invade and settle land not adjacent to their own national borders. Among the Nordic nations, the Danish-Norwegian union, and then Denmark alone, practised this form of colonialism in the Caribbean, in Africa and in Asia, but also and importantly in the North Atlantic, Greenland, the Faroe Islands and Iceland.[14] Sweden also has a history of overseas colonialism in North America and the Caribbean, but this nation, as well as Finland and Norway, was more involved in another less spectacular form of colonialism that is often, and problematically, termed 'internal colonialism'. This colonialism focused on Sápmi and did not demand an overseas journey. Because it was conducted within borders already claimed by a nation state it appeared, and still appears, as internal expansion by those who recognise the authority of this nation state.

Both of these basic forms of colonialism are mediated by Nordic Gothic and exist within virtually all Nordic nations in many languages. In consideration of the tension that still exists between colonised and coloniser in the Nordic region, this writing is produced from two different vantage points. Some Gothic writers identify as Danes, Norwegians or Swedes whereas others identify as Icelandic, Greenlandic, Inuit or Sámi. There are also writers that utilise Gothic to discuss migration from the Global South into the Nordic region from different points of origin. In this writing, Gothic can again be used both to fortify conservative and even racist positions, or it can be employed to address racist ideologies and practises rooted in the colonial enterprise. While the scope of this chapter does not make it possible to substantially address writing written by, or about, diasporic communities in the Nordic region, the existence of such communities and their representation in Gothic literature should be mentioned.

Denmark and Norway

To look first at Danish and Norwegian Gothic, these two nations, often operating as a coalition, had a greater stake in overseas colonialism than Sweden or Finland. The Dano-Norwegian empire comprised, typically with Denmark at the helm, extensive and long-lasting slave colonies in the Danish West Indies, minor colonial settlements and trading stations in India and Africa, and complete colonial control over Iceland, Greenland and the Faroe Islands. This long colonial history has given rise to the aforementioned postcolonial Gothic tradition that emerges along with postcolonial writing in other parts of the world. Just like the non-Gothic, postcolonial novel, this Gothic novel is written in an effort to respond to a long tradition of colonial writing seemingly designed to lend support to the gendered and racial categories that informed and stimulated colonialism. To this particular tradition belongs Icelandic author Halldór Laxness' extraordinary, absurd and at times Gothic *Kristnihald undir Jökli/Christianity Under Glacier* (1968; *Under the Glacier*, 1972). The premise of *Kristnihald undir Jökli* is not unlike that of Joseph Conrad's *Heart of Darkness*: a young man is sent by the Bishop of Reykjavik to a village at the foot of the remote Snæfellsjökull Glacier to investigate what the pastor of the village is doing. Arriving at the glacier, he finds that the door to the church has been nailed shut and that the pastor, like Conrad's Kurtz, appears to have lost his moorings and abandoned civilisation in the traditional sense. The difference is that, even if the pastor has gone native and given up Christianity for a much wider theosophical system of belief, he is no Kurtz huddling among shrunken heads. Rather, it is the bishop's great need to contain the possible dissolution of Christianity, and of the colonial order that it represents, that appears as abject in the novel.

The critique of colonial practise is more straightforward in Peter Høeg's bestselling and often overtly Gothic *Frøken Smillas fornemmelse for sne* (1992; *Miss Smilla's Feeling for Snow*, 1993). This novel is generally classified as crime fiction, but its use of terror and the supernatural means that it crosses the border into Gothic. It tells the story of Smilla Jasperssen, the daughter of a female Greenlandic Inuit hunter and a wealthy Danish doctor. Largely due to this hybrid identity, Smilla leads a lonely life in Copenhagen, befriended only by the boy Isaiah, a similarly lonely child who is also an Inuit and who has lost his father and now lives with his alcoholic mother. This friendship ends suddenly when the child falls to his death. Because of her 'feeling' for snow, Smilla understands that his death is suspicious and begins to investigate. Relentless in her pursuit of the truth, indeed a hunter like her mother, she discovers a strange conspiracy that leads her back to her native Greenland. For decades, an enterprise known as the Cryolite Corporation of Denmark, headed by the novel's main villain Tørk Hviid, has been investigating a highly unusual meteor that crashed into Greenland in the 1960s. In the water that surrounds the still active meteor, tropical, parasitical worms swim. It was these worms that killed the child Isaiah's father. Isaiah had been infected by his father and also carries the worms. It is because of this infection and of his knowledge of the location of the meteor that Isaiah is killed.

As Sheena Patchay, among others, observes, Høeg's book deals extensively with 'postcolonial issues of identity formation and the power imbalances extant in any colonialist system'.[15] The novel is driven by the conflict between Greenlandic and Danish interests. The Cryolite Corporation, a representative of Danish as well as global capitalism, is a predatory organisation that does to late twentieth-century Greenland what the commercial institutions in the major European empires have always been doing: walking over indigenous corpses to acquire natural (or, in this case, unnatural) resources. In exploring this neocolonial context, the novel sides strongly with the inventive, relentless, but not always likeable, Smilla.

Like in much other postcolonial writing, the novel's project is intersectional, it and seeks to concurrently investigate related issues of class, gender, race and ethnicity. As Ann McClintock has argued: '[i]mperialism cannot fully be understood without a theory of gender power. Gender power was not the superficial patina of empire, an ephemeral gloss over the more decisive mechanics of class and race. Rather gender dynamics were from the outset, fundamental to the securing and maintenance of the imperial enterprise.'[16] It is therefore not strange that many of the texts that explore Nordic colonialism pay particular attention to gender, and that the more critical texts often place a young female character, rather than a white male, at its centre. To make Smilla, an indigenous woman, the protagonist of the novel is thus a subversive move. However, while the novel evidently seeks to sabotage the dominance of the white male, and thus the symbolic order of Empire, it also invests Smilla with almost uncanny powers. Her feeling for snow, acquired while a child on Greenland but also seemingly inherited from her Inuit mother, turns Smilla into something slightly alien. Like the discursive tropes of 'the magical negro' or 'the magical Indian' that are often used in American popular culture, Smilla becomes not only a champion of indigeneity, but also a strange and not entirely human entity: an Other.[17]

Unlike Peter Høeg, the Norwegian born Kim Leine lived for a long time in Greenland, a period he accounts for in the autobiographical *Kalak* (2007). While he cannot claim to write from the position of the indigenous, he strongly sides, like Høeg, with the decolonial perspective. His award winning and extraordinary *Profeterna i Evighetsfjorden* (2012; *The Prophets of Eternal Fjord*, 2015) follows the life of the missionary priest Morten Pedersen, a Norwegian by birth, who studies theology and medicine, reads Rousseau and imbibes the Enlightenment heritage in Copenhagen in the 1780s, and who eventually becomes a missionary on Greenland. If the missionary priest is one central character in Nordic Gothic, the Enlightenment scientist is the other. As with the missionary, this figure is central to both postcolonial and Gothic literature. In English Gothic, Frankenstein as well as Robert Walton – the Arctic explorer who receives the monster on board his ship frozen into the ice – represent the scientist. In *Profeterna i Evighetsfjorden*, the missionary and the scientist merge in Pedersen, but he often seems more interested and preoccupied with biology and medicine than with theology. He studies 'Linnaeus's great nomenclature… and to a certain extent he feels he becomes one with his image of the young Linnaeus'.[18] Also, like Frankenstein, he collects dead human bodies for dissection and then watches as the professor: '[m]akes his incisions with casual exactness, exposes the greenly glistening muscles of the dead, layer by layer, allowing the shameful smells to be released into the air as the students snigger uneasily or exchange jokes in Latin, and the iridescent tinge of the intestines becomes, little by little, reflected on their own faces.'[19]

Pedersen is consumed by this vision of uncompromising mortality. Watching pre-adolescent girls skipping rope in white dresses he is appalled and considers how '[in] a few short years they will be drawn into the stall and impregnated, swell and give birth, amid ejaculations of blood and slime and stifled gasps, into handkerchiefs splashed with anaesthetic alcohol and perfume'.[20] This vision of the human body as abject and mortal is certainly Gothic, and the novel constantly returns to the human body as concurrently recognisably human and uncanny, forced into unintended shapes by different forms of violence.

comes from the snow reflecting what little light there is from the moon and the stars or from the Aurora Borealis. Because of the seasons and the climate, the region is host to plant and animal life very different from that found in southern parts, and much of the area is elevated, with Scandinavia's highest mountains found here. This is where the borders of Norway, Sweden and Finland converge, and it is also where Sápmi is located, spread over a vast land mass that stretches across territory claimed by four different nations.

Sápmi has been inhabited by the Sámi since before the formation of powerful nation states and economies in Scandinavia. The relationship between Swedes and the Sámi was first characterised by regular or intermittent trade and there is little recorded conflict. With the discovery that Sápmi was very rich in timber and iron ore, gold and silver, and with the establishment of economically and territorially ambitious nation-states in need of these natural resources, efforts were made to colonise the region and to establish firm borders between Norway, Sweden, Finland and Russia so that these nations could divide these resources between themselves. Colonisation of Sápmi was at times violent, but still far from the genocide that marked European colonisation of North or South America, Australia or Africa. However, as in these parts of the world, it was accompanied with an attempt to eradicate as much of the language, culture, customs and religion of the indigenous population as possible. During the eighteenth and nineteenth century, Sápmi was imagined in scholarly as well as fictional writing as a repository of Otherness, a sublime and wild landscape, and a site of tremendous resources that the indigenous population was squandering. Through exploratory journeys such as Carl von Linnaeus' investigatory trip to Sápmi, resulting in the work *Flora Lapponica* (1732), the nation of Sápmi was mapped, while the Sámi themselves were increasingly racialised. In the nineteenth century, people from Scandinavia and from all over Europe began to measure and map the Sámi body. They collected Sámi crania and skeletons, and they compiled collections of Sámi artefacts and traditions, even as these artefacts and traditions were outlawed in Sápmi. During the beginning of the twentieth century, the Sámi remained second-class citizens, exposed to various forms of racism, mapped and segregated by the state-sponsored eugenics movement, and deprived of much of the land that they depended on for both cultural and physical survival.[25]

Sápmi is the location of a number of Nordic Gothic texts, many of which comment extensively on the past and present history of the Sámi as described above. Kerstin Ekman's early and noticeably Gothic crime novel *De tre små mästarna* (1961; *Under the Snow* 1997) takes place in Sápmi and gives Sámi traditions a crucial role in the story. For a part of the novel, the reader is encouraged to believe that the crime has a supernatural element and that the Sámi are to blame, but in the end it is revealed that the violence was committed by a native Swede. In Anders Fager's short story 'Den brutne mannens önskan' (The Broken Man's Wish) from the Lovecraftian collection *Svenska Kulter* (2009, *Swedish Cults*), Gothic horror enters the narrative in ways that makes the story teeter precariously between imperial and postcolonial Gothic. The historically anchored story describes how Swedish soldiers belonging to the fragmented army of the recently deceased Charles XII of Sweden plunder Norwegian farms as they head back towards the Swedish border in the early eighteenth century. The story is focalised through a Norwegian farmer who sees his family murdered, his house plundered and who is horribly tortured by starving and miserable soldiers. As he lies broken, dying, his mother-in-law – an old Sámi woman – persuades him to blow into a strange pipe that she once collected from her shaman father. The pipe calls the ancient and evil frost creature '*Ittakva*' who destroys the retreating Swedish army. In this way, the short story gives significant agency to the Sámi, and imagines a terrible destruction of the murdering, miserable servants of Swedish empire. At the same time, the Sámi is represented as fundamentally Other, agents of witchcraft connected to ancient and evil forces. The supernatural violence that the Sámi woman conjures may be just, but it is still abject and marks her, as in late-Victorian Imperial Gothic novels such as Richard Marsh's *The Beetle* (1897) or Bram Stoker's *Dracula* (1897), as inherently Other and vengeful.

The most widely read Nordic Gothic novels that take place in Sápmi are Stefan Spjut's *Stallo* (2012) and its sequel *Stalpi* (2017). As discussed in Chapter 6, the plot revolves around an amateur cryptozoologist who comes into contact with the Stallo of the title, a race of shape-shifting trolls that inhabit Sápmi alongside the humans. Ann-Sofie Lönngren has argued in 'Trolls!! Folklore Literature and "Othering" in the Nordic Countries' (2015) that the troll 'is made up of an intersection of different axes of power and can thus be understood in light of a postcolonial world order, the development of the Nordic welfare states in the twentieth century, and modern, Western standards relating to gender and sexuality' and as such it 'challenges the Enlightenment's concept of human as a stable entity that is once and for all established'.[26] In *Stallo*, this non-normativity is connected to indigeneity in many different ways. The Stallo have long lived alongside the Sámi, even interbreeding with them on occasion. In the novel, the Sámi again appear as potentially abject and Other. This is also the case in Andre Øvrelid's found-footage, mock horror film *Trolljegeren* (2010; *Troll Hunter*). As discussed by Höglund in 'Revenge of the Trolls: Norwegian (Post) Colonial Gothic', the trolls in this film are clearly an indigenous population, and as in *Stallo*, they merge symbolically and mythologically with the Sámi who are strangely absent from the narrative.[27] In this way, the troll has become a way for Nordic authors to discuss Nordic colonialism, but also to imagine the Sámi as fundamentally different, even as a violent threat to Nordic state power and Nordic citizens.

There are no trolls in *Idjabeaivváš*, but this eight-episode crime thriller still makes extensive and overt use of Gothic effect. It was written and directed by Måns Mårlind and Björn Stein who are no strangers to visual Gothic. They have collaborated in a number of projects, including episodes of the critically acclaimed Nordic Noir *Bron/Broen* (2011, 2013–4; *The Bridge*) and they have also co-directed the Gothic vampire action movie *Underworld: Awakening* (2012). In addition, they have for a long time been involved in turning Fager's *Svenska Kulter* into a feature film. In *Idjabeaivváš*, Mårlind and Stein set out to make a TV series that would be interesting to a vast, international audience eager for more Scandinavian crime stories, but that also sheds light on the history of Sápmi and the past and present plight of the Sámi people. The result has much in common with Høeg's aforementioned *Frøken Smillas fornemmelse for sne*, in that it pits a fundamentally colonial and capitalist modernity against a marginalised indigeneity armed primarily with a sense of justice and an almost supernatural understanding of nature and time. The representation of the Sámi as mysterious and in possession of seemingly paranormal powers has caused considerable controversy and, as will be discussed, critics remain divided on the series as a colonial/postcolonial intervention.

In the dramatic opening of the series, an unconscious man has been strapped to the rotor blades of a helicopter not far from the city of Kiruna in northern Sweden. As he wakes up, the blades start moving, the engine drowning out the man's screams until he is ripped apart and thrown into the heath that surrounds the helicopter. This scene is replaced by the series' title and credit sequence. To the sound of a *jojk*, the traditional song of the Sámi, the camera rushes over a vast body of water towards a low sun framed by the rolling mountains of Sápmi. The title of the series then appears, first in Northern Sápmi as *Idjabeaivváš* then in French as *Jour Polaire*, in English as *Midnight Sun* and in Swedish as *Midnattssol*.[28] The fact that the Sápmi titles comes first signals the series' aim to make the Sámi central to the narrative.

Because the man who has died is discovered to be a French citizen, the young and ambitious French police officer Kahina Zadi is sent to Kiruna to liaise with the Swedish police. Because Kahina is an outsider, she gives the opportunity for the series to explain the geography, climate and ongoing power struggle between the Swedish and the Sámi in the region. Moreover, Kahina is also second-generation Algerian Berber and has first-hand experience of the racism that colonialism produces. She is picked up by chief prosecutor Rutger Burlin and together they travel in a helicopter towards the crime scene. As they pass over the great Kiruna mine, nicknamed 'mother' by the locals, Kahina is told that the mine produces enough iron ore every single day for six Eiffel towers. She is also informed that because the mining process has begun to threaten the integrity of the city of Kiruna, the entire city is being moved. While the Sámi are not mentioned in this particular exchange, it is clear that the mine is a locus of power in the region: 'Without her, there is nothing.' During another trip, Kahina spots a herd of reindeer and learns that they belong to the Sámi: 'This land belonged to them before the Swedish came and grabbed everything. They took everything except the reindeer probably because it's such hard work.' When Kahina asks if the Sámi have held on to their 'traditional way of life' she is informed that some do and some don't and that many are ashamed 'because they have been treated like shit for the past 400 years'. The colonial history and the present that form the context of this series is thus thoroughly established.

Before the first episode is over, two more people are murdered. The first is a local helicopter pilot who, naked, bleeding and bound by chains, is attacked and killed by wolves. The other is chief prosecutor Burlin who has been sickly throughout the episode and who is suddenly struck by hallucinations of Kiruna collapsing around him. He keels over and dies on the street. His death thrusts assistant prosecutor Anders Harnesk into the role of primary investigator. Harnesk is himself half-Sámi and also a closeted homosexual. Like Smilla, and a bit like the troll, his position is thus non-normative and transgressive. He is also very well placed to explain the peculiar geographical and cultural terrain that forms the background of the increasingly Gothic plot to both Kahina and the audience.

A few episodes into the series, mounting evidence shows first that there is a strange connection between the French state and the people working at the Kiruna mine, and also that the murders have been committed by someone who is either Sámi or who has an extensive understanding of Sámi culture and traditions. At each gruesome murder scene, Sámi artefacts have been left behind. This prompts Kahina and Harnesk to investigate the local Sámi population, in particular those who are not entirely integrated, but also to speak to the few French people that live in the area. Their investigation brings them into contact both with a retired French CEO and one of the local Sámi Nåjds, a shaman. In this way, the series brings the violence inherent in Swedish colonialism in Sápmi to the surface and also connects it to French global power.

At this point in the series, it is clear that *Idjabeaivváš* is Gothic in several different ways. Burlin's hallucination and morbid death were brought on by poison that had been fed to him for an extended period of time and that was derived from plants in the area. Another man is found tortured to death in an outdoor, Sámi storage space, his heart pierced long after death by a Sámi spear. Like the climate, the landscape – with its low forests, barren and wolf-inhabited open spaces, blood sucking mosquitos, and its gaping mine that is devouring an entire city – is both sublime in the traditional sense and a constant source of uncanny Gothic terror. As in von Trier's seminal *Riget*, there is a profound conflict between, on the one hand, the ancient landscape and the people who belong to the landscape, and, on the other hand, what is buried deep in the ground or erected on top of it. Also, and controversially, *Idjabeaivváš* invests Sámi traditions, and the people that practise these traditions, with an uncanny, even paranormal, understanding of space and time. The key figure here is the Nåjd, played by Sámi musician and activist Sofia Jannok, one of many Sámi actors in the series.

In their efforts to figure out how the poison that killed Burlin was acquired, Kahina and Harnesk travel by helicopter to the isolated cabin where the Nåjd lives with her brother. Harnesk is eventually allowed into the cabin and offered coffee by the Nåjd. The Nåjd informs him enigmatically that: 'Since I was a child, I've had the feeling that something is going to happen. Something wicked... and this feeling I still call: The great suffering.' As in many Gothic classics, a sense of foreboding and a vague prophecy of doom informs the story. Yet, the most Gothic moment transpires outside the cabin, where Kahina has just received a neck massage from the helicopter pilot. The viewer again sees hands reaching for Kahina's shoulders, rubbing them, but when she shakes them off and says she is fine, she and the viewer sees the helicopter pilot reclining in the distance. The body to which the hands belong cannot be seen anywhere. Disturbed by the uncanny experience, Kahina insists that the interview with the Nåjd should continue at the police station. Once there, the Nåjd stops talking, but when three elderly men, evidently Sámi and also identified as Nåjds, gather outside the station and begin to sing the traditional *jojk*, she joins in. As they sing in unison, the overcast sky begins to move quickly across the heavens, signalling their strange connection to, and even partial control over, Sápmi space time.

The Gothicisation of Sápmi and the Sámi further intensifies when Eddie, a young and bullied Sámi in his mid-twenties, enters the story. Eddie is the brother of the Sámi poet and activist Evelina Geatki, a role that is also filled by a well-known Sámi activist: the actress, rapper and *jojk* singer Maxida Märak. Geatki is believed to have killed herself by throwing herself down a waterfall, but her body has never been found. Thus, it comes as no great surprise when Geatki appears to be in hiding from the world in her brother's old house. What is surprising is the discovery that seemingly kind and mild-mannered Eddie is, in fact, the murderer. He has learnt that a group of miners working one of the shifts at the mine have received a substantial sum of money to bury radioactive waste from a French nuclear bomb in a sealed-off part of the Kiruna mine. Eddie has now begun killing all the people involved in this deed to avenge the pollution of Sápmi, seemingly egged on by his sister.

Yet, Eddie is also driven by a wish for personal vengeance. In the penultimate episode, the skeletal remains of Evelina Gaetki's body are discovered. The figure that has accompanied, conversed and conspired with Eddie must therefore be a ghost or a figment of Eddie's bereaved mind, or perhaps both. Evelina is with him, asking for comfort, helping out with his vengeance, yet he knows that his sister is dead. She was killed after a joint decision by the miners because she accidentally learned about the conspiracy to hide the waste. Eddie knows about this because of a video message Evelina sent him shortly before she was killed, and after torturing one of the conspirators, the victim found in the storage space with a spear through his heart. Evelina is dead, yet she has returned and is with her brother, helping him avenge her own death.

Again, Sápmi becomes a location where time and space follow other trajectories, where the border between life and death is less absolute than in the nation-state Sweden. The Nåjd has told Harnesk that, for him 'the mountain' is 'open', that what they are 'looking for is invisible', like a 'crack', and that he 'must find the borders'. Indeed, a Gothic fissure

7.1 The ghost of Evelina urging Eddie on in his project of vengeance (SVT/Canal+, 2016, *Idjabeaivváš/Jour Polaire/Midnight Sun/Midnattssol*).

divides Sápmi from the rational world that Sweden has embraced. This does not mean that the Nåjd has helped to engineer or even support the violence being done to the miners who helped hide the French radioactive material. She aids the investigation in various ways, but cannot, or will not, prevent the cataclysmic ending to the story. In the final episode, Eddie engineers a partial flooding of the mine, and perishes with the remaining miners. He has left behind a video where he calls for a Sápmi uprising. Sitting in traditional Sámi dress, on a mountain overlooking the Kiruna mine, he holds a spear before him and repeatedly tells the unseen viewer: 'Seize this spear, and take back our Sápmi.'

This video recording and the fact that Kahina and Harnesk fail to prevent the death of the miners, indicate that the true crime of *Idjabeaivváš* is not in fact the murder of the miners, but the colonisation of Sápmi; the destruction of the land first by the Swedish state and then by French neocolonial interests. In the series, the true revelation is that Sweden and France have both ruthlessly exploited Sápmi, stealing its natural resources, destroying the land and the culture, and dumping the refuse of neocolonial ambitions beneath the surface. The series makes this devastating exploitation plain in many different ways, but mostly by tying together French and Swedish colonialism by aligning Kahina's Algerian Berber identity with that of the Sámi. Interrogating a young Sámi named Kristoffer, a member of the activist organisation Young Sámi, Kahina explains: 'I am French, but I am also Berber… Indigenous

7.2 Eddie urging the viewer to seize the spear and take back Sápmi (SVT/Canal+, 2016, *Idjabeaivváš/Jour Polaire/Midnight Sun/Midnattssol*).

people, like you. And I know what it feels like when people stare, because of your colour, your name… I know, I've had it all my life. I understand you, Kristoffer.' Thus, the audience is not encouraged to mourn for the more than 20 miners that perish in the mine, but for land stolen and destroyed and for cultures suppressed and torn apart. Eddie's call for a Sápmi insurrection is buried by Harnesk, proud that the language of the Sámi has no word for war, but at the same time it is voiced by the series itself.

Both the indictment of Swedish and French colonialism and the Gothicisation of Sápmi and the Sámi in *Idjabeaivváš* created controversy. The Swedish critic Gunilla Brodrej argued that:

> The Sámi are depicted either as militant young activists or as strange oddballs who appear suddenly with a *jojk* and something very mysterious in their eyes. Clairvoyant and peculiar, the nåjd (the musician Sofia Jannok) sits at a table and speaks in riddles, long since abandoned by the director. The hip hopper Maxida Märak figures as the city's long-lost Sámi icon. Through this wretched arrangement, majority society keeps limiting the role of the Sámi in society. First as reindeer herder. Now as a prop.[29]

Indeed, and as in Peter Høeg's *Frøken Smillas fornemmelse for sne*, a certain Othering, perhaps even a form of exotism, appears to be at work in the series. The Nåjd's preternatural connection with time and space, her refusal or inability to speak plainly, can be seen as evidence of a still existing agency unacknowledged by post-Enlightenment society, but she also brings the log lady of *Twin Peaks* to mind. Just like the owls are not what they seem in upstate Washington, the reindeer of Sápmi also function as a connection to a different and Gothic reality.

Some Sámi voices have seconded Brodrej's critique, while others have dismissed it. Unsurprisingly, Märak and Jannok, the activists and actors who play key roles in the series, stress the fact that *Idjabeaivvá*š sheds light on the long history of Swedish colonialism in Sápmi. 'Many Swedes are completely uninterested or know little about the political situation of the Sámi, and in these cases, popular culture is a good way to reach an audience. It is our most effective weapon',[30] Märak declares in an interview. Also, the Sámi Johan Sandberg McGuinne argues that Brodrej's article exemplifies exactly the kind of stereotypical understanding of the Sámi that she says she seeks to undo. By arguing for a certain understanding of the Sámi, she builds her argument around an image 'that is just as colonial, one-dimensional and stereotypical as the one we have been granted by Sweden.'[31]

Nordic (Post)colonial Gothic

The object of the analysis of *Idjabeaivvá*š has not been to determine whether it succeeds or fails as a (post)colonial or decolonial interrogation of Swedish racist attitudes or of state exploitation of Sápmi.[32] The focus here is to show how deeply informed this particular Gothic narrative is by past and present colonialism. Indeed, as the analysis of the Høeg, Leine, Spjut and Fager texts shows, Nordic Gothic revolves, much like Anglophone or Francophone Gothic, around images of race and comments frequently on Empire. Colonialism may have been written out of Nordic history, but it haunts its Gothic fiction just as it haunts Nordic society. Similar to the more established Gothic traditions, Nordic Gothic is sometimes imperial. As such, it is arguably capable of mobilising Gothic in the service of Empire and colonialism by casting the indigenous Other as a monstrous, hostile, transformative entity; as a malign troll or witch.

However, there is also a Nordic Gothic that seeks to dismantle colonialism, even normativity itself, through stories that identify neoliberal modernity as the true destructive force, and that imagine progressive and liberating alternatives to stale and heteronormative formations of culture. *Idjabeaivvá*š and Lindqvist's 'Gräns' are examples of texts that clearly propose that what haunts society is not an abject and uncivilised indigeneity, but capitalism, modernity and the heteronormative masculinity that, as Mrinali Sinha is one of many to have observed, underpinned the colonial project.[33]

Much modern Nordic Gothic, like a great number of modern international Gothic texts, gets lost in these negotiations, or simply refuses to take sides, even as it reproduces the ideological stakes in question. As in international Gothic texts, many narratives exist concurrently across the entire ideological scale that moves from conservative, heteronormative and imperial Gothic to anti-imperial, post-colonial, and non-normative Gothic. In this way, Nordic Gothic is both dependent on, and a critic of, the international Gothic canon. It haunts the Imperial Gothic of *Dracula*, but it is also haunted by it. It dismisses the notion that indigeneity is abject and Other even as it rehearses this very trope. In the process, it opens up new roads to understanding Nordic colonialism as it occurred both within the territory claimed by Nordic nation states and outside it. Any account of Nordic Gothic must acknowledge the presence of these roads, regardless of where they lead.

Notes

1 As Gurminder Bhambra argues in *Rethinking Modernity: Postcolonialism and the Sociological Imagination*, the 'histories of imperialism, colonialism, and slavery that enabled Europe and the West' are crucial to any understanding of how Europe and the Global North became modern (London: Palgrave Macmillan, 2007), pp. 145–6. See also W. Mignolo, *The Darker Side of Western Modernity: Global Futures, Decolonial Options* (Durham: Duke University Press, 2011).
2 A. Smith and W. Hughes (eds), *Empire and the Gothic: The Politics of Genre* (London: Palgrave Macmillan, 2003), p. 1.
3 See also P. Brantlinger, *Rule of Darkness: British Literature and Imperialism, 1830–1914* (Ithaca: Cornell University Press, 1988); T. Khair, *The Gothic, Postcolonialism and Otherness: Ghosts from Elsewhere* (Basingstoke: Palgrave MacMillan, 2009); C. Sugars and G. Turcotte (eds), *Unsettled Remains: Canadian Literature and the Postcolonial Gothic* (Waterloo: Wilfrid University Press, 2009); T. Khair and J. Höglund (eds), *Postcolonial and Transnational Vampires: Dark Blood* (Basingstoke: Palgrave Macmillan, 2012); J. Höglund, *The American Imperial Gothic: Empire, Culture, Violence* (Farnham: Ashgate, 2014); and J. D. Edwards and S. Vasconcelos (eds), *Tropical Gothic in Literature and Culture* (Abingdon: Routledge, 2016).
4 Khair, *The Gothic, Postcolonialism and Otherness*, p. 6.
5 R. Duncan, *South African Gothic: Anxiety and Creative Dissent in the Post-apartheid Imagination and Beyond* (Cardiff: University of Wales Press, 2018).
6 K. L. Piper argues in 'Inuit Diasporas: Frankenstein and the Inuit in England' that Shelley's *Frankenstein* 'appeared to be timed to coincide with the advent of… infamous expeditions to the North. Besides being captivated by the expeditions themselves, the English public had long been fascinated by Greenlandic Inuits and Eskimos… in *Frankenstein*, the creature himself came to represent these inhabitants of the

North, as well as the threat of their arrival in England if increased communication were to occur. Just as John Sackhouse had once arrived as a stowaway on British shores, so *Frankenstein*'s creature is a stranger who must be incorporated in – or rejected from – European culture', *Romanticism*, 13:1 (2007), pp. 63–75, 63.
7   N. Feuz, *Horrora Borealis* (Paris: Livre de Poche, 2018).
8   E. Oxfeldt, *Nordic Orientalism: Paris and the Cosmopolitan Imagination 1800–1900* (Copenhagen: Museum Tusculanum Press, 2005).
9   Smith and Hughes, *Empire and the Gothic*, p. 4.
10 Brantlinger, *Rule of Darkness*, p. 227.
11 S. Keskinen, S. Tuori, S. Irni and D. Mulinari (eds), *Complying with Colonialism: Gender, Race and Ethnicity in the Nordic Region* (Farnham: Ashgate, 2009), p. 1.
12 See E. Donaghue *Black Women/White Men. The Sexual Exploitation of Female Slaves in the Danish West Indies* (Bloomington: Authorhouse, 2006); L. Körber and E. Volquardsen (eds), *The Postcolonial North Atlantic: Iceland, Greenland and the Faroe Islands* (Berlin: Nordeuropa Institut der Humboldt Universität, 2014); A. Svalastog and G. Fur (eds), *Visions of Sápmi* (Røros: Arthub Publisher, 2015); M. Naum and J. M. Nordin (eds), *Scandinavian Colonialism and the Rise of Modernity. Small Time Agents in a Global Arena* (New York: Springer, 2013).
13 A. Loomba, *Colonialism/Postcolonialism* (Abingdon: Routledge, 1998), p. 8.
14 See K. Loftsdóttir and L. Jensen (eds), *Whiteness and Postcolonialism in the Nordic Region* (Farnham: Ashgate, 2012).
15 S. Patchay, 'Not Just a Detective Novel: Trauma, Memory and Narrative Form in *Miss Smilla's Feeling for Snow*' *JLS/TLW*, 26:4 (2010) 17–35. DOI: 10.1080/02564718.2010.529311.
16 A. McClintock, *Imperial Leather: Race, Gender, and Sexuality in the Colonial Contest* (New York: Routledge: 1995), pp. 6–7.
17 See M. W. Hughey 'Cinethetic Racism: White Redemption and Black Stereotypes in "Magical Negro" Films', *Social Problems*, 56:3 (2009), pp. 543–77, DOI:10.1525/sp. 2009.56.3.543, and J. Kilpatrick *Celluloid Indians: Native Americans and Film* (Lincoln: University of Nebraska Press, 1999). Smilla is noticeably different from the trope of the 'magical negro' and 'magical Indian' in that her powers are not used to transform a white, male protagonist.
18 K. Leine, *Prophets of Eternal Fjord* (London: Atlantic Books, 2016), p. 13.
19 Leine, *Prophets of Eternal Fjord*, p. 22.
20 Leine, *Prophets of Eternal Fjord*, p. 24.
21 The name '*Sukkertoppen*' partly accomplishes the same deeply ironic work as the name of 'Sweet Home' used to designate the slave plantation on which the protagonists live in Toni Morrisson's *Beloved* (1980). At the same time, it signals a desire for the Greenlandic settlement to yield the same kind of colonial bounty as the early European colonies in America where white sugar, along with cotton and tobacco, was central to the early triangular trade.
22 L. Jensen 'Postcolonial Denmark: Beyond the Rot of Colonialism?', *Postcolonial Studies*, 18:4 (2015), pp. 440–52, 448. DOI:10.1080/13688790.2015.1191989.
23 See C. Lundström, *White Migrations: Gender, Whiteness and Privilege in Transnational Migration* (Basingstoke: Palgrave Macmillan, 2014).
24 See J. Höglund's 'Wither the Present, Wither the Past: The Low-Budget Gothic Horror of Stockholm Syndrome Films', in J. D. Edwards and J. Höglund (eds),

B-Movie Gothic: International Perspectives (Edinburgh: Edinburgh University Press, 2018), pp. 122–38.
25 See C. G. Ojala and J. M. Nordin, 'Collecting Sápmi: Early modern collecting of Sámi material culture', Nordisk Museologi 2 (2015), pp. 114–22; L. Andersson Burnett, 'The "Lapland" Giantess in Britain' in D. Brydon, P. Forsgren and G. Fur (eds), Concurrent Imaginaries, Postcolonial Worlds: Toward Revised Histories (Leiden: Brill, 2017), pp. 123–43; R. Kvist, 'The Racist Legacy in Modern Swedish Saami Policy', Canadian Journal of Native Studies, 14:2 (1994), pp. 203–20.
26 A. Lönngren, 'Trolls!! Folklore Literature and "Othering" in the Nordic Countries' in A. Lönngren, H. Grönstrand, D. Heede and A. Heith (eds), Rethinking National Literatures and the Literary Canon in Scandinavia (Newcastle upon Tyne: Cambridge Scholars Publishing, 2015), pp. 205–30, p. 205.
27 J. Höglund, 'Revenge of the Trolls: Norwegian (Post) Colonial Gothic', Edda, 117:2 (2017), pp. 115–29. DOI: 10.18261/issn.1500-1989-2017-02-03.
28 This naming of the series is significant. By first presenting the title in Northern Sápmi, and by moving the Swedish title to the end, it inverts the traditional linguistic order and the power structure that accompanies it.
29 'Samerna porträtteras antingen som militanta unga aktivister eller underliga kufar som plötsligt dyker upp med en jojk och något gravt gåtfullt i blicken. Synsk och sällsam sitter nåjden (musikern Sofia Jannok) vid ett bord och talar i gåtor, för länge sedan övergiven av regissören. Hiphoparen Maxida Märak figurerar som stadens mystiskt försvunna samiska ikon. Genom detta usla upplägg fortsätter majoritetssamhället att begränsa samens roll i samhället. Först som renskötare. Nu som rekvisita.' G. Brodrej, 'Samisk exotism i SVT:s thrillerserie' Expressen (13 November 2016), www.expressen.se/kultur/gunilla-brodrej/samisk-exotism-i-svts-thrillerserie/.
30 'Många svenskar är helt ointresserade eller dåligt insatta i samernas politiska situation och då är populärkultur ett bra sätt att nå ut. Det är vårt mest effektiva vapen' Maxida Märak cited in J. Andersson, 'Premiär för SVT:s blodiga morddrama' Göteborgsposten (23 October 2016), www.gp.se/kultur/tv/premi%C3%A4r-f%C3%B6r-svt-s-blodiga-morddrama-1.3890859.
31 'Denna bild är precis lika kolonial, endimensionell och stereotyp som den vi alltid fått oss tilldelad av Sverige.' J. Sandberg McGuinne, 'Gunilla Brodrej vet inte hur samer har det', Expressen (18 November 2016), www.expressen.se/kultur/gunilla-brodrej-vet-inte-hur-samer-har-det/.
32 Indeed, any attempt to settle such a debate by a Swedish academic writing as an employee of a University in Southern Sweden would be problematic.
33 See M. Sinha, Colonial Masculinity: The 'Manly Englishman' and The 'Effeminate Bengali' in the Late Nineteenth Century (Manchester: Manchester University Press, 1995).

8

Maria Holmgren Troy

Lost (and gained) in translation: Nordic Gothic and transcultural adaptation

'As openly acknowledged and extended reworkings of particular other texts, adaptations are often compared to translations.'[1]

Lars von Trier's Danish TV series *Riget* (DR 1994, 1997, four plus four episodes; *The Kingdom*) and John Ajvide Lindqvist's Swedish novel *Låt den rätte komma in* (2004; *Let the Right One In*, 2007) are arguably the two most significant and influential examples of Nordic Gothic in the boom of Gothic productions in the Nordic region around and after the turn of the century. Von Trier's TV series about a haunted hospital in Copenhagen and Lindqvist's vampire novel set in a Stockholm suburb quickly gained international recognition. The popularity of Lindqvist's novel was further boosted when it was adapted into what became an internationally acclaimed Swedish film: *Låt den rätte komma in* (2008; *Let the Right One In*). Lindqvist wrote the screenplay himself for this film adaptation and it was directed by Tomas Alfredson.

Riget and *Låt den rätte komma in* have also spawned American adaptations, which will be discussed together and compared with von Trier's and Lindqvist's Nordic Gothic productions in this chapter. Based on von Trier's TV series, Stephen King developed *Kingdom Hospital* (ABC 2004, thirteen episodes) with von Trier as one of the executive producers. *Kingdom Hospital* was the first American adaptation of a Danish TV series,[2] and it has been followed by American adaptations of Nordic Noir police-procedural series such as Danish *Forbrydelsen* (2007–2012; *The Killing*), adapted into the American series *The Killing* (2011–2014), and Swedish-Danish *Bron/Broen* (2011–2018), adapted into *The Bridge* (2013–2014), set on the border between the United States and Mexico. The popularity of Nordic Noir is also evidenced in the Swedish 2009 film adaptations of the novels in Stieg Larsson's Millennium trilogy (2005, 2006, 2007), the American-Swedish adaptation of the first novel in the trilogy, *Män som hatar kvinnor* (2005; *The Girl with the Dragon Tattoo*, 2008), into the film *The Girl with the Dragon Tattoo* (2011), and the American-Swedish film *The Girl in the Spider's Web* (2018), an adaptation of the first novel in the new Millennium trilogy, David Lagercrantz' *Det som inte dödar oss* (2015; *The Girl in the Spider's Web* 2015). The American film, *Let Me In* (2010), with a screenplay and direction by Matt Reeves, acknowledges both the novel and the Swedish film as sources for this adaptation of *Låt den rätte komma in*. Nordic Gothic might appear to be surfing on an international wave of interest in Nordic Noir, but the American adaptations of von Trier's TV series and Lindqvist's novel and film actually preceded all of the American adaptations of the Nordic Noir productions mentioned above.

Adaptation is one way in which Nordic Gothic circulates across media and national borders. It should be noted, however, that Danish *Riget* and Swedish *Låt den rätte komma in* had reached an international audience long before the release of the American adaptations.[3] Although some critics have attempted to argue that they have a more global appeal or relevance than the Nordic versions,[4] these adaptations were first and foremost targeting a national, American audience as evinced by their use of 'Americanisation' as a 'transculturating' adaptation strategy.[5] In *A Theory of Adaptation* (2013), Linda Hutcheon suggests that 'there is a wide range of reasons why adapters might choose a particular story and then transcode it into a particular medium or genre… [T]heir aim might well be to economically and artistically supplant the prior works. They are just as likely to want to contest the aesthetic or political values of the adapted text as to pay homage'.[6] From Stephen King's and Matt Reeves' perspectives, the American adaptations are at least partly meant to pay homage to the Nordic Gothic precursors, which is visible in quite a few direct audio-visual 'quotations' of the Nordic versions in the American productions. Beyond King's and Reeves' personal admiration for and interest in adapting *Riget* and *Låt den rätte komma in*, there were unsurprisingly also American economic interests at play. ABC, one of the big traditional US networks, needed to improve its viewer ratings in a changing TV landscape, which I will comment on below, and hoped that King's *Kingdom Hospital* would be the answer to that challenge, whereas Reeves had been the director of the found-footage horror movie *Cloverfield* (2008), a profitable box office hit. However, despite Stephen King pronouncing it 'the best American horror movie in the last 20 years',[7] *Let Me In* did not meet economic expectations; and with falling ratings *Kingdom Hospital* failed to run for a second season.

In this chapter, I will examine certain aspects of *Riget* and *Låt den rätte komma* – both the novel and the Swedish film adaptation – in conjunction with the American adaptations. This examination will show how these Nordic and American productions relate to the Gothic and the uncanny in different ways. In connection with the transculturating of adaptations, Hutcheon observes that '[a]n adaptation, like the work it adapts, is always framed in a context – a time and a place, a society and a culture' and that, '[i]n the name of relevance, adapters seek the "right" resetting or recontextualizing'.[8] A number of thematic aspects that are dealt with in other parts of *Nordic Gothic* are thus of interest here, such as the representation of the history of the setting and the provincial versus the urban. Hutcheon also suggests that there is frequently 'an accompanying shift in the political valence from the adapted text to the "transculturated" adaptation', and that '[s]ometimes adapters purge an earlier text of elements that their particular cultures in time or place might find difficult or controversial'.[9] This chapter will underline some ideological specificities particular to the different cultures under scrutiny, as well as some differences between the Nordic and American productions that are related to Gothic humour. In the case of *Riget* and *Kingdom Hospital*, the adaptation is made within the same medium, and in my discussion of the settings I will pay attention to one of the media-specific framings that guide the viewers' perception of the two TV series: the pre-credit sequences. To provide a background, I will first briefly present television's relation to horror and Gothic and how von Trier, King and Lindqvist have moved between different media.

Moving between media

Novels, films and TV series are different media with different challenges and possibilities, some of which have considerable impact on adaptations. These media have also had varying statuses in different national and regional contexts over time. For instance, *Twin Peaks* (ABC 1990–1991), which influenced Danish art film writer and director Lars von Trier's foray into that medium, was an unusual instance at the time of an American film director making a TV series.[10]

Although, as Helen Wheatley argues in *Gothic Television* (2006), television may be the perfect medium for Gothic due to its uncanny potential, as it, like the genre, 'is deeply concerned with the domestic',[11] television's relation to horror and Gothic has historically also been complicated precisely by the medium's 'deep-rooted links to the safety of hearth and home'.[12] In *The Pleasures of Horror* (2005), which includes comments on both *Riget* and *Kingdom Hospital*, Matt Hills makes a distinction between 'TV horror' and 'Gothic TV': 'TV horror' in Hills' definition is 'associated with gore and low culture' whereas 'Gothic TV' is connected to 'high(er) cultural versions of horror *literature*' and can thereby be 'approximated to period drama or literary adaptation'.[13] Hills suggests that the classic horror monster, if shown on television, was often made less monstrous by the historical distance of the setting or by it being an anachronism whose affective power was reduced.[14] What eventually made TV horror legitimate and lent it cultural value around the turn of the century was partly the targeting of niche or fan audiences and partly discourses of authorship.[15]

The development of American television in the 1980s and early 1990s, which resulted in new types of television drama and new channels, has been called 'television's second golden age': it created a tradition of quality television that includes '*auteurism*, genre hybridity, a new and heightened sense of realism, niche marketing and a slightly more provocative content'.[16] Andreas Halskov points to similar developments in parts of Scandinavia during that period.[17] According to Halskov, DR (the Danish broadcasting corporation) bought *Twin Peaks* in 1990, not in order to gain high viewer ratings but because, through its association with 'arthouse director David Lynch, *Twin Peaks* could strengthen DR's image as a producer of quality television for a Danish audience that was, at best, ambivalent when it came to American TV shows'.[18]

Riget played a similar role for DR as *Twin Peaks*: it was quality branding and not ratings that counted. And, as Halskov puts it, '[i]f one were to mention only one TV show as the catalyst for *the second golden age* of Danish television drama, one would unflinchingly point to Lars von Trier's miniseries *Riget* (*The Kingdom*)'.[19] The TV series also changed the general impression of von Trier in Denmark 'from obscure, provoking outsider to our own provoking outsider'.[20] Earlier, while being celebrated as an *auteur* in other parts of Europe, von Trier was not appreciated in Denmark, where he was seen as an impossible figure both in terms of attitude and aesthetics.[21] Indeed, *Riget* was a breakthrough for von Trier that made him popular not only in Denmark but also in Sweden.[22]

Riget and *Kingdom Hospital* are examples of 'authored TV'; the names Lars von Trier and Stephen King stand for some kind of quality that audiences recognise.[23] This quality is different in each case: King is regarded as the master of mainstream Gothic, while von Trier is recognised precisely for not being mainstream. Although King complained in 1981 about network television's censorship restrictions, which made showing horror on television difficult, if not impossible,[24] since then his attitude has changed with the changes in television and he now prefers to adapt his novels and short stories for the small rather than the large screen.[25] Against the background of the second golden age of television as outlined above, it makes sense that King has found television an increasingly suitable medium for his work. He has, however, chosen to work primarily with networks, usually ABC, instead of more niche TV channels.[26] In *TV Horror* (2013), Lorna Jowett and Stacy Abbott propose that 'King's work has proved ideally suited to mainstream television because its hybridity [a combination of horror, American gothic and New England folk fiction] already downplays the horror'. They point out that 'the genre of Stephen King is more gothic than horror, more suggestive than graphic, and more character- than action-based'.[27] Like Hills, then, Jowett and Abbott make a distinction between TV horror and Gothic TV. They also mention that '[w]hile horror is often defined by gore and splatter, even on TV, at the other end of the spectrum are productions that delight in surrealism and strangeness, evoking the fantastic through art-house emphasis on visuality',[28] placing *Twin Peaks*, *Riget* and *Carnivàle* (HBO, 2003–2005) at the latter end of the spectrum as examples of '*auteur* TV' where an arthouse director brings artistic style and vision to a TV series.[29]

Also moving between different media, John Ajvide Lindqvist worked as a scriptwriter for a Swedish comedy TV series (1999–2001) and a drama series (2005), as well as a magician and stand-up comedian, before his debut as a novelist with *Låt den rätte komma in*; and he insisted on writing the screenplay for the Swedish adaptation of his novel. According to the director, Tomas Alfredson, Lindqvist did this surprisingly well,[30] most likely due to his earlier experiences of writing for television. After being courted by a great many interested parties after the resounding success of his vampire novel, Lindqvist very deliberately chose Alfredson as director for the film adaptation.[31] By then, Alfredson had worked both as a TV and film director in Sweden, and was a member and the director of a Swedish group of comedians, Killinggänget. Lindqvist had seen Alfredson's film *Fyra nyanser av brunt* (2004; *Four Nuances of*

Brown),[32] which includes a scene where a boy considers suicide to the sound of the religious song 'Han är min sång och min glädje' ('He is my Song and my Joy'); this scene convinced Lindqvist that Alfredson was the 'right one'.[33] A dark sense of humour is thus important common ground for Lindqvist and Alfredson.[34]

Lindqvist compares Alfredson to Lars von Trier: he sees them both as being able to 'subtly evoke strong emotions without it becoming pathetic'.[35] Lindqvist also sees similarities to von Trier's work in what he himself tries to achieve as a writer: 'I want to write high quality entertainment literature. Or as I call it: functioning melodrama. As Lars von Trier's films for example… They never feel cold or calculating…'[36] As a writer of Gothic fiction, Lindqvist is often compared to Stephen King, but he claims to be much more inspired by Clive Barker,[37] who wrote and directed the classic horror movie *Hellraiser* (1987) – a film that is based on his novella *The Hellbound Heart* (1986). Barker's works are considered as central contributions to the splatterpunk genre, and, as I have argued elsewhere, Lindqvist includes splatterpunk elements in his novel *Låt den rätte komma in*.[38]

These graphic aspects of Lindqvist's novel are to a great extent lost in the translation of the novel into film and so is much of the humour in Lindqvist's novel, which is Gothic in the sense that it is mostly related to horrific elements including the explicit paedophilia. Humour and horror are not that far apart, according to Lindqvist:

> "It's about taking a normal situation and placing something anomalous in it", Lindqvist explains. "Comedy becomes more comical with a straight man as a counterbalance. Horror works in similar ways".
>
> "The funniest", he says, "is comedy when it is balancing on the edge of horror, when you build up anxiety that ends in liberating laughter".[39]

His thoughts on the connections between horror and laughter are relevant not only regarding *Låt den rätte komma in*, but also to Gothic humour in *Riget*. What I call 'Gothic humour' is thus related to body horror, the abject, the grotesque and the macabre; a combination of Gothic or horror and laughter.

Lost in translation? – Gothic humour in *Låt den rätte komma in* and *Riget*

Låt den rätte komma in features a bullied twelve-year-old boy, Oskar, who lives with his divorced mother in an apartment complex in

Blackeberg, a Stockholm suburb. His life changes when he befriends a vampire child called Eli who, together with the adult human helper Håkan, moves in next door. This adult male character is one of the novel's focalisers, which means that the reader gets first-hand insights into the reasoning of someone with paedophilic inclinations.

Gothic humour in Lindqvist's novel is evident in the treatment and development of Håkan. After having thrown acid over himself when being caught at an unsuccessful attempt at acquiring fresh human blood for Eli and subsequently offering up his own blood to his 'beloved' while in the hospital, Håkan is transformed into an undead disfigured, brain-dead monster with a constant erection. Escaping from the morgue, what drives this monster is finding Eli, whom he traps in the basement of an apartment building. The vampire child is at first afraid of this grotesque version of his former helper, who 'emits an overpowering sense of threat', but then he sees the undead monster's erection which he masturbates: 'Eli imagined one of those obscene dolls that you wound up with a key; a monk whose cape went up and then he started masturbating as long as the mechanism allowed./ *clickety-click, clickety click* ... / Eli laughed, was so occupied with the crazy image that he didn't notice when Håkan stepped into the room, uninvited.'[40] This may be seen as an text-internal illustration of what Lindqvist calls comedy 'balancing on the edge of horror' but with a dark twist since the 'liberating laughter' is cut short and Eli is severely physically abused and violently raped by Håkan.[41]

The glue-sniffing teenager Tommy, who does not have a part in the two film adaptations, is also in the basement and overhears the interaction between Eli and the monstrous Håkan. Tommy is in the dark clasping a shooting trophy, a small statuette, that he has stolen from a police officer dating his mother. When he tries to move from the corner where he has been hiding, he stumbles over what he first irrationally believes to be his father's corpse. It is actually the undead Håkan who has finally been blinded and overpowered by Eli, who has managed to escape. Tommy's fear and its abject consequences are described in graphic detail before he 'drew back, away from the corpse, with excrement clinging to his buttocks, and thought for a moment that he could *see in the dark* as his sound impressions transformed into vision and he *saw* the corpse rise up in the darkness, a yellowish shape, a constellation.'[42] As Tommy tries to get away, fragments from a popular Swedish children's TV show, *Fem myror är fler än fyra elefanter* (1973–1974; *Five ants are more than four elephants*), appear in his mind and he almost 'started to sing out loud.'[43] Slowly he realises that the living corpse that is chasing him is blind and he manages to use the statuette as a club to knock it down. However, it keeps its erection and refuses to stay down so Tommy hits the remains of the undead Håkan again and again, singing *'An elephant balancing on the little, little thread of a spider web!'*, a Swedish song for pre-school children. The dark, situational comedy is strengthened when the owner of the shooting trophy finally finds Tommy covered in blood and tissue scraps singing *'Two-hundred and seventy-five elephants / On a teensy spider weee – ...'* in a broken voice as he continues to hit 'the butchered remains', which are still moving, with the base of the trophy.[44] Thus, Gothic humour in this example includes body horror, the abject, the grotesque and the bizarre.

In the Swedish film adaptation, which does not include Håkan's undead rampage, the humour mainly resides in his clumsy ineptness as a provider of blood for Eli. The viewer is treated to his foray into a forest area to find a suitable victim, where his doings are watched for a while by a white poodle, and to another failed attempt in a locker room at the public pool where he acts as a lethal peeping Tom. In the American adaptation, in which care has been taken to rid the vampire child's adult male human helper of any suspicions of paedophilic desires,[45] the humour is further toned down. Casting Richard Jenkins in this part may possibly be seen as an allusion to the Gothic comedy of the American TV series *Six Feet Under* (HBO 2001–2005), in which he plays the deceased but still present father. In a 2010 interview, however, Reeves and the interviewer agree that choosing Jenkins for this unnamed part that they both refer to as 'the father', in combination with the use of cinematic techniques and plot development, bestows on this character a 'tragic dimension' and helps the audience sympathise and even identify with 'someone who is essentially a serial killer'.[46] This figure in the American adaptation is thus very far removed from Håkan and his development as a character in the novel, and there are arguably very few, if any, traces of Gothic humour in *Let Me In*.

Comedy and humour of different kinds are among the most prominent traits of *Riget*. As Gunhild Agger suggests, it is actually the humorous spirit (*den humoristiske ånd*) that keeps all of the diverse genres, storylines and details together in the Danish TV series. This humorous spirit, as Agger points out, ranges over gallows humour, situational comedy, farce, practical jokes, satire, wit, sarcasm, irony, absurdity and the grotesque.[47] Here I will focus on a few instances of Gothic humour in *Riget* and comment briefly on how these elements have fared in the American adaptation. Gothic humour in these TV series, I would suggest, is primarily based on body horror, the abject, the grotesque and, in *Kingdom Hospital*, 'the whimsical macabre'.[48]

Body horror fits perfectly into the hospital setting, which is the obvious locus for realistic as well as Gothic fears connected to the invasion or mutilation of the human body. For example, both series include a medical student or a nurse, who regularly faints when she sees blood. In *Kingdom Hospital*, there is nurse Carrie von Trier, a playful reference that combines the name of the title character of King's first published novel, *Carrie* (1974), with 'von Trier'. In *Riget*, the fainting medical student, Sanne, who cannot stand being present at an autopsy, is later shown absorbed in watching slasher movies on video, possibly as some kind of antidote to her phobia. She is also very briefly involved in the ongoing storyline about the severed head that the medical student Mogge, who is the chief of staff's daft son, sets in motion as a bizarre attempt at courting the director of the sleeping lab. The head looks like Mogge's, which, among other things, turns this storyline into a humorous take on the Gothic trope of the double. After meandering and appearing at different points in the first season of *Riget*, Lars von Trier as horror-show host holds it up as he comments on episode four.[49]

Riget's horror host is a rip-off from the American TV anthology series *Alfred Hitchcock Presents* (CBS, NBC, 1955–1965), although von Trier does not introduce but concludes each episode. Holding up the severed head is in line with Hitchcock's introductions which 'often featured odd puns, bad jokes and sight gags (playing with a noose, appearing with a knife lodged in his back), and emphasised the amusement potentially offered by the material he was presenting. Often this meant responding to the story in a flip manner.'[50] Although Stephen King appears in a cameo part as the custodian Johnny B. Goode in *Kingdom Hospital*,[51] there is no equivalent in the American TV series to von Trier's horror-host appearances at the end of each episode. *Kingdom Hospital* does, however, include a version of the severed-head story including the Gothic double motif. The headless body in this version, however, does not stay still in the morgue. Instead it rushes around looking for its head like a chicken without a head, bumping into things because it obviously cannot see. If there is such a thing as 'Gothic slapstick', this is it.

The turn to voodoo and the zombification of doctor Krogshøj in *Riget* also include elements of Gothic humour, as does Krogshøj's love interest Judith's grotesque birth of a baby in the shape of full-sized Udo Kier – who not only plays the baby but also his evil, supernatural father – at the end of the first season and the baby's continuing abnormal growth in the second season. Here, Gothic humour is connected to uncanny ambiguity, which is mostly lost in the American adaptation. In her comparison of the two series, Agger notes that good and evil are to a much larger extent presented as absolute contrasts or oppositions in the American series. She compares doctor Krogshøj, who is an 'ambivalent figure' (*'ambivalent figur'*) with increasingly 'diabolical' (*'diabolske'*) traits, with his counterpart doctor Hook in *Kingdom Hospital* whom she describes as 'a less dubious and more serious person' (*'en mindre dubiøs og mere seriøs person'*), and she also mentions that the story about the grotesque baby, Lillebror, is omitted in the American version. Both characters are examples of what she calls 'strange mixed forms of good-evil and evil-good' (*'mærkelige blandformer mellem det gode-onde og det onde-gode'*) in the Danish version.[52] Here, I would add that von Trier's delightful horror-host commentary encourages the audience to embrace this mixture: 'to take the good with the evil', which is an inversion of the Swedish and Danish expression '*ta det onda med det goda*' which means that one should take the bad with the good, the rough with the smooth.

In *Kingdom Hospital*, the most ambiguous character is actually the creature Antubis, which has the shape of a monstrous anteater due to the ghost girl Mary Jensen's mispronunciation of Anubis, the Egyptian god of death and regeneration that often is depicted as a jackal. Antubis claims to be both good and evil but mainly helps the protagonists and often appears at Mary's side as an oversized threatening pet. This creature is an example of what Catherine Spooner has called the 'whimsical macabre', which 'deliberately fuses the cute, fanciful and quirky with the gloomy, gruesome and morbid. It brings together images of, or associated with, childhood... with Gothic and horror iconography, to create a gently comic effect'.[53] The same could be said of the opening credits with its musical theme that sounds like a lullaby, while the accompanying Gothic images are fanciful and quirky as well as gloomy and morbid. This credit sequence is reminiscent of that of *Six Feet Under* and very different from that of *Riget*, which has more in common with those of the American police procedurals *Homicide: Life on the Street* (NBC, 1993–99) and *NYPD Blue* (ABC, 1993–2005).

Setting and resetting Gothic and the uncanny: Riget and Kingdom Hospital

Riget and *Kingdom Hospital* are primarily set in the present time of their production and engage with space, history and geography in various

the use of a pre-credit sequence in TV series was common but the repetition of the same sequence for all episodes is quite unusual. For instance, the two American TV series *Homicide* and *NYPD Blue*, whose grainy and jumpy documentary-like style served as an inspiration for the use of camera and cutting in *Riget*, used the pre-credit sequence to introduce some issue or aspect of the plot of each episode, which means that each pre-credit sequence is different. Moreover, in *Riget*, the images of water, slow-moving bodies and cloth together with the measured tones of the Danish voice-over have a peculiar, hypnotic effect.[60]

> The Kingdom Hospital rests on ancient marshland where the bleaching ponds once lay. Here the bleachers moistened their great spans of cloth. The steam evaporating from the wet cloth shrouded the place in permanent fog. Centuries later the hospital was built here. The bleachers gave way to doctors and researchers, the best brains in the nation and the most perfect technology. To crown their work they called the hospital The Kingdom. Now life was to be charted and ignorance and superstition never to shake the bastions of science again. Perhaps their arrogance became too pronounced and their persistent denial of the spiritual. For it is as if the cold and damp have returned. Tiny signs of fatigue are appearing in the solid, modern edifice. No living person knows it yet, but the gateway to the Kingdom is opening once again.[61]

Rigshospitalet in Copenhagen is actually located on Blegdamsvej 9 ('9 Bleaching Pond Road'). The bleaching ponds were moved to this area, which was outside the ramparts of the city, in the 1660s, at which time the road was also constructed.[62] The bleachers disappeared from this area in the middle of the nineteenth century, roughly around the same time as Denmark – after two centuries of royal absolutism – became a constitutional monarchy, industrialisation began in Copenhagen, and the city grew beyond the old ramparts. The hospital was founded in 1910, and the sixteen-storey central building shown in the TV series was completed in the 1970s. So, although the bleaching at the bleaching ponds had gone on for centuries before the hospital was built, the period between this industry disappearing and the founding of the hospital was relatively short. However, the statement 'Centuries later the hospital was built here' intoned over the suggestive sepia-coloured images lends a mythological aspect to this historical site.

The rest of the pre-credit sequence is a brilliant illustration of what scholars have seen as the Enlightenment's and modernity's production of the Gothic and the uncanny.[63] The voice-over of this sequence highlights the conflicts between scientific reason and the supernatural, between modern technology and the spiritual. This discord is obviously one of the main themes of the TV series, and is personified in the antagonistic relationship between Swedish Dr. Helmer and the psychic Mrs. Drusse, an elderly woman who is a would-be patient and who takes on the role as detective with a focus on the supernatural. At the end of the pre-credit sequence, the camera leaves the bleachers and their wet environment to delve into the ground beneath them, where finally a pair of hands breaks through the earth as an illustration to the statement: 'No living person knows it yet, but the gateway to the Kingdom is opening once again'. The Gothic implications here are that the dead are not only still active, but also that they know something that the living will soon discover, and that the gateway is opening between the hospital, which can also be seen as a microcosm of the modern Danish nation, and that which has been repressed – the past, the supernatural, spirituality – by what the hospital stands for: rationality, modern science and perfect technology. The hands uncannily signal the return of the repressed.

The pilot of American *Kingdom Hospital* uses a similar structure to that of the Danish series: it begins with a pre-credit sequence with a voice-over that briefly outlines a historical scenario for the place on which the modern hospital is built. The sequence, which is shown only in this episode, is in some ways reminiscent of *Riget*'s pre-credit sequence, but it employs a different, darker colour scheme and sharper images than von Trier's deliberately blurry ones:

> A hundred and fifty years ago, the Gates Falls Mill stood here. It employed 200 men and women. Good Yankees, all. Sixteen-hour shifts during the Civil War when the Gates Falls Mill made uniforms for the Union Army. The job of the men wearing those uniforms was to end the peculiar institution. The peculiar institution being slavery. When the mill burned in 1869 most of them got out. The fire started on the first floor. Most of the adult mill workers escaped. Most of the children... Most of the children did not. This is the realm of darkness.

The pre-credit sequence thus brings up two social issues in nineteenth-century America: child labour and slavery.

Children were exploited as workers in the nineteenth-century American textile industry, and in King's TV series they die while their adult counterparts escape the 1869 fire that destroys the mill. The children appear to have been locked in since they are banging on a closed door, trying but failing to escape. In *Kingdom Hospital*, in general as well as in the pre-credit sequence, fire is an element of destruction, unlike in the watery *Riget*. There is, however, a similar movement down through the ground and hands breaking through the earth at the end of the

American TV series' pre-credit sequence. The accompanying words are different, though: 'This is the realm of darkness.' This, I would suggest, is a movement from the details of the American past at a particular time and place – historical and fictive – to a more diffuse sense of Gothic horror in the guise of repressed or forgotten local history.

Although Gates Falls Mill or Gates Mill, as it is called in the final episode of the series, is as fictional as Kingdom Hospital itself, Lewistown in Maine was in fact an important mill town from the 1820s until well into the twentieth century, and its textile industry played a significant part during the Civil War. The mill owners in Lewistown stocked up on cotton at the beginning of the war, which proved to be a wise move since the Civil War lasted longer than mill owners in other towns had expected and the war 'disrupted cotton supplies for New England in general'.[64] Where the cotton came from in the first place is not mentioned, although one can assume that it had its origin at Southern plantations, grown and harvested by slaves. There is more than the cotton and the uniforms for the Union soldiers that connects Lewistown's history to the 'peculiar institution' or slavery, as the voice-over ever so helpfully clarifies. Indeed, the very existence of the state of Maine is linked to slavery: having been a part of Massachusetts called the District of Maine, it was made a non-slavery or free state in 1820 to balance the entrance of Missouri into the union as a slave state. While slavery is not overtly addressed again in *Kingdom Hospital*, the emphasis on it at the very beginning makes sense in setting the scene for a Gothic TV series that is an adaptation expressly 'developed for US television' as the credits announce: as Teresa A. Goddu argues in *Gothic America* (1997), 'slavery haunts the American gothic'.[65] In this TV series, though, the history of slavery is at least partly overwhelmed by the atrocities performed in the old Kingdom hospital that was burnt to the ground in 1939, which serves as a Gothic historical and physical layer between the nineteenth-century mill and the current Kingdom Hospital.

Whereas the 1869 Lewistown mill fire in *Kingdom Hospital* appears to be entirely fictional, Lewistown's historical relationship to Boston may have influenced the choice to transform Swedish Dr. Stig Helmer into Dr. Stegman, who comes from and longs to be back in Boston. From the mid-eighteenth century, Boston-based capitalists were in charge of Lewistown's rapid development as a mill town and into a 'company town'. These capitalists 'dominate[d] the city's financial institutions, its political life, and its religious and intellectual activities'.[66] Nevertheless, the relationship between Lewistown and Boston, or between Maine and Massachusetts, is obviously no direct equivalent to that between the two Scandinavian countries.

As indicated, the relationship between Denmark and Sweden in *Riget* is portrayed in Swedish Dr. Helmer's negative attitude towards his Danish colleagues, Rigshospitalet and Denmark in general. He repeatedly expresses his disapproval and most famously in the first episode when, on the roof of the hospital, he ends a monologue celebrating Sweden in comparison with Denmark by shouting '*Danskjävlar!*' ('Bloody Danes!' or literally 'Danish devils!'). Here von Trier plays with Danish stereotyping of Swedes and Sweden,[67] as the figure of Dr. Helmer invokes the stereotypical Danish perception of Swedes as people who take themselves 'too seriously... having no sense of humour' and 'Sweden as a modern, but centralist and controlling society' with 'an excessive tendency to issue bans and prohibitions'.[68] Dr. Helmer clearly represents the idea of the 'formal, reserved and conformist Swede, who hasn't got the natural individualism and humour of the typical Dane', but his narcissistic egoism and love of hierarchies contradict the stereotypical notion of Sweden as 'more collective and social democratic than Denmark'.[69] According to stereotypical views of Swedishness in Denmark in the 1990s, he also regards himself and Sweden as standing for 'quality, safety and success'.[70] Nevertheless, before the present events in the series he has already failed to uphold these qualities in the disastrous brain operation of the girl Mona and his professional reputation is shown to rest on academic theft.

Copenhagen is moreover the capital of the nation-state or kingdom of Denmark and Rigshospitalet is the Danish national hospital, while Lewistown is neither the state capital nor the largest city in Maine, which could also be regarded as a peripheral state in the United States, being small and bordering on Canada. Boston, on the other hand, is the state capital of Massachusetts and very important in terms of American national history and cultural development. Consequently, the geographically informed tension between Dr. Stegman and just about everybody else in Stephen King's TV series is connected to this physician's strong sense of being much more sophisticated than the provincial environment and people of Lewistown – and especially Kingdom Hospital – deserve.

Ironically, Kingdom Hospital's chief of staff, Jesse James,[71] is played by Ed Begley Jr. who also played Dr. Victor Ehrlich in the medical drama series *St. Elsewhere* (1982–1988),[72] set in the underequipped and underrated fictional hospital St. Eligius in the poor southern part of Boston.

That Boston hospital could not be farther from what Dr. Stegman has in mind. Like his counterpart Einar Moesgaard in *Riget*, Jesse James is engaged in promoting 'Operation Morning Air', but not in order to create a congenial working environment and thus impress government officials, as is the case in the Danish series, but to make Kingdom Hospital more commercially attractive to a potential buyer, an aspect that points to different ideologies in the two series.

Setting and resetting Gothic and the uncanny: *Låt den rätte komma in* and *Let Me In*[73]

The film adaptations of *Låt den rätte komma in* are very similar both in terms of the time of adaptation, 2008 and 2010, and the time of the setting, the early 1980s, but the place differs: Reeves' Hollywood film *Let Me In* is set in American Los Alamos in New Mexico instead of in Swedish Blackeberg. In Lindqvist's novel, as Sofia Wijkmark observes, the rational and well-organised place seems to be the prerequisite for the free play of horror.[74] In the Swedish film, too, '[t]he setting is recognizably Blackeberg in the 1980s, to a Swedish audience both familiar and mundane'.[75] Similarly, in *Let Me In*, the horror hinges on the ordinariness and familiarity of the surroundings. As I have argued elsewhere, the geographical setting is essential to the uncanny atmosphere and horror of the novel and the two films, since the uncanny concerns the intrusion or eruption of the unfamiliar in the familiar or vice versa.[76]

Both *Låt den rätte komma in* and *Let Me In* create an uncanny atmosphere by introducing the unfamiliar in the shape of the vampire child and the murderous helper in a familiar setting. In the American movie, the familiar is also present in the centrality of cars, which here serve as the hunting ground for the vampire's human helper, while, in *Låt den rätte komma in*, his Swedish counterpart uses public transport and locates his victims on foot in a forest area and in the locker room of a public swimming pool. The depictions of the familiar in the American and Swedish versions are thus ideologically divergent: the individualist American society where car ownership is central, and the more communally oriented Swedish society of the early 1980s.

Blackeberg and Los Alamos were built in the mid-twentieth century by Stockholm City and the US government, respectively. Blackeberg, finished in 1952, preceded the Million Programme (*miljonprogrammet*) that the Swedish government implemented 1965–1974, whose goal was to provide affordable modern housing for an increasingly urban Swedish population. The novel begins by describing the suburb Blackeberg as history-less, rational and modern: 'That tells you something about the modernity of the place, its rationality. It tells you something of how free they were from the ghosts of history and of terror. It explains in part how unprepared they were.'[77] The rest of the novel can be read as a meditation on the shortcomings of this image of rationality and modernity: the Swedish welfare state. Besides vampirism, murder and bullying, social problems depicted in Lindqvist's novel are theft, fencing, shoplifting, glue sniffing and alcoholism. In the novel and the Swedish film, a few socially marginal characters, most of them drinking regularly at the local Chinese restaurant, play important parts in the plot. These characters are nowhere to be seen in the American film, which depicts only middle-class characters.

Los Alamos, New Mexico, is connected to rationality through science: the US government constructed it in 1942 for the Los Alamos National Laboratory, home of the Manhattan Project during the Second World War and still an important site related to nuclear warfare and national security issues. Los Alamos as a setting, then, stands for the kind of scientific rationality – with a deadly twist – that has produced the uncanny ever since the eighteenth century. Because of the secrecy involved in the research and development geared towards warfare during and after the Second World War, Los Alamos moreover represents the other side of *heimlich* that Freud traces in his discussion about the uncanny (*das Unheimliche*): 'what is concealed and kept out of sight',[78] as opposed to *heimlich* in the sense of what is familiar or homelike. John Beck suggests that Los Alamos, as a setting in novels, 'has come to represent the concealment of power in its most deadly military form, a power folded into the deep time of the Southwestern landscape.'[79] In his book on the Manhattan Project in post-Cold War New Mexico, anthropologist Joseph Masco actually uses the phrase 'nuclear uncanny' to describe 'the material effects, psychic tensions, and sensory confusion produced by nuclear weapons and radioactive materials'.[80] That Reeves' film is set in Los Alamos carries uncanny potential in this national, historical context.

To conclude, the American geographical settings in *Let Me In* and *Kingdom Hospital* could thus be seen as the outcomes of Reeves' and King's search for the right framing or context for their adaptations of the Nordic Gothic productions. In both cases, they have actually chosen not only to move the story to an American setting, but also to place it in a smaller town, Los Alamos and Lewistown, which is a significant move away from the central location of *Riget* in the Danish capital and the only slightly more marginal one of a Stockholm suburb in *Låt den rätte komma in*. In that sense, these two iconic Scandinavian texts represent a kind of urban Nordic Gothic, whereas the American adaptations pertain to a kind of small-town American Gothic of which Stephen King is currently the main and most celebrated proponent.

The TV series engage with the local history of the setting in their pre-credit sequences in ways that evoke the Gothic and the uncanny. *Kingdom Hospital*'s pre-credit sequence focuses on one incident, the fire in a textile mill after the Civil War, a clear instance of American Gothic. Invoking a very different temporality with mythical overtones, *Riget*'s recurring, suggestive pre-credit sequence gives glimpses of a now obsolete Danish vocation that went on for centuries on the grounds of the modern hospital. The voice-over outlines the tension between modern technology and the supernatural, between scientific reason and the spiritual, and ends with the return of the repressed turning this particular, Danish situation and location into a perfect example of modernity's relationship to Gothic and the uncanny in general.

Låt den rätte komma in and *Let Me In* are set in places that lack a long history and are strongly connected to science and rationality around and after the Second World War. The uncanny atmosphere is created by the introduction of the unfamiliar in a familiar 1980s setting in both the Swedish and the American versions. The ideological difference between the individualist American society and the more communal Swedish one is, for example, shown in the use of cars in the American adaptation. Moreover, the socially marginal characters of *Låt den rätte komma in* are not part of *Let Me In*. Similarly, ideological differences between *Riget* and *Kingdom Hospital* are evident in the different aims of the chief of staff's 'Operation Morning Air' in the two series, which also points to Danish Riget being a public hospital while American Kingdom Hospital is private.

Another aspect of *Riget* and Lindqvist's novel that has in part been changed or lost in translation is Gothic humour. Body horror tied to Gothic humour is used both in *Riget* and *Kingdom Hospital*, but the American series tends more towards the whimsical macabre and Gothic slapstick than the grotesque. In the Danish TV series and the Swedish novel Gothic humour is deeply invested in the grotesque, the abject and even splatterpunk features. Indeed, in excluding elements such as grotesque births, paedophilia and ambiguous good-evil characters, the American adaptations have also eliminated a great deal of what could be termed Nordic Gothic humour.

Notes

1. L. Hutcheon, with S. O'Flynn, *A Theory of Adaptation* (London: Routledge, 2nd edn, 2013), p. 16.
2. G. Agger, 'I transformationernas rige: Fra *Riget* til *Kingdom Hospital*', in P. Stein Larsen, P. Kaj Pedersen, E.-U. Pinkert and B. Sørensen (eds), *Interaktioner. Om kunstarternes productive mellemværender* (Aalborg: Aalborg Universitetsforlag, 2009), p. 18.
3. See Introduction for a brief discussion of the international reception.
4. See S. Peacock, 'Two *Kingdoms*, Two Kings', *Critical Studies in Television* 4:2 (2009), pp. 24–36; and C. Siegel, 'Let a New Gender In? American Responses to Contemporary Scandinavian Gothicism', in C. L. Crow (ed.), *A Companion to American Gothic* (Chichester: Wiley Blackwell, 2014), pp. 547–58.
5. Regarding American (Hollywood) adaptations of non-American works, Hutcheon outlines two different strategies of transculturating: the most common is Americanising; the other is trying to appeal to an international audience by 'de-emphasizing any national, regional, or historical specificities', in *Theory of Adaptation*, pp. 146–7.
6. Hutcheon, *Theory of Adaptation*, p. 20.
7. R. Adams, 'Stephen King: *Let Me In* "is the best American horror film in the last 20 years"', *Awardsdaily*, www.awardsdaily.com/2010/10/08/stephen-king-let-me-in-the-best-american-horror-film-in-the-last-20-years/. Accessed 17 December 2018.
8. Hutcheon, *Theory of Adaptation*, pp. 142, 146
9. Hutcheon, *Theory of Adaptation*, pp. 145, 147.
10. A. Halskov, *TV Peaks: Twin Peaks and Modern Television Drama* (Odense: University Press of Southern Denmark, 2015), p. 33.
11. H. Wheatley, *Gothic Television* (Manchester: Manchester University Press, 2006), p. 1.
12. M. Hills, *The Pleasures of Horror* (London: Continuum, 2005), p. 119. See also L. Jowett and S. Abbott, *TV Horror: Investigating the Dark Side of the Small Screen* (London: I. B. Tauris, 2013), p. xiii.
13. Hills, *Pleasures of Horror*, p. 120.
14. Hills, *Pleasures of Horror*, pp. 121–4.
15. Hills, *Pleasures of Horror*, p. 126.
16. Halskov, *TV Peaks*, p. 41. Halskov refers to Robert J. Thompson's *Television's Second Golden Age* (1996).
17. In 1988 the monopoly of DR (the Danish broadcasting corporation) was broken by the new broadcast network TV 2. The year before, the Swedish public service monopoly, which had included two channels (TV 1 and TV2) from 1969, had also been broken. In contrast, the Norwegian broadcasting corporation NRK's second channel only appeared in the mid-1990s.
18. Halskov, *TV Peaks*, p. 37. The first episode of *Twin Peaks* was aired in Norway and Sweden in November 1990, and in Denmark and Finland in February 1991. *Imdb*, www.imdb.com/title/tt0098936/releaseinfo?ref_=tt_ql_dt_2. Accessed 11 September 2018.
19. Halskov, *TV Peaks*, p. 198.
20. N. Thorsen, *Geniet Lars von Trier: Liv, Filmer och Fobier*, trans. T. Andersson (Stockholm: Arkad, 2013), p. 264. 'från obskyr, provocerande särling till allas vår egen provocerande särling.' My translation from Swedish.

ways. *Riget* is set in the actual hospital in Copenhagen, Rigshospitalet or Riget, which in von Trier's TV series is haunted by ghosts as well as medical malpractice, Kafkaesque bureaucracy and awkward attempts at New Public Management.[54] This hospital provides a labyrinthine and multi-layered setting equivalent to the castle or the haunted house in earlier Gothic narratives.[55] It is a liminal space that registers clashes and serves as a conduit between the past and the present, between scientific rationality and the supernatural,[56] which is also very much the case with the American Kingdom Hospital. Moreover, *Riget* highlights tensions cast as international between the Danish hospital staff and a Swedish physician who perceives his Danish colleagues as irrational and unscientific and who longs to be back in Sweden. In King's adaptation, the fictive Kingdom Hospital is placed in Lewistown, Maine, and the physician at odds with the rest of the hospital staff is from Boston, Massachusetts, not from another country.

There is actually more than one reason why *Kingdom Hospital* is set in Maine rather than any other location in the United States. Hutcheon claims 'that adapters must have their own personal reasons for deciding first to do an adaptation and then choosing which adapted work and what medium to do it in'.[57] In this case, I would add 'place' to adapted work and medium. Hutcheon argues that these personal reasons, as well as 'culturally and historically conditioned reasons', are worth considering in the study and theorising of adaptations.[58] Generally speaking, Maine is Stephen King's state of choice: he was born, grew up and lives there, and his fiction is usually set in Maine, but unlike *Kingdom Hospital* in imaginary rather than actual towns. Maine, in other words, is King's preferred Gothic location. That the hospital is set in Lewistown is based on King's personal experience of spending time at the hospital in Lewistown in 1999 after having been hit by a minivan and severely injured. This autobiographical incident is transposed and integrated into *Kingdom Hospital* through a new central character: the painter Peter Rickman, whose last name is an amalgam of Stephen King's pseudonym Richard Bachman.[59]

Regarding setting, the pre-credit sequences of *Riget* and *Kingdom Hospital* – that is, the sequence that comes before the opening credits – do significant work. In both cases, this sequence places the location of the hospital in a historical context using both images and voice-over. The pre-credit sequence also serves to relate the two TV series to the Gothic and the uncanny in specific, but different ways.

In the Danish series, the same sepia-coloured pre-credit sequence is repeated at the beginning of each of the eight episodes. In the 1990s,

21 Thorsen, *Geniet Lars von Trier*, p. 220.
22 According to the *IMDb*, *Riget* was not released in Finland until 1996 and in Norway until 1997. In 1997, *Riget II* was also screened at the Reykjavik Film Festival. www.imdb.com/title/tt0108906/releaseinfo?ref_=tt_ql_dt_2. Accessed 11 September 2018.
23 Jowett and Abbott, *TV Horror*, p. 168.
24 Jowett and Abbott, *TV Horror*, p. 70.
25 Jowett and Abbott, *TV Horror*, p. 71.
26 Jowett and Abbott, *TV Horror*, p. 71.
27 Jowett and Abbott, *TV Horror*, p. 73.
28 Jowett and Abbott, *TV Horror*, p. 156.
29 Halskov, *TV Peaks*, pp. 12–13.
30 L. Lagerström, 'Tomas – den rätte', *Film i skolan*, Svenska filminstitutet (November 2008), www.filminstitutet.se/filmiskolan. Accessed 18 September 2017.
31 Lindqvist had received thirty-plus offers to film his novel before he settled for Alfredson. Lagerström, 'Tomas – den rätte'.
32 *Fyra nyanser av brunt* with Killinggänget employs a slightly surreal heightened realism. The film has four interwoven storylines that were broken into separate parts when the film was made into a TV series (four episodes) and shown on Swedish television in 2005.
33 Lagerström, 'Tomas – den rätte'.
34 L. Lagerström, 'Författare med guldläge', *Film i skolan*, Svenska filminstitutet (November 2008), www.filminstitutet.se/filmiskolan. Accessed 18 September 2017.
35 Lagerström, 'Författare med guldläge'.
36 J. Weithz, 'Skräckmästaren', *Flamman* (18 June 2008), http://flamman.se/a/skrackmastaren. Accessed 5 July 2017. 'Jag vill skriva högkvalitativ underhållningslitteratur. Eller som jag själv kallar det: fungerande melodram. Som Lars von Triers filmer till exempel. De är så jävla mycket, överlastade, men man köper det. De känns aldrig kalla eller beräknande, de berör.' My translation.
37 Weithz, 'Skräckmästaren'.
38 M. H. Troy, 'Predator and Prey: The Vampire Child in Novels by S. P. Somtow and John Ajvide Lindqvist', *Edda*, 104:2 (2017). DOI: 10.18261. See also Sofia Wijkmark's 'John Ajvide Lindqvist's *Little Star*: Gothic Horror as Remediation of Video Nasties', *Gothic Studies* 18:1–2 (2018), pp. 77–94. DOI: 10.7227/GS.0036.
39 E. Redvall, 'Skräckmästaren förvånad över framgången', *Sydsvenskan* (20 October 2005), www.sydsvenskan.se/2005-10-19/skrackmastaren-forvanad-over-framgangen. Accessed 5 July 2017. '-Det handlar om att ta en normal situation och placera något avvikande i den, förklarar John Ajvide Lindqvist. Komiken blir mera komisk med en straight man som motvikt. Skräcken fungerar på ungefär samma sätt./ Allra roligast, säger han, blir komiken om den balanserar på skräckens yttersta gräns, när man bygger upp en oro som får sin förlösning i skrattet.' My translation.
40 Lindqvist, *Let the Right One In*, pp. 431–2.
41 Redvall, 'Skräckmästaren förvånad över framgången'. For a discussion of the rape scene in terms of splatterpunk, see Troy, 'Predator and Prey', pp. 141–2.
42 Lindqvist, *Let the Right One In*, p. 443.
43 Lindqvist, *Let the Right One In*, p. 444.
44 Lindqvist, *Let the Right One In*, pp. 459–60.

45 See M. H. Troy, 'Dealing with the Uncanny? Cultural Adaptation in Matt Reeves's Vampire Movie *Let Me In*', *American Studies in Scandinavia* 48:1 (2016), pp. 38–9.
46 M. Reeves, 'Matt Reeves Explains How Steven Spielberg Helped Shape *Let Me In*', interview by P. Hall, *Moviefone*, 5 October 2010, http://news.moviefone.com/2010/10/05/matt-reeves-explains-how-steven-spielberg-helped-shape-let-me-in/. Accessed 27 October 2014.
47 G. Agger, 'Hoved-, humor- og genrehistorier: En analyse af *Riget*', *K&K* 80 (1996), p. 155.
48 C. Spooner, *Post-Millennial Gothic: Comedy, Romance and the Rise of Happy Gothic* (London: Bloomsbury, 2017), p. 104.
49 For an elaboration on the use of the head, heads and brains in *Riget* in connection with humour and genre, see Agger, 'Hoved-, humor- og genrehistorier'.
50 T. Jones, *The Gothic and Carnivalesque in American Culture* (Cardiff: University of Wales Press, 2015), p. 141.
51 For comments on the play with names, see M. Browning, *Stephen King on the Small Screen* (Bristol: Intellect, 2011), p. 122; and Peacock, 'Two *Kingdoms*, Two Kings', p. 29.
52 Agger, 'I transformationernas rige', p. 28.
53 Spooner, *Post-Millennial Gothic*, p. 104.
54 Agger points out that the same management culture that is under satirical attack in *Kingdom Hospital* in the context of a private hospital is also satirically castigated in *Riget*, although the Danish situation at that point was far from the American. 'I transformationernas rige', p. 32. For *Riget* as a critique of the Danish welfare state see T. R. Tangherlini, 'The Ghost in the Machine: Supernatural Threat and the State in Lars von Trier's *Riget*', *Scandinavian Studies* 73:1 (2001), pp. 1–24.
55 Agger stresses that both TV series have labyrinthine plots. 'I transformationernas rige', pp. 23, 36. For a thorough discussion of grotesque and uncanny elements in *Riget*, see C. Bainbridge, *The Cinema of Lars von Trier: Authenticity and Artifice* (London: Wallflower Press, 2007).
56 For a reading of the different parts or layers of the hospital as representing the rational, scientific and modern and irrational, spiritual and uncanny, see G. Creeber, 'Surveying *The Kingdom*: Explorations of Medicine, Memory and Modernity in Lars von Trier's *The Kingdom* (1994)', *European Journal of Cultural Studies* 5:4 (2002), pp. 392–5.
57 Hutcheon, *Theory of Adaptation*, p. 92.
58 Hutcheon, *Theory of Adaptation*, pp. 95, 107.
59 Peacock, 'Two *Kingdoms*, Two Kings', p. 28.
60 Ove Christensen and Claus K. Kristiansen trace von Trier's interest in hypnosis in the films and even a commercial that he made before *Riget*, as well as provide an excellent discussion of what they call *hypnoseanæstetik* in the TV series in 'Porten til *Riget*', in E. Jørholt (ed.), *Ind i Filmen* (København: Medusa, 1995). See in particular pp. 299–307.
61 Translation taken from the English subtitles.
62 'Blegdamme på Blegdamsvej', *Dengang* (13 October 2009), www.dengang.dk/artikler/2050. Accessed 25 August 2018.
63 See T. Castle, *The Female Thermometer: Eighteenth-Century Culture and the Invention of the Uncanny* (New York: Oxford University Press, 1995); D. L. Hoeveler, *Gothic Riffs: Secularizing the Uncanny in the European Imaginary, 1780–1820* (Columbus:

Ohio State University Press, 2010); and J. E. Hogle, 'Introduction: Modernity and the Proliferation of the Gothic', in J. E. Hogle (ed.), *The Cambridge Companion to Modern Gothic* (Cambridge: Cambridge University Press, 2014), pp. 3–19.

64 J. S. Leamon, *Historic Lewistown: A Textile City in Transition*, Produced for the Lewistown Historical Commission (Auburn: Maine, 1976), p. 12 www.lewistonmaine.gov/DocumentCenter/Home/View/1191. Accessed 25 August 2018.

65 T. A. Goddu, *Gothic America: Narrative, History, and Nation* (New York: Columbia University Press, 1997), p. 3.

66 Leamon, *Historic Lewistown*, p. 10.

67 For Danish stereotypical views of Swedes in the 1990s, see M. Cardel Gertsen and C. Werther, 'The Mote in Thy Brother's Eye – Swedes in Danish Ads', *Advances in Consumer Research* 26 (1999), pp. 678–83.

68 Cardel Gertsen and Werther, 'The Mote in Thy Brother's Eye', p. 678.

69 Cardel Gertsen and Werther, 'The Mote in Thy Brother's Eye', p. 681.

70 Cardel Gertsen and Werther, 'The Mote in Thy Brother's Eye', p. 681.

71 For comments on the name Jesse James see Browning, *Stephen King on the Small Screen*, p. 122; and Peacock, 'Two *Kingdoms*, Two Kings', p. 29.

72 *St. Elsewhere* includes grainy shots tending towards brownish-orange of the hospital that are reminiscent of those of Rigshospitalet in *Riget*.

73 This section draws on Troy, 'Dealing with the Uncanny?', pp. 25–41.

74 S. Wijkmark, 'Naturen och det Kusliga: Nedslag i Samtida Svensk Skönlitteratur', *Tidskrift för Litteraturvetenskap* 1 (2012), p. 9. See also Helena Karlsson on Blackeberg in 'The Vampire and the Anxieties of a Globalizing Swedish Welfare State: *Låt den rätte komma in (Let the Right One In)* (2008)' *EJSS* 43:2 (2013), pp. 189–90. DOI 10.1515/ejss-2013–0010.

75 R. Wright, 'Vampire in the Stockholm Suburbs: *Let the Right One In* and Genre Hybridity', *Journal of Scandinavian Cinema* 1:1 (2010), p. 58.

76 Troy, 'Dealing with the Uncanny', p. 28. The following discussion of the settings partly overlaps with pp. 28–9 in this article.

77 J. A. Lindqvist, *Let the Right One In*, trans. E. Segerberg (London: Quercus, 2009), p. 2.

78 S. Freud, 'The "Uncanny" (1919)', in Volume 17 (1917–1919) of *The Standard Edition of the Complete Works of Sigmund Freud*, trans. J. Strachey (London: Hogarth Press, 1955), pp. 224–5.

79 J. Beck, *Dirty Wars: Landscape, Power, and Waste in Western American Literature* (Lincoln: University of Nebraska Press, 2009), p. 103.

80 J. Masco, *The Nuclear Borderlands: The Manhattan Project in Post-Cold War New Mexico* (Princeton: Princeton University Press, 2006), p. 28.

Johan Höglund

Nordic Gothic new media

While Horace Walpole's *The Castle of Otranto* (1764) is typically perceived as the birth of Gothic, Walpole did not conceive of this particular mode as simply a literary genre. Walpole also found expression for Gothic in his ambitious architectural transformation of his house Strawberry Hill, from modest cottage to neo-Gothic castle complete with ramparts and battlements. The art of Henry Fuseli and Francisco Goya produced during the late eighteenth and early nineteenth centuries is also central to early Gothic and has illustrated countless reprints of the classic Gothic novels. In addition to this, as Francesca Saggini shows in *The Gothic Novel and the Stage: Romantic Appropriations* (2015), the theatre picked up the Gothic trend very quickly. Saggini claims that the Gothic movement is not simply from page-to-stage but also takes place in the opposite direction, so that Matthew Lewis in *The Monk* (1796) appropriated a 'variety of contemporary spectacular forms and conventions taken from the fringe world of pantomime and visual shows' when he wrote his novel.[1] When the moving image is invented and early film turned from the simple recording of everyday scenes to telling stories in the beginning of the twentieth century, these early films frequently turned to classic Gothic texts such as *Frankenstein* and *Dracula*. In this way, Gothic is multimodal and intermedial from its earliest beginnings and it invades virtually all new forms of artistic communication as these are invented. When computers and digital communication enabled what has been termed 'new media', Gothic moved with it, taking the form of hypertexts, or what Espen J. Aarseth termed 'ergodic literature', and games.[2]

This chapter maps and analyses new Gothic media developed in the Nordic region. Before the discussion of the actual media, the chapter considers what the notion 'new media' entails and what the concepts 'Gothic' and 'Nordic' actually mean when the focus is new media rather than literature or cinema. An analysis follows of four of the more important and widely disseminated games and a consideration of the interactive stories that they tell in relation to a Nordic geographical, ideological and cultural landscape. The first two of these games, Finnish *Alan Wake* (2010) and Swedish *Little Nightmares*, are what is often referred to as AAA games – games with a considerable production budget and a large, international audience. The other two, Swedish *Year Walk* (2013) and Norwegian *Through the Woods* (2016), are independent games that may look for wide dissemination, but keep much closer to Nordic themes and settings.

Regarding the concept of new media, it should be noted that most of the material in this chapter consists of games, and they will be referred to as such. Even so, new media is a useful concept since it acknowledges that games have both a performative, ludological component and a narrative aspect that is at times dominant.[3] Indeed, the games discussed below are most properly described as interactive, digital narratives and encourage the person who operates them to focus on the narrative rather than on the gaming element. Indeed, few of the independent games are competitive or can be 'won' in the conventional sense. Even in the cases when the games discussed can be properly won, the narrative element may be as important as the ludological component. For example, in *Alan Wake*, the ludological element is strong and often involves the gamer in fierce and complicated combat, but they must also watch a great number of cinematic cut-scenes that, when added together, comprise a full-length feature film.

Turning to the notion of Gothic in games, Michael Hancock has argued, building on Fred Botting's observation that the early Gothic novel and video games have many things in common, that 'video games as a medium can be usefully thought of as inherently gothic in the way they are predicated on doubling and repetition'.[4] From this perspective, the very act of gaming has a Gothic quality, since it disturbs the notion of a single, rational self. In particular, I will focus on media that has notably Gothic content and that involve the gamer in what can be termed 'Gothic performance'. By Gothic content, I refer to Gothic figures such as the ghost, the zombie or the cyborg, the haunted house or castle, the devilish villain and the innocent victim in distress. By Gothic performance,

I refer to the exploration of labyrinthine spaces, the pursuit of order and sanity in a world that seems to resist both, the confrontation with Gothic figures, and the discovery of a divided and perhaps even monstrous self. Some of the games that I discuss revolve constantly around this content and this performance, others are more properly defined as genre mash-ups that combine Gothic, horror, science-fiction and war, melodrama and comedy, and move in and out of the Gothic mode.

The concept of Nordic in Nordic Gothic new media is arguably more problematic than in more conventional media. What this book refers to as the Nordic Gothic novel is typically written in one of the Nordic languages and routinely placed within the geographical remit of the North. Similarly, while some Nordic directors of Gothic and horror cinema operate outside the Nordic region and make films in English, most Nordic Gothic films are linked to the Nordic region through language and scenography. The game industry works differently in this respect. There are indeed Gothic games that have a very clear connection to the histories, geographies and Gothic traditions of the Nordic region, but even those will typically use English as the mode of communication. Alongside these games, most of which can be termed independent as they are not distributed by one of the major game production studios, there are a number of large Nordic game developers that make AAA games for the big international game production companies. These games can be notably Gothic, but they usually have no obvious relationship to Nordic languages, histories, traditions or geographies. To give a fair account of Nordic Gothic new media, it is necessary to consider both independent games that clearly reference the Nordic context, and the big-budget games made for a large, international audience.

In terms of analytical approach, I discuss Nordic Gothic new media by considering its relationship to recognisably Nordic geographies, cultures and traditions, but also by considering what can be described as a central ideological tension in Gothic culture between Gothic that seeks to undo dominant ideologies and Gothic that works to maintain them. As mentioned, independent games typically take place in Nordic spaces, but most games distributed by the major, international game studios do not. In these cases, I will consider how the ideological tension connects these games to what can perhaps be termed the 'Nordic ideological landscape'.

The existence of ideological tension, as such, has been noted by many critics of Gothic. Teresa Goddu has observed in *Gothic America: Narrative, History, and Nation* that 'the gothic can remain continuous with official narratives, even when it apparently contradicts them'.[5] Thus, the 'gothic may unveil the ideology of official discourse, but its transformative power can be limited'.[6] Gothic is sometimes profoundly reactionary and seeks to erect the same intellectual, societal, imperial and patriarchal borders that it is often understood to seek to dismantle. From these two perspectives, and as discussed in other chapters of this book, Gothic is capable of assuming both profoundly radical and deeply conservative positions so that individual Gothic texts, including games, can be understood as existing on an ideological scale that stretches from radical anti-modern and critical attitudes to firmly conservative, patriarchal and pro-modernity stances.

Like global Gothic in general, Nordic Gothic moves across this entire spectrum, but it arguably appears to prefer to tell stories that problematise modernity and question normative notions of gender and race. Daniel Brodén has argued in a number of studies that recent Swedish crime film 'has not only reflected the dark sides of modernity in a general sense, but specifically the cultural anxieties and contradictions of the developing post-war welfare state'.[7] Because the present chapter investigates only four Nordic Gothic horror games, it is impossible to make any general conclusions regarding where these games exist on this ideological spectrum, and if they perform the same kind of work as Nordic crime fiction. Even so, it is useful to consider the relationship of these games to this dominant movement in Nordic Noir. As Yvonne Leffler's chapter on Nordic Gothic crime shows, there is a strong connection between Nordic Crime and Nordic Gothic, and the two genres sometimes converge. Also, as discussed in several other chapters of this book, Nordic Gothic and horror such as that produced by, for example, Peter Høeg, John Ajvide Lindqvist, Mats Strandberg and Johanna Sinisalo reveal a profound discomfort with specifically Nordic formations of modernity, with normative, stable notions of individuality, and with an understanding of the world as conveniently divided into good and evil. Thus, this chapter will investigate the possibility that Nordic Gothic games critically explore the same ideological terrain.

New Nordic media developers: *Alan Wake*

While this chapter is the first study of Nordic Gothic new media as such, there have been attempts at mapping European Gothic and horror games. In 'European Horror Games: Little Red Riding Hood's Zombie BBQ and the European Game Industry' (2013), Kara Andersen and

Karra Shimabukuro list one Danish, four Finnish and eight Swedish horror games, and also note that 'by an overwhelming percentage, these [and other European] games are set in American settings'.[8] The reason is financial: '[a]nnexing images, storylines, and tropes associated with American Hollywood images is a sound marketing strategy'.[9] While there is, as will be discussed below, also a market for games that explore the Nordic as a setting for Gothic and horror, the most financially viable and widely circulated games produced in the Nordic region are, like most of the international game industry, made for a US/global market. This market expects games to communicate effortlessly in English and to be exceptionally well produced. It also expects gamers to be comfortable with tropes and gaming interfaces made popular in the first generation of horror-themed action games that were produced in the United States in the 1990s and early 2000s. This was the time when today's major genres such as strategy and role playing, the first-person shooter and the third-person action or adventure were established, and also when the major Gothic and horror franchises were born, including *Alone in the Dark* (1992), *Wolfenstein* (1992), *Doom* (1993) and *Resident Evil* (1996).

Game producers in the Nordic region began making Gothic-themed games at the end of the 1990s and produced a number of internationally successful titles during the first decade of the new millennium. Some of the most notable game developers in Sweden include Frictional Games, which produced and published the *Penumbra* series (2007–2008), the *Amnesia* series (2010–2013) and *Soma* (2015), and MachineGames, which has developed well-received and controversial games for the AAA *Wolfenstein* franchise since 2014. In Denmark, IO Interactive is responsible for the successful and sometimes Gothic third-person shooter *Hitman: Codename 47* (2000). In Finland, Finnish Housemarque is known for the third-person zombie shooter *Dead Nation* (2010), and Remedy Entertainment is the developer of the inventive and the award-winning AAA games *Alan Wake* (2010) and *Alan Wake's American Nightmare* (2012). These games have all reached a wide, international audience and many were developed with substantial budgets, setting them apart from some of the other games discussed below.

Of the titles mentioned above, *Alan Wake* is arguably the most Gothic and also one of the most ambitious. Following the successful first-person shooter *Max Payne* (2001), Remedy Entertainment developed *Alan Wake* for Microsoft Game Studios over a five-year period. *Alan Wake* is Gothic on several levels, and while the intended audience is clearly one

9.1 The gaming interface of *Alan Wake* (Remedy Entertainment, 2010, *Alan Wake*).

inundated with American popular culture, and American Gothic and horror fare in particular, it also contains some references to Nordic traditions. The game has a notably strong narrative element and the essentially linear story is told through a number of cut-scenes and scripted sequences. Before exploring the complex story that unfolds in the game, it is useful to first consider the ludological dimension.

The game can be characterised as belonging to the third-person survival horror genre, where the gamer can always see her or his avatar slightly to the left of the centre of the screen, and must operate this avatar to find clues, solve puzzles and either escape or engage various enemies in combat. The third-person perspective separates the gamer from the avatar more clearly than the first-person perspective where the avatar's eyes are also the gamer's eyes. In other words, it is always clear to the gamer that the figure on the screen is an avatar and not the gamer. At the same time, the third-person perspective can increase suspense, in that the gamer can see things being done to the avatar. If a threat approaches from the back of the avatar, the gamer will see this, unlike in the first-person perspective. In addition, the gamer can also perceive how the avatar reacts to disturbing situations (perhaps by falling over, perhaps by standing paralysed). Thus, the avatar is at the same time the gamer, and the character in a story that unfolds before the gamer's eyes.

This is one of many doubling effects that games cause, and *Alan Wake* purposely makes use of it to create a troubling and overtly Gothic gaming experience. As the gamer tries to keep the avatar alive, they invest time, energy and affect into the game character. Yet, every time that the avatar dies or when the gamer loses control over the avatar for some other reason, the established bond is broken, only to have to be restored again in the game sequence that follows the resurrection of the character or the cut scene. As Michael Fuchs has argued, 'some self-aware Gothic texts, including *Alan Wake*, turn redundancy and repetition (and, thus, contemporary Gothic's derivativeness) into semantically loaded stylistic devices'.[10] Indeed, the avatar of *Alan Wake* dies repeatedly and similar scenes play out again and again, but with slight changes, and the combat is notably repetitive. Time and time again, the gamer will lose agency as the main character is wrested from her or his control. From a Gothic perspective, this is not simply a game mechanic, but a disturbing and uncanny 'lived experience'.

While the gameplay itself is arguably Gothic in this way, it is the setting, the complex and multi-layered narrative, as well as the game's many citations of Gothic and horror literature and film that makes it a truly Gothic game. *Alan Wake* tells the story of an eponymous writer of horror who, in the game's prologue, runs over a hitchhiker. This opening clearly cites Hollywood slasher *I Know what You did Last Summer* (1997), especially when the hitchhiker suddenly comes alive and begins to chase Alan with a large axe, asking him how it feels to be hunted by his own creation. The scene grows increasingly strange when an incorporeal presence suddenly appears and explains how he can fight back; by shining a light on the attacking entity and then shooting it. In the next moment, Alan wakes up (Alan Wake is a play on the word 'awake') out of what turns out to be a recurring nightmare. Throughout the game, Alan is constantly plunged into waking and dreaming states, a repetitive process that continually asks Alan and the gamer if the action is real or a Poesque dream within a dream.

The person waking Alan up is his wife, Alice, and in the game's first episode we learn that Alan has been suffering from writer's block and that the two have escaped to the Pacific northwest for a holiday. They arrive on a ferry at a small town named Bright Falls, and the first stop is a diner where a coffee-loving sheriff, a blonde waitress and a strange middle-aged lady cradling a lantern in her arms strongly recall David Lynch's first season of *Twin Peaks* (1990). To again cite Fuchs, this exemplifies how the game is replete 'with scenes and moments that function as doubles of past Gothic texts. In this way, the game text constantly summons up the ghost of the Gothic'.[11] *Alan Wake* is a game that wants the gamer to recognise the many references to other Gothic texts and thereby inhabit the Gothic space that they conjure. Thus, these references are not simply a homage to gothic and horror classics, but an attempt to build a collage where they are brought to bear on the story. The game becomes a site where the Gothic and horror canon is both encountered and performed.

Alan and Alice are in the Bright Falls diner to rent a cabin from the proprietor, but they are tricked by a veiled and ghostly lady to instead take residence in a house on a small island outside the city. Once there, an alien force drags Alice into the lake. Alan jumps in after her but quickly loses consciousness. When he wakes up he is sitting in his car, wrecked against a tree, and a week has passed that he cannot remember. When he explains to the police that his wife has been lost and tries to show the sheriff where she was dragged into the water, the entire island on which their house was located has disappeared. Locals informs Alan that it sank during an earthquake back in the 1970s.

This is the beginning of Alan's attempt to find out what happened to his wife, regain his memories of the lost week, avoid increasingly inquisitive law-enforcement agents and keep at bay a horde of nightmarish tool murderers, clearly reminiscent of Michael Myers' of *Halloween* (1978) or Jason Voorhees' of *Friday the 13th* (1980), who beset him during nightly explorations. These various outside forces constitute a great challenge to Alan, but his internal turmoil and schizophrenic mind are equally difficult to manage. During his exploration, he finds the pages of a new novel called *Departure* that is apparently authored by him but which he cannot remember having written. He is also contacted by someone who demands these pages in exchange for his wife, but his attempt to hand them over and retrieve his wife collapses in a nightmarish, violent and uncanny confrontation.

Alan again loses and regains consciousness only to find himself locked in a mental institution. At this stage, the possibility that he has gone insane seems plausible even to the gamer. He is treated by a psychiatrist named Hartman who specialises in artists and explains to Alan that his wife has in fact drowned and that Alan is 'torn apart by guilt, suffering from hallucinations, paranoid delusions, and obsession about light and darkness'. This analysis strongly recalls Dennis Lehane's 2003 novel *Shutter Island*, where the protagonist appears to be living inside a paranoid fantasy in order to shield himself from the terrible actions that he committed and is trying to suppress. Even when Alan confronts the psychiatrist and escapes the institution, again pursued by a gathering of axe-wielding psychopaths, this possibility remains. The entire game is so replete with a sense of schizophrenic doubling that the gamer – despite directing most of Alan's movements with the help of the keyboard – is often forced to abandon any sense of being in control.

During the game's final episodes, this Gothic sense of doubling and this lack of agency remain. Alan keeps collecting pages from the book he cannot remember writing, compiling them into a disturbing novel that seems to describe horrific incidents that he either has just experienced or which he is about face. Then, during a delirium induced by moonshine, he finds that he is able to remember parts of the week that he lost after the disappearance of his wife. It appears that a dark entity inhabits the lake and that this entity can enter the bodies of human beings. Currently, it inhabits the body of a Barbara Jagger, the woman who lured Alan and his wife to the island cabin. The lake into which Alice disappeared has the power to change reality through the creative machinations of an artist. The dark entity/Jagger is trying to force Alan to provide them with more agency and power through his writing. The novel *Departure* is the text that they have ordered.

In this way, the game is ultimately about the creative process as a Gothic practice. The protagonist produces the nightmarish reality which he inhabits. The psychiatrist's analysis that Alan is the victim of paranoia triggered by guilt is correct, but in ways that the psychiatrist could not have understood: the world of horror that Alan inhabits is not a delusion created by creative paranoia, it is a reality created through this paranoia. By playing this game, the gamer also becomes caught in this world as they direct Alan through the Gothic reality that envelops him. The gamer is constantly forced to try to determine whether the reality that the game shows is 'real', an illusion created by the entity that beset Alan, or a figment of Alan's own disturbed imagination.

The ending does not resolve these queries. In the final chapter of the game, Alan reaches what appears to be another dimension under water. Inside this dimension, he encounters increasingly strange phenomena, his own doppelgänger and, finally, within the sunken house, the veiled Barbara Jagger who is host to the dark entity. Using a light switch given to him as a child to dispel his fear of the dark, he destroys her by letting loose a tremendous white light. He then sits down in front of his typewriter that apparently remains in the house and finishes the novel. This ending allows his wife to swim out of the lake into which she was pulled by the dark entity. However, rather than returning to the surface with his wife, Alan remains in the house with the dark presence that still lives there, writing on his typewriter. Is he holding on to the agency that helped him destroy the body controlled by the dark presence at the bottom of the lake, or has he become the new corporeal vessel for darkness?[12]

Perhaps because it is made for a US market, *Alan Wake* never declares its Nordic provenance within the game. As Yvonne Leffler has observed in this book and elsewhere, the wilderness is 'a very central generating *locus* of horror' in Scandinavian narrative fiction.[13] In this way, the focus on the wilderness is possibly a Nordic characteristic, but American Gothic, from Nathaniel Hawthorne's 'Young Goodman Brown' (1835) to *The Blair Witch Project* (1999), has also often taken place in dark, labyrinthine forest landscapes. *Alan Wake's* oblique references to Nordic mythology are more obviously Nordic. During the gameplay, Alan comes across the Anderson brothers, two old rock-musicians that form the band Old Gods of Asgard. Diagnosed with drug-induced dementia, these brothers are also confined to the psychiatric clinic where Alan is imprisoned for a short while. Anderson is, of course, a Scandinavian family name, and to further enhance the Nordic connection, the brothers have renamed themselves Tor and Odin, with Tor sporting a plastic toy hammer and Odin, like the god, missing an eye. However, this link to the Nordic region is also potentially weak. Since Marvel Comics' introduction of Nordic gods into the US superhero canon, they have also become part of the US cultural landscape. Even so, the presence of Nordic gods in the game should be noted, since many other Nordic Gothic texts also reference this pagan past.

New Nordic media developers and the major studios: *Little Nightmares*

Unlike much other survival horror, *Alan Wake* involves the gamer in constant combat with the various threats that confront the avatar/gamer, which can be said to be typical of a dominant American narrative and ludic tradition informed by hypermasculinity and gun violence. Other national or transnational Gothic gaming paradigms seldom give the gamer access to guns and they do not involve the gamer in the performance of hypermasculinity. For instance, Japanese and other Asian third-person survival horror most often does not encourage the gamer to resolve issues through combat or violence and will often force the avatar to flee from confrontation.[14] The survival horror game genre emerged out of Japan in the late 1980s and early 1990s and migrated to other national and international contexts. Nordic game developers have also created games that belong to it and such a game is the critically

Nordic Gothic new media

9.2 Six running to avoid the long arms of the janitor in *Little Nightmares* (Tarsier Studios, 2017, *Little Nightmares*).

well-received *Little Nightmares* (2017) by Swedish Tarsier Studios, distributed by Japanese Bandai Namco Entertainment.

The avatar of *Little Nightmares* is not the white, gun wielding man of *Alan Wake*, but instead a miniscule, pre-adolescent girl named Six, clad in a yellow, hooded raincoat. When the game begins, she is huddled in a piece of luggage in the bowels of what eventually turns out to be a large ship ominously named The Maw. Controlling Six, the gamer must negotiate the obstacle that the ship itself constitutes, as well as a number of threats in the form of immense and monstrous humanoid creatures: a seemingly blind janitor with impossibly long arms, a pair of immensely fat chefs who prepare enormous amounts of red meat, a large gathering of similarly obese guests who voraciously consume this meat, and who will enthusiastically seize and eat Six if given the opportunity, and a ghostly and supremely hostile female apparition. Throughout the game, Six has no access to weapons that she can use to fend off these threats. During gameplay, the gamer can only avoid capture and certain death by hiding and running.

At the start of the game, the aesthetics and narrative are notably European and reminiscent of the Gothic and proto-steampunk environments of Terry Gilliam's *Brazil* (1985) or of Marc Caro and Jean-Pierre Jeunet's *La Cité des Enfants Perdus* (1995). As in the latter of these two films, Six is one of several children who have been kidnapped and taken to a labyrinthine structure on the ocean. However, the further the game proceeds, the clearer the inspiration from Japanese popular culture becomes. In particular, the game draws on productions by Japanese animated film company Studio Ghibli. Halfway into the game, the ship appears as a particularly nightmarish version of the bath house in *Spirited Away* (2001). In this film, similarly long-armed creatures, semi-demonic beings and voracious eating abound. The final enemy, referred to as 'the Lady', is not a Ghibli figure though, but the thin, white-faced, dark-haired and sinister female ghost figure endemic to Japanese and South Korean horror film.

While the game's aesthetic and basic plot clearly draws on previous European and Japanese film by making the gamer move a small, brave and resourceful child through a hostile and notably Gothic environment, the game surprises by complicating the child's seeming innocence. The gamer is likely to grow attached to the beautifully animated Six in her yellow raincoat, and the abject nature and appearance of the creatures that assail her further encourages this affective engagement. However, as the gamer moves further and further into the game, Six's character shows increasingly disturbing tendencies. From time to time, Six will be seized by hunger cramps. It is evident that she must eat to be able to move on. When this occurs, the gamer loses control over the avatar and can only observe a seamless cut-scene where Six finds nourishment from her immediate surroundings. The first time this happens, Six comes across another captive child, who reaches through bars to provide Six with something to eat. The next time Six gets hungry, the only thing near is a piece of raw meat from a mouse trap. The willingness of Six to consume this type of food signals that she is not the innocent creature that her appearance suggests. As the game proceeds, Six feeds off a dying rat caught in another mouse trap and then sates her hunger with small

9.3 Six feeding off a gnome that has attempted to hand her the sausage that lies ignored to the left (Tarsier Studios, 2017, *Little Nightmares*).

gnome, a creature of her own size and who was trying to provide her with a sausage.

Here, the game clearly deviates from the cinematic models that it cites. Six is small and essentially defenceless, but somehow also demonic. When she reaches the final enemy of the game, the Lady, the gamer discovers that this enemy cannot abide mirrors. Fortunately, Six finds a mirror and the gamer's challenge is to repeatedly hold this up to the Lady when she attacks Six. Eventually, the Lady collapses on the floor, breathing shallowly with her long, white neck exposed. Again, Six's hunger pains set in and it comes as no great surprise when she bites into the suddenly defenceless woman and feeds to discordant music. It appears that this act transforms Six in some manner. A strange, dark smoke ominously circles her. In the final cut-scene of the game, Six makes her way through the vast room where the obese guests sit gorging themselves. Only this time, Six is not running frantically across the tables to avoid the fat paws that try to grab her; she instead strides confidently down the floor space that separates the tables, the light bulbs in the ceiling lanterns popping and exploding in her wake. Like before, the guests turn hungrily after her and stretch out their arms to grab and consume her, but in doing so, their faces turn ashen and their bodies distort to the sound of bones popping and breaking. Six walks unmolested into the bright daylight leaving death in her wake.

The game thus complicates, as much Gothic fiction does, the simple binaries of good and evil. Six is certainly a mostly defenceless and sympathetic avatar, and the ship that she traverses is definitely a hellish place inhabited by grotesque and demonically hungry beings. Yet, she also harbours an insatiable appetite and a capacity for destructive violence. This is obviously not a new trope in Gothic, as monstrous hunger and death in the figure of a (demonic) child occur in *The Exorcist* (1973), *The Omen* (1976), several of Steven King's novels and short stories, in the Japanese film *Ju-On: The Grudge* (2002) and, of course, in John Ajvide Lindqvist's *Let the Right One In* (2004).[15] These and similar texts posit the demonic child as the abject other and describe how forces of good seek to undo them. *Little Nightmares* revises this model by encouraging the gamer to identify with the demonic child. Thus, through the association between the avatar and the gamer who steers the avatar through the narrative, the game can be said to encourage the gamer to also discover this in herself or himself. As discussed above, this is a theme that can be discerned in much Nordic Gothic new media. *Little Nightmares* is thus one of several Nordic texts that disturbs established notions of good and evil, and that makes the gamer engage with an avatar that is complex and Other.

Independent games: *Year Walk*

While the Nordic games that sell the most copies are distributed by international game producers and appeal to large, international audiences, there is another category of games that, like Nordic Gothic literature, draw from Nordic mythology and place their games within Nordic settings. Most of these games are independently developed and not distributed by any of the large publishers, but by using English to interact with the gamer, and through distribution platforms such as AppStore, Steam or Origin, they can still reach a reasonably large and international audience.

To this category belongs Malmö-based Simago AB, which has produced a series of Gothic-themed games for mobile devices such as the iPhone and iPad. The most successful and critically acclaimed game of this kind is *Year Walk* (2013). This game uses a simple interface that makes it possible for the gamer to navigate using only their fingers. *Year Walk* is a rough translation of the Swedish concept 'Årsgång'. According to this ancient practice, it is possible to see into the future through nightly walks during certain days of the year. In *Year Walk*, the gamer is told in the first few screens that this walk was conducted in particular 'To see if they would be wealthy / To see if they would be happy / To see if they would live / To see if they would be loved'. The game then places the gamer in the body of a young man called Daniel Svensson who travels through a snowy yet recognisably Swedish landscape to a windmill where a young woman is waiting. From their brief conversation, it becomes clear that Daniel and the woman have had an affair but that the woman

9.4 The recognisably Swedish house where Daniel can be assumed to live in *Year Walk* (Simago, 2013, *Year Walk*).

has now received a proposal to marry. Despite being warned not to, Daniel decides to investigate the future by conducting a year walk.

During this nightly walk, Daniel encounters a series of beings from Nordic mythology, including the Hulder, the brook horse, the Myling, the Night Raven and the Church Grim.[16] The gamer who controls Daniel progresses through the game by keeping track of various numerical patterns in the game and making use of these to resolve a series of puzzles. At the end of what can be termed the game's first section, the gamer manages to complete the Year Walk and receives the following enigmatic prediction: 'It's too late now / It can't be changed / The decision has already been made / You must stop coming here', and then, appearing word for word, 'I don't love you anymore'.

This screen then shifts back to daytime. The landscape has also changed, the ground is green and pollen, rather than snowflakes, flows in the air. The gamer moves through this spring-like landscape until they come across the young woman, now lying still on the grass as if sleeping. As the gamer watches, the grass is coloured red by blood that wells from the centre of the body. Following this, credits roll to what sounds like an old psalm, but at the end of them, new cryptic words appear: 'I have written it all down, everything that happened, it can be changed, we must deliver the message, my notes, hidden, the companion, the year is the passcode, 1894, remember, 1894'. This message sends the gamer on to a new Gothic quest. The word 'companion' refers to another app by Simago: *Year Walk Companion*. This is both an addition and a continuation of the first game. When the gamer downloads the app, new material, most of it in the form of descriptions of Nordic traditions and mythological creatures, appears. If the gamer enters the passcode, they are given access to a set of journal notes by a man called Theodore Almsten who has been researching the Year Walk and has become consumed by the tradition. The journal also provides a new passcode that can be used to unlock a more detailed ending to the game. This comes in the form of a set of newspaper clippings that explain the presence of the Mylings in the game and describe how Daniel was executed for the murder of Stina Nilsson. The destinies of Theodore and Daniel now seem to collide in strange ways. When the words 'You can save her. You know what you must do' and a knife appears, it is unclear what follows. Who is the 'you' addressed here? The gamer, Daniel or Theodore, or all at the same time? Will Theodore/Daniel attempt to save Stina by killing her? Will Theodore kill Daniel, somehow reaching through time to do so, or will he kill himself as a way of obliterating Daniel?

Again, Gothic doubling informs the narrative. The gamer is both Daniel Svensson, the man who, the gamer discovers, was executed for the murder of Stina Nilsson, and Theodore Almsten, a student in the present who is obsessively trying to understand and engage in the occult ritual of the Year Walk. Like in much Gothic fiction, the attempt to understand the process of occult detection is both enlightening and ultimately futile. As in *Alan Wake*, the resolution remains mysterious and ambiguous. While the murder of Stina Nilsson is explained, the reasons why she was murdered remain obscure. Did the ritual of the Year Walk prompt the violence? Was Daniel simply deranged? Will Theodore perform similar violence, or will his intervention somehow change what happened more than 100 years ago? Also, the avatar Theodore in the second part of the game is, as in *Little Nightmares*, potentially both a heroic figure at the end of a long struggle and a monster.

The slow pace of Year Walk is very different from the often-frantic gameplay of *Alan Wake*, or the practical resolution of puzzles in *Little Nightmares*. However, *Year Walk* is similar to these games, and to *Little Nightmares* in particular, through the slow revelation that the avatar is monstrous. From the initial meeting with Stina in the windmill, to the newspaper clipping that explains that Daniel murdered her and will be executed for this crime, the character follows a downward Gothic spiral both guarded over and accelerated by haunting Nordic mythological creatures. At the end of this descent, Daniel, but also Theodore, encounters the ultimate darkness of his own destructive potential.

Independent games: *Through the Woods*

In 2014–2015, independent Norwegian studio Antagonist crowdfunded the third-person survival horror game *Through the Woods* and released it via the Steam platform in 2016. At the beginning of the game, the gamer is informed that the location of the game is Western Norway, and anyone who has spent time in the region should have no difficulties recognising the area from the pine trees, the fjord and the dramatic, rock-strewn mountains. The game is set in present-day Norway and revolves around the blonde and Scandinavian-looking Karen, mother of the pre-adolescent Espen. Karen and Espen have moved into a cabin located by a fjord and the gamer soon learns that Karen is not the best mother. She works through the night and sleeps during the day, leaving her son understimulated, bored and alienated. Indeed, Karen herself expresses a sadness at her perceived failure as a mother throughout the

9.5 Karen entering one of the derelict Viking settlements on the island in *Through the Woods* (Antagonist, 2016, *Through the Woods*).

game, and provides more and more detail on this failure as the game proceeds.

The lack of stimulus in the house drives Espen to venture out on the rickety lake pier, and Karen comes out of the house just in time to see him kidnapped by a man in ancient Norwegian garb. In a similarly antiquated Norwegian long boat, the man disappears to a mist-shrouded island full of deserted and dilapidated Viking settlements. Inside these houses, Karen finds notes, conveniently for the gamer written in English, that describe how the villagers try to survive the onslaught of a host of hostile creatures from Scandinavian folklore, while at the same time being deprived of their children.

As Karen moves through the labyrinthine and hilly island, from settlement to settlement, through caves and dense forests, she encounters a number of the creatures that have assailed the villagers. Armed only with a torch, she can do little to keep the Trolls, Nøkken, the Hulder, the Wergen and other monsters from tearing her to shreds (something that occurs with regularity in the game). Visually, these beings are strikingly similar to how they have been depicted in recent independent Norwegian horror films such as *Troll Hunter* (2010) and *Thale* (2013). To survive, Karen must tread quietly through the forest, while at the same time learning more about the monsters and the horrific plight of the island. Many of the houses she enters are full of bones eaten clean by unknown predators. Shouted arguments and violent encounters between neighbours and spouses appear frozen in time and reach Karen's ears as she walks past the houses. In some places, survivors actually remain, but they have been driven insane by grief, clutching dead babies to their chests. Apparently, the children have been euthanised by their parents before being stolen by a man referred to as Erik. Karen realises that Erik is the same man as the one who kidnapped Espen and that her son is to be sacrificed for some dark reason.

Karen now appears to the gamer as a vulnerable but utterly dedicated mother who vows to rescue her beloved son from Erik. However, through two voice-overs – one occurring in real time when Karen comments on things that she sees or hears, and the other apparently recorded at some point in the future, looking back on what happens in the game as if this action is already concluded – we learn more about her. Karen's estranged husband appears to have committed suicide at some point. Karen is appalled by the monsters that have killed so many of the inhabitants on the island, but still strikes a deal with two Wergen – large supernatural wolves who speak Norwegian to each other – setting them free to prey on the remaining villagers so that they will let her continue looking for Espen. As in *Alan Wake*, *Little Nightmares* and *Year Walk*, the gamer is left in doubt of what truly motivates the avatar that they control. Towards the end of the game, the gamer understands that Karen has a dark personal history. She was once an abusive mother who broke the arm of her son Espen in a fit of anger. When her husband wanted custody, she blamed the injury on him. Shut out of his son's life, her husband killed himself.

While Karen seems to have regretted her role in this troubled past, the conclusion of the game draws an even darker picture of her character. Once she manages to catch up with Erik and Espen, she discovers that her son walks willingly to his sacrifice. The reason why Erik has sacrificed thousands of children over the years (sacrifices morbidly noted in a ledger stored in a cave), is so that the Fenris Wolf, the harbinger of Armageddon in pre-Christian Nordic traditions, shall not break free of the chains that bind him. This situation recalls Drew Goddard's horror film *The Cabin in the Woods* (2012), where gods known as the Ancient Ones demand yearly sacrifices or they will rise and obliterate humanity. In this game, these hungry gods have been replaced by the Nordic Fenris Wolf.

Despite his young age, Espen recognises the need to keep the wolf at bay and willingly jumps to his death to keep the world from collapsing. In a drawn-out and melodramatic scene, the gamer helps Karen to try

9.6 Karen approaches the site where Erik is about to sacrifice Espen to the Fenris Wolf. The jagged mountains in the background are the wolf's gigantic, open jaws (Antagonist, 2016, *Through the Woods*).

to bring him back to life through CPR, an attempt that cannot succeed in the game. In the confrontation, Erik has also died, and, to make sure that Espen's sacrifice was not in vain, Karen now vows to continue Erik's work. She will be the one kidnapping children to appease the hunger of the Fenris wolf. When this occurs, the gamer has reached the point when Karen's second narrative was recorded and realises that the story they just played through was always in the past, that the gamer has helped Karen to complete a journey from being a loving if inadequate mother to becoming a serial child-murderer.

Despite a well-constructed game engine that makes the gamer's journey through the beautiful rendition of the Norwegian landscape seem realistic, *Through the Woods* is an awkward game. The gamer frequently gets lost in the labyrinthine hills and forests, Trolls and Huldra appear out of nowhere, or cannot be seen at all. The writing is overly melodramatic and the main character's voice actor, speaking with a clear Norwegian accent, is unnecessarily wooden. Yet the game manages to pull the gamer in through its complex and inherently Gothic storyline, where the uncovering of horror that reaches back thousands of years is accompanied by the slow revelation of a dark and guilt-ridden personal past. Like in *Alan Wake*, *Little Nightmares* and *Year Walk*, the game's avatar, and by extension the gamer, enacts an inherently Gothic narrative. At the end of the game story lies not the happy resolution of a completed adventure, but the inevitable conclusion to the avatar's own dark and ambiguous past history.

Conclusion: Nordic Gothic new media

A study of four games cannot make general claims about what sets Nordic Gothic new media apart from Gothic digital content developed in other parts of the world. Even if a much larger body of material had been investigated it would remain difficult precisely because new media and games in particular are produced for a global, mostly English-speaking marketplace. This does not mean, however, that the specifically Nordic does not have an impact on Gothic new media developed in the North. In a fiercely competitive marketplace, local content is potentially a way to compete. It is clear that the Nordic – its nature, mythologies and traditions – does serve as a source of inspiration for game developers based in the North. Above all, independent games refer to Nordic history and traditions. Unlike AAA games, but like much Nordic literature and film, the independent games discussed here are set within recognisably Nordic forest landscapes, providing the gamer with a clear sense of place. It should be noted that, for games, this is an aesthetic rather than a financial choice. Whereas Nordic Gothic television or film turns to the forest to save money (the scenography is virtually for free in the wilderness), Nordic games turn to Nature not for budget reasons, but precisely because of its potential to act as a Gothic locale haunted by pagan pasts, pre-Christian creatures and mythologies, and buried injustices.

If the focus on wilderness is one central characteristic that informs Nordic Gothic new media, as it does novels and films, the other is arguably the tendency to complicate the notion of good and evil and to problematise authority. In a study of Nordic Noir television, Glen Creeber agrees with Brodén's aforementioned reading of Nordic Noir when he argues that while the shows he studies provide a form of closure through the disentangling of the crime, 'the moral, political and social problems that produced' the crime remain unresolved.[17] As a number of the chapters that make up this book demonstrate, Nordic Gothic is similarly complex and addresses a comparable moral, political and social dynamic. *Through the Woods* and *Year Walk* both contain extensive documentation that reveals a confrontation between political and social institutions and Gothic. In *Through the Woods*, the avatar's custody battle with her husband – including deliberations in the court room – play out in front of the gamer. In *Year Walk*, the gamer is provided with extensive information regarding the local government's punishment of the avatar. *Little Nightmares* tells a very different story, but also revolves around how a vast institution consumes subjects. The ship that constitutes the gaming universe in *Little Nightmares* is a voracious and horrifically hostile entity that preys on the weak in order to feed a frenzied and similarly voracious adult community. However, the avatars that move through these troubled game worlds, which challenge and (partly) destroy them, are also ravenous and monstrous. While the destruction they accomplish may be necessary, even welcome, there is little sense that a better world is dawning in its wake. Of course, Gothic outside of the Nordic region is also deeply ambiguous and frequently revolves around protagonists that are both attractive and monstrous. Gothic thrives on unresolved moral issues and on problematising modernity. The point here is not that Nordic Gothic new media is the only form of Gothic to describe a world loosened from its moral moorings, but that moral uncertainty and a discomfort with modernity are particularly strong tendencies in Nordic Gothic new media

Notes

1 F. Saggini, *The Gothic Novel and the Stage: Romantic Appropriations* (London: Pickering & Chatto: 2015), p. 3.
2 As argued by Espen Aarseth, this is a form of interactive literature that requires 'non-trivial effort' to read. In other words, ergodic literature is interactive and cybertextual; by choosing among different possible continuations supplied in the text, the reader can actually influence how the narrative proceeds and concludes. E. Aarseth, *Cybertext: Perspectives on Ergodic Literature* (Baltimore: Johns Hopkins University Press, 1997), p. 1.
3 Since the emergence of formal game studies in the 1990s, game scholars have noted that most games consist of two elements: games are narratives telling a story and a performative negotiation of various obstacles. The term often used for research that investigates this performative element is 'ludology' (from the Latin word for games: *ludus*). During the early 2000s, there was a sometimes fierce discussion regarding whether games should be studied as primarily an (apolitical) performative negotiation of game objects, or whether the important aspect was still the (political) narratives that games conveyed. Today, game scholarship tends to discuss both ludological and narratological aspects of games, and often considers both as informed by a political context.
4 M. Hanckock, 'Doppelgamers: Video Games and Gothic Choice' in J. Faflak and J. Haslam (eds), *American Gothic: An Edinburgh Companion* (Edinburgh: Edinburgh University Press, 2016), pp. 166–86, p. 166.
5 T. A. Goddu, *Gothic America: Narrative, History, and Nation* (New York: Columbia University Press, 1997), p. 2.
6 Goddu, *Gothic America*, p. 2.

7 D. Brodén, 'The dark ambivalences of the welfare state: Investigating the transformations of the Swedish crime film', in *Northern Lights: Film and Media Studies Yearbook*, 9:1 (2011), pp. 95–109, p. 98.
8 K. Andersen and K. Shimabukuro, 'European Horror Games: Little Red Riding Hood's Zombie BBQ and the European Game Industry', in D. Och and K. Strayer (eds), *Transnational Horror Across Visual Media: Fragmented Bodies* (Abingdon: Routledge, 2013), pp. 86–105, p. 95.
9 Andersen and Shimabukuro, 'European Horror Games', p. 95.
10 M. Fuchs, 'A Different Kind of Monster: Uncanny Media and Alan Wake's Textual Monstrosity', in C. Duret and C-M. Pons (eds), *Contemporary Research on Intertextuality in Video Games* (Hershey PA: IGI Global, 2016), pp. 39–53, p. 40.
11 Fuchs, 'A Different Kind of Monster', p. 40.
12 Additional, downloadable content called *The Signal* and *The Writer* continues the story and provides different, yet also inconclusive and ambiguous answers to these questions.
13 Y. Leffler, 'The Devious Landscape of Scandinavian Horror', in P. M. Mehtonen and M. Savolainen (eds), *Gothic Topographies: Language, Nation Building and 'Race'* (Abingdon: Routledge, 2013), pp. 141–52, p. 151.
14 There are notable exceptions to this, such as Japanese Capcom's *Resident Evil* (1996), a trend-setting, violent shooter game that has spawned a number of sequels and movie adaptations.
15 For a discussion on the Gothic child, see E. Hanson. "Knowing Children. Desire and Interpretation in *The Exorcist*" in S. Bruhm and N. Hurley (eds), *Curiouser. On the Queerness of Children* (Minneapolis: University of Minnesota Press, 2004), pp. 107–36; E. Pifer, *Demon or Doll. Images of the Child in Contemporary Writing and Culture* (Charlottesville: University Press of Virginia, 2000); and M. H. Troy 'Predator and Prey: The Vampire Child in Novels by S. P. Somtow and John Ajvide Lindqvist', *Edda*, 117:2 (2017), pp. 130–44. DOI: 10.18261/issn.1500-1989-2017-02-04.
16 Hulder is a female being of the forest and named *Huldra* or *Skogsrå* in Swedish; the brook horse is named *Bäckahästen* and also exists in Scottish mythology where it functions as a way to move between worlds; the Myling is also known as Utburd and is essentially the ghost of an abandoned, unbaptised child not given a Christian burial and therefore doomed to roam the land until given a proper resting place; and the Night Raven is referred to as Nattramn, and, like the Myling, it is possibly the ghost of an unbaptised child or a suicide. Finally, the Church Grim is called *Kyrkogrimmen* in Swedish and this is the animal ghost guardian of a creature buried alive underneath a church cornerstone.
17 G. Creeber, 'Killing us Softly: Investigating the Aesthetics, Philosophy and Influence of Nordic Noir Television', *Journal of Popular Television*, 3:1 (2015), pp. 21–35, 32.

Appendix: Nordic Gothic fiction

Films

Antichrist (Lars von Trier, 2009)
Besökarna (Joakim Ersgård, 1988)
Blödaren (Hans Hatwig, 1983)
Cirkeln (Levan Akin, 2015)
De dødes tjern (Kåre Bergstrøm, 1958)
Det sjunde inseglet (Ingmar Bergman, 1957)
Død snø (Tommy Wirkola, 2009)
Fritt fall (Roar Uthaug, 2006)
Gräns (Ali Abassi, 2018)
Harpoon: Reykjavik Whale Watching Massacre (Július Kemp, 2009)
Häxan (Benjamin Christensen, 1922)
Jungfrukällan (Ingmar Bergman, 1960)
Körkarlen (Victor Sjöström, 1921)
Låt den rätte komma in (Tomas Alfredson, 2008)
Madness (Sonny Laguna, David Liljeblad, Tommy Wiklund, 2010)
Månguden (Jonas Cornell, 1988)
Nattevagten (Ole Bornedal, 1994)
Persona (Ingmar Bergman, 1966)
Rymdinvasion i Lappland (Virgil W. Vogel, 1959)
Thale (Aleksander L. Nordaas, 2013)
Trolljegeren (Andre Øvredal, 2010)
Svart Lucia (Rumle Hammerich, 1992)
Valhalla Rising (Nicholas Winding Refn, 2009)
Valkoinen peura (Erik Blomberg, 1952)
Vampyr (Carl Theodor Dreyer, 1931–1932)
Vargtimmen (Ingmar Bergman, 1968)
Villmark (Pål Øie, 2003)
Vittra (Sonny Laguna, Tommy Wiklund, 2012)

Games

Alan Wake (Remedy Entertainment, 2010)
Alan Wake's American Nightmare (Remedy Entertainment, 2012)
Amnesia (Frictional Games, 2010–2013)
Dead Nation (Housemark, 2010)
Hitman: Codename 47 (IO Interactive, 2000)
Little Nightmares (Tarsier Studios, 2017)
Max Payne (Remedy Entertainment, 2001)
Penumbra (Frictional Games, 2007–2008)
Soma (Frictional Games, 2015)
Through the Woods (Antagonist, 2016)
Year Walk (Simago, 2013)

Literature

Almqvist, Carl Jonas Love. *Skällnora kvarn* (1838)
Andersen, Hans Christian. 'Den lille havfrue' (1837)
––. 'De røde sko' (1847)
––. 'De vilde Svaner' (1838)
––. 'Dyndkongens datter' (1858)
––. *Fodreise* (1829)
––. 'Skyggen' (1847)
––. 'Snedronningen' (1844)
Blicher, Steen Steensen. *Præsten i Vejlbye* (1829)
Blixen, Karen. *Seven Gothic Tales/Syv Fantastiske Fortællinger* (1934/1935)
––. 'The Supper at Elsinore'/'Et familieselskab i Helsingør' (1934/1935)
Ekman, Kerstin. *De Tre Små Mästarna* (1961)
––. *Händelser vid vatten* (1993)
––. *Herrarna i skogen* (2007)
––. *Rövarna i skuleskogen* (1988)
Elfgren, Sara Bergmark. *Norra Latin* (2017)
Elfgren, Sara Bergmark, Mats Strandberg, Kim. W. Andersson, Karl Johansson and Lina Neidestam. *Berättelser från Engelsfors* (2013)
Fager, Anders. *Svenska Kulter* (2009)
Hagberg, Mattias. *Rekviem för en vanskapt* (2012)
Hansen, Maurits Christopher. *Mordet på maskinbygger Roolfsen* (1839)
Höglund, Panu Petteri and S. Albert Kivinen. *The Book of Poison: Stories Inspired by H. P. Lovecraft* (2014)
Høeg, Peter. *Frøken Smillas fornemmelse for sne* (1992)
Ibsen, Henrik. *Gengangere* (1881)
Ingemann, Bernhard Severin. *Sfinxen* (1820)
––. *Varulven* (1834)
Jensen, Caroline L. *Vargsläkte* (2011)
Jølsen, Ragnhild. *Rikka Gan* (1904)
Kaaberbøl, Lene. *Blodsungen* (2012)
––. *Fjendeblod* (2013)

—. *Genkommeren* (2014)
—. *Ildprøven* (2011)
—. *Kimæras hævn* (2011)
—. *Viridians blod* (2011)
Kandre, Mare. *Aliide, Aliide* (1991)
—. *Bestiarium* (1999)
—. *Bübins unge* (1987)
Lagercrantz, David. *Det som inte dödar oss* (2015)
Lagerlöf, Selma. *Anna Svärd* (1928)
—. 'Bortbytingen' (1908)
—. *Charlotte Löwensköld* (1925)
—. 'De fågelfrie' (1892)
—. *En herrgårdssägen* (1899)
—. 'Frid på jorden' (1917)
—. *Gösta Berlings saga* (1891)
—. *Herr Arnes Penningar* (1903)
—. *Körkarlen* (1912)
—. *Löwensköldska ringen* (1925)
—. 'Stenkumlet' (1892)
—. 'Värmländsk naturskönhet' (1933)
Lagerkvist, Pär. *Dvärgen* (1944)
—. 'Far och jag' (1924)
—. *Onda sagor* (1924)
Larsmo, Ola. *Swede Hollow* (2016)
Larsson, Stieg. *Män som hatar kvinnor* (2005)
—. *Millennium* (2005–2007)
Laxness, Halldór. *Kristnihald undeir Jökli* (1968)
Leine, Kim. *Profeterna i evighetsfjorden* (2012)
Linderholm, Helmer. *De ulvgrå* (1972)
Lindqvist, John Ajvide. 'Gräns' (2006)
—. *Hanteringen av odöda* (2005)
—. *Låt den rätte komma in* (2004)
—. *Lilla stjärna* (2010)
—. *Människohamn* (2008)
—. *Rörelsen. Den andra platsen* (2015)
Lindqvist, John Ajvide, Johan Theorin and Åke Edwardson. *De odöda. Skräckberättelser av John Ajvide Lindqvist, Johan Theorin, Åke Edwardson* (2012)
Livijn, Claes. 'Samwetets fantasi' (1821)
Ljungstedt, Aurora. 'Harolds skugga' (1861)
—. *Hin ondes hus* (1853)
Lundgren, Åke. *Långa lappflickan – sägnen om Stor-Stina* (1981)
Lundström, Janne. *De Ofria* (2016)
Niemi, Michael. *Fallvatten* (2012)
—. *Koka Björn* (2017)
Nordin, Magnus *Djävulens märke* (2018)
Ohlmarks, Åke. *Gengångare* (1971)
—. *Slottsspöken* (1973)

Rydberg, Viktor. *Vampyren* (1848)
Sigurðardóttir, Yrsa. *Auðnin* (2008)
---. *Þóra Guðmundsdóttir* (2010)
Sinisalo, Johanna. *Ennen päivänlaskua ei voi* (2000)
Spjut, Stefan. *Stallo* (2012)
---. *Stalpi* (2017)
Stagnelius, Erik J. *Riddartornet* (1821)
Strandberg, Mats. *Hemmet* (2017)
Strandberg, Mats and Sara Bergmark Elfgren. *Cirkeln* (2011)
---. *Eld* (2012)
---. *Nyckeln* (2013)
Strindberg, August. *Spöksonaten* (1907)
---. 'Tschandala' (1889)
Theorin, J. *Blodläge* (2010)
---. *Nattfåk* (2008)
---. *Rörgast* (2013)
---. *Skumtimmen* (2007)
Topelius, Zacharias. 'En natt och en morgon' (1843)
Trotzig, Birgitta. *Dykungens dotter: En barnhistoria* (1985)

TV series

Ängelby (Johan Kindblom and Thomas Tivemark, 2015)
Bron/Broen (Hans Rosenfeldt, 2011–2018)
Forbrydelsen (Søren Sveistrup, Torleif Hoppe and Michael W. Horsten 2007–2012)
Idjabeaivváš (Måns Mårlind and Björn Stein, 2016)
Jordskott (Henrik Björn and Anders Engström, 2015, 2017)
Kullamannen (Leif Kranz, 1967–1968)
Riget (Lars von Trier and Nils Vørsel, 1994, 1997)

Bibliography

Aarseth, E. *Cybertext: Perspectives on Ergodic Literature*. Baltimore: Johns Hopkins University Press, 1997.
Adams, R. 'Stephen King: Let Me In "is the best American horror film in the last 20 years"'. *Awardsdaily*. www.awardsdaily.com/2010/10/08/stephen-king-let-me-in-the-best-american-horror-film-in-the-last-20-years/. Accessed 17 December 2018.
Adkins, R. *The 'Monstrous Other' Speaks. Postsubjectivity and the Queering of the Normal*. Oregon: UMI Dissertations Publishing, 2010.
Agger, G. 'Hoved-, humor- og genrehistorier: En analyse af *Riget*'. *K&K*, 80 (1996), 135–58.
—. 'I transformationernas rige: Fra *Riget* til *Kingdom Hospital*', in P. Stein Larsen, P. Kaj Pedersen, E-U. Pinkert and B. Sørensen (eds), *Interaktioner. Om kunstarternes productive mellemværender*. Aalborg: Aalborg Universitetsforlag, 2009, pp. 17–36.
Alkestrand, M. *Magiska möjligheter: Harry Potter, Artemis Fowl och Cirkeln i skolans värdegrundsarbete*. Göteborg: Makadam förlag, 2016.
—. 'Walking in Someone Else's Shoes: The Body Switch in the Engelsfors Trilogy', *Barnboken* 40 (2017), 1–19.
Andersen, H. C. *Fairy Tales*. Trans. T. Nunnally, ed. and intro. J. Wullschlager. London: Penguin, 2004.
—. *Fodreise fra Holmens Canal til Østpynten af Amager i Aarene 1828 og 1829*. Copenhagen: DSL/Borgen, 1986.
—. 'The Little Mermaid', in H. C. Andersen *Fairy Tales*, pp. 67–87.
—. 'The Snow Queen', in H. C. Andersen *Fairy Tales*, pp. 175–204.
—. 'The Wild Swans', in H. C. Andersen *Fairy Tales*, pp. 107–21.
Andersen, K. and K. Shimabukuro. 'European Horror Games: Little Red Riding Hood's Zombie BBQ and the European Game Industry', in D. Och and K. Strayer (eds), *Transnational Horror Across Visual Media: Fragmented Bodies*. Abingdon: Routledge, 2013, pp. 86–107.
Andersson, J. 'Premiär för SVT:s blodiga morddrama'. *Göteborgsposten*, 23 October 2016. www.gp.se/kultur/tv/premi%C3%A4r-f%C3%B6r-svt-s-blodiga-morddrama-1.3890859. Accessed 30 January 2019.

Andersson Burnett, L. 'The "Lapland" Giantess in Britain', in D. Brydon, P. Forsgren and G. Fur (eds), *Concurrent Imaginaries, Postcolonial Worlds: Toward Revised Histories*. Leiden: Brill, 2017, pp. 123–43.

Ankarloo, B. 'Witch Trials in Northern Europe 1450–1700', in B. Ankarloo, S. Clark and W. Monter (eds), *Witchcraft and Magic in Europe: The Period of the Witch Trials*. London: Athlone Press, 2002, pp. 53–95.

Arnstad, M. 'Hem ljuva folkhem'. *Språktidningen*, January 2016. http://spraktidningen.se/artiklar/2015/12/hem-ljuva-folkhem. Accessed 4 January 2019.

Bainbridge, C. *The Cinema of Lars von Trier: Authenticity and Artifice*. London: Wallflower Press, 2007.

Beck, J. *Dirty Wars: Landscape, Power, and Waste in Western American Literature*. Lincoln: University of Nebraska Press, 2009.

Bhambra, G. *Rethinking Modernity: Postcolonialism and the Sociological Imagination*. London: Palgrave Macmillan, 2007.

'Blegdamme på Blegdamsvej'. *Dengang*, 13 October 2009. www.dengang.dk/artikler/2050. Accessed 25 August 2018.

Botting, F. *Gothic*. London and New York: Routledge, 1996.

Brantlinger, P. *Rule of Darkness: British Literature and Imperialism, 1830–1914*. Ithaca: Cornell University Press, 1988.

Brodén, D. 'The dark ambivalences of the welfare state: Investigating the transformations of the Swedish crime film'. *Northern Lights: Film and Media Studies Yearbook*, 9:1 (2011), 95–109.

---. *Folkhemmets skuggbilder: En kulturanalytisk genrestudie av svensk kriminalfiktion i film och TV*. Stockholm: Ekholm & Tegebjer, 2008.

Brodrej, G. 'Samisk exotism i SVT:s thrillerserie', *Expressen*, 13 November 2016. www.expressen.se/kultur/gunilla-brodrej/samisk-exotism-i-svts-thrillerserie/. Accessed 30 January 2019.

Browning, M. *Stephen King on the Small Screen*. Bristol: Intellect, 2011.

Cardel Gertsen, M. and C. Werther. 'The Mote in Thy Brother's Eye – Swedes in Danish Ads'. *Advances in Consumer Research* 26 (1999), 678–83.

Castle, T. *The Female Thermometer: Eighteenth-Century Culture and the Invention of the Uncanny*. New York: Oxford University Press, 1995.

Christensen, O. and C. K. Kristiansen. 'Porten til Riget', in E. Jørholt (ed.), *Ind i Filmen*. København: Medusa, 1995, pp. 285–309.

Clover, C. *Men Women and Chain Saws: Gender in the Modern Horror Film* (1992). Princeton: Princeton University Press, 2015.

Creeber, G. 'Killing us softly: Investigating the Aesthetics, Philosophy and Influence of Nordic Noir Television'. *Journal of Popular Television* 3:1 (2015), 21–35.

---. 'Surveying *The Kingdom*: Explorations of Medicine, Memory and Modernity in Lars von Trier's *The Kingdom* (1994)'. *European Journal of Cultural Studies* 5:4 (2002), 387–406.

Day, W. P. *In the Circles of Fear and Desire: A Study of Gothic Fantasy*. Chicago and London: University of Chicago Press, 1985.

Del Principe, D. 'Introduction: The EcoGothic in the Long Nineteenth Century', *Gothic Studies*, 16:1 (2014), 1–8.

Demker, M., Y. Leffler and O. Sigurdsson (eds). *Culture, Health and Religion: Sweden Unparadised*. New York: Palgrave Macmillan, 2014.

Dijkstra, B. *Idols of Perversity. Fantasies of Feminie Evil in Fin-de-Siècle Culture*. New York: Oxford University Press, 1986.
Donaghue, E. *Black Women/White Men: The Sexual Exploitation of Female Slaves in the Danish West Indies*. Bloomington: Authorhouse, 2006.
Dryden, L. *The Modern Gothic and Literary Doubles: Stevenson, Wilde and Wells*. Basingstoke: Palgrave Macmillan, 2003.
Duncan, R. *South African Gothic: Anxiety and Creative Dissent in the Post-apartheid Imagination and Beyond*. Cardiff: University of Wales Press, 2018.
Edelson, C. D. *Siting Horror: Place and Space in American Gothic Fiction*, Diss. University of California Riverside, 2007.
Edwards, J. D. and S. Vasconcelos (eds). *Tropical Gothic in Literature and Culture*. Abingdon: Routledge, 2016.
Ekman, K. *The Forest of Hours*. Trans. Anna Paterson. London: Chatto & Windus, 1996.
—. *Herrarna i skogen*. Stockholm: Bonniers, 2007.
Ekman, S. *Writing Worlds, Reading Landscapes: An Exploration of Setting in Fantasy*. Diss. Lund University: Centre for Language and Literature, 2010.
Elfgren, S. B. and M. Strandberg. *The Circle*. Trans. P. Carlsson. London: Hammer, 2012.
—. *Fire*. Trans. A. Paterson. London: Hammer, 2013.
—. *The Key*. Trans. A. Paterson, London: Hammer, 2015.
Fahl, H. '"Cirkeln" – en svensk "Twilight"?', *Dagens Nyheter*, 31 March 2011. www.dn.se/dn-bok/cirkeln-en-svensk-twilight/. Accessed 3 February 2018.
—. 'En ort som gjord för mörk magi'. *Dagens Nyheter*, 23 April 2012. www.dn.se/dn-bok/en-ort-som-gjord-for-mork-magi/. Accessed 3 February 2018.
Freud, S. 'The Uncanny' [1919], in *The Standard Edition of the Complete Psychological Works of Sigmund Freud. Vol 17 (1917–1919). An Infantile Neurosis and Other Works*. Trans. J. Strachey. London: Hogarth Press, 1955, pp. 217–56.
Friedan, B. *The Fountain of Age*. New York: Simon and Schuster, 1993.
Fuchs, M. 'A Different Kind of Monster: Uncanny Media and Alan Wake's Textual Monstrosity', in C. Duret and C-M. Pons (eds), *Contemporary Research on Intertextuality in Video Games*. Hershey: IGI Global, 2016, pp. 39–53.
Fyhr, M. *De mörka labyrinterna. Gotiken i litteratur, film, musik och rollspel*, Stockholm, Lund: Ellerström, 2003.
—. *Svensk skräcklitteratur 1: Bårtäcken över jordens likrum*. Lund: Ellerström 2017.
Goddu, T. A. *Gothic America: Narrative, History, and Nation*. New York: Columbia University Press, 1997.
Gregersdotter, K. 'The Scandinavian Zombie and the Welfare State: A Reading of John Ajvide Lindqvist's *Handling the Undead*', in Jane Fernandez-Goldborough (ed.), *Making Sense of Pain: Critical and Interdisciplinary Perspectives*. Oxfordshire: Inter-Disciplinary Press, 2010, pp. 211–18.
Gustavsson, T. 'Slasher in the Snow: The Rise of the Low-Budget Nordic Horror Film', in Tommy Gustafsson and Pietari Kääpä (eds), *Nordic Genre Film: Small Nation Film Cultures in the Global Marketplace*. Edinburgh: Edinburgh University Press, 2015, pp. 189–202.
Hadenius, S. *Modern svensk politisk historia: Konflikt och samförstånd*. Stockholm: Hjalmarsson & Högberg, 2003.
Haelfe-Thomas, A. *Queer Others in Victorian Gothic: Transgressing Monstrosity*. Cardiff: University of Wales Press, 2012.

Haglund T. 'Fankulturen förlänger fantasins universum'. *Svenska Dagbladet*, 22 February 2015, part 3, 6–7. www.svd.se/fankulturen-forlanger-fantasins-universum. Accessed 30 January 2019.

Halskov, A. *TV Peaks: Twin Peaks and Modern Television Drama*. Odense: University Press of Southern Denmark, 2015.

Hancock, M. 'Doppelgamers: Video Games and Gothic Choice', in J. Faflak and J. Haslam (eds), *American Gothic: An Edinburgh Companion*. Edinburgh: Edinburgh University Press, 2016, pp. 166–84.

Hanson, E. 'Knowing Children. Desire and Interpretation in *The Exorcist*', in S. Bruhm and N. Hurley (eds) *Curiouser: On the Queerness of Children*. Minneapolis: University of Minnesota Press, 2004, pp. 107–36.

H. C. Andersen Centret. http://andersen.museum.odense.dk/eventyr/start.asp?sprog=dansk. Accessed 18 October 2018.

Haraway, D. *The Companion Species Manifesto: Dogs, People and Signinficant Otherness*. Chicago: Prickly Paradigm, 2003.

––. *When Species Meet*. Minneapolis: University of Minnesota Press, 2008.

Haugen, T. (ed.). *Literære skygger. Norsk fantastisk literature*. Oslo: Landslaget for norskundervisning, 1998.

Hills, M. *The Pleasures of Horror*. London: Continuum, 2005.

Hirdman, Y. *Att lägga livet tillrätta: Studier i svensk folkhemspolitik*. Stockholm: Carlssons, 1989.

Hjørnager Pedersen, V. *Ugly Ducklings?: Studies in the English Translations of Hans Christian Andersen's Tales and Stories*. Odense: University Press of Southern Denmark, 2004.

Høeg, P. *Frøken Smillas fornemmelse for sne*. København: Rosinante & Co, 1992.

Hoeveler, D. L. *Gothic Riffs: Secularizing the Uncanny in the European Imaginary, 1780–1820*. Columbus: Ohio State University Press, 2010.

Hogle, J. E. 'Introduction: Modernity and the Proliferation of the Gothic', in J. E. Hogle (ed.), *The Cambridge Companion to Modern Gothic*. Cambridge: Cambridge University Press, 2014, pp. 3–19.

––. 'Introduction: The Gothic in Western Culture', in J. E. Hogle (ed.), *The Cambridge Companion to Gothic Fiction*. Cambridge: Cambridge University Press, 2002, pp. 1–20.

Höglund, J. *The American Imperial Gothic: Empire, Culture, Violence*. Farnham: Ashgate, 2014.

––. and Khair, T. (eds) *Postcolonial and Transnational Vampires: Dark Blood*. Basingstoke: Palgrave Macmillan, 2012.

––. 'Revenge of the Trolls. Norwegian (Post) Colonial Gothic', *Edda*, 104:2 (2017), 115–29. DOI: 10.18261/issn.1500-1989-2017-02-05.

––. 'Wither the Present, Wither the Past: The Low-Budget Gothic Horror of Stockholm Syndrome Films', in J. D. Edwards and J. Höglund (eds), *B-Movie Gothic: International Perspectives*. Edinburgh: Edinburgh University Press, 2018. pp. 122–38.

Horner, A. and S. Zlosnik. *Gothic and the Comic Turn*. Basingstoke: Palgrave MacMillan, 2005.

Hughes, W. and A. Smith (eds). *Ecogothic*. Manchester: Manchester University Press, 2013.

Hughey, M. W. 'Cinethetic Racism: White Redemption and Black Stereotypes in "Magical Negro" Films'. *Social Problems*, 56:3 (2009), 543–77. DOI:10.1525/sp.2009.56.3.543.

Hume, R. 'Gothic versus Romantic: A Revaluation of the Gothic Novel'. *PMLA*, 84:2 (1969), 282–289.
Hurley, K. *The Gothic Body: Sexuality, Materialism and Degeneration at the Fin-de-Siècle*. Cambridge: Cambridge University Press, 1996.
Hutcheon, L., with S. O'Flynn. *A Theory of Adaptation*. 2nd edn. London: Routledge, 2013.
Iversen, G. 'Between Art and Genre: New Nordic Horror Cinema', in M. Hjort and U. Lindqvist (eds), *A Companion to Nordic Cinema*. Malden: Wiley Blackwell, 2016, pp. 332–50.
Jackson, R. *Fantasy: The Literature of Subversion*. London: Methuen, 1981.
Jägerfeld, J. 'De har nyckeln till tonårens magi'. *Modern Psykologi* 1 (2015). https://modernpsykologi.se/2015/02/16/de-har-nyckeln-till-tonarens-magi/. Accessed 30 January 2019.
Jakobson, L. 'På de avvisade trollens sida'. *Svenska Dagbladet* (13 August 2006). www.svd.se/pa-de-avvisade-trollens-sida. Accessed 27 March 2019.
Jakobsson, A. 'Horror in the Medieval North: The Troll', in K. Korstophine and L. R. Kremmel (eds), *The Palgrave Handbook to Horror Literature*. Palgrave Macmillan, 2018.
Jarvis, C. 'School is Hell: Gendered Fears in Teenage Horror'. *Educational Studies* 27:3 (2001), 43–52. DOI: 10.1007/s10583-007-9058-0.
Jensen, L. 'Postcolonial Denmark: Beyond the Rot of Colonialism?'. *Postcolonial Studies*, 18:4 (2015), 440–52. DOI:10.1080/13688790.2015.1191989.
Jenzen, O. 'Social Realism and the Paranormal in Scandinavian Fiction', in O. Jenzen and S. R. Munt (eds), *The Ashgate Research Companion to Paranormal Fiction*. Farnham: Ashgate, 2013, pp. 227–39.
Johnsson, H. *Strindberg och skräcken: skräckmotiv och identitetstematik i Strindbergs författarskap*. Umeå: H:ström Text Kultur, 2009.
Jones, T. *The Gothic and Carnivalesque in American Culture*. Cardiff: University of Wales Press, 2015.
Jowett, L. and S. Abbott. *TV Horror: Investigating the Dark Side of the Small Screen*. London: I. B. Tauris, 2013.
Kääpä, P. *Ecology and Contemporary Nordic Cinemas: from Nation Building to Cosmopolitanism*. New York: Bloomsbury Academics, 2014.
Karlsson, H. 'The Vampire and the Anxieties of a Globalizing Swedish Welfare State: *Låt den rätte komma in* (*Let the Right One In*) (2008)'. *EJSS* 43:2 (2013), 184–99. DOI: 10.1515/ejss-2013-0010.
Kastbjerg, K. M. 'Reading the Surface: The Danish Gothic of B. S. Ingemann, H. C. Andersen, Karen Blixen and Beyond'. University of Washington, 2013. https://digital.lib.washington.edu/researchworks/handle/1773/25006.
Keskinen, S., S. Tuori, S. Irni and D. Mulinari (eds). *Complying with Colonialism: Gender, Race and Ethnicity in the Nordic Region*. Farnham: Ashgate, 2009.
Khair, T. *The Gothic, Postcolonialism and Otherness: Ghosts from Elsewhere*. Basingstoke: Palgrave MacMillan, 2009.
Kilpatrick, J. *Celluloid Indians: Native Americans and Film*. Lincoln: University of Nebraska Press, 1999.
Kjellström, R. 'Staloproblemet i samisk historia', in Jørn Sandnes (ed.), *Folk og resurser i nord. Foredrag fra Trondheims-symposiet om midt- og nordskandinavisk kultur*, 1982.

Körber, L. and E. Volquardsen (eds). *The Postcolonial North Atlantic: Iceland, Greenland and the Faroe Islands*. Berlin: Nordeuropa Institut der Humboldt Universität, 2014.
Kvist, R. 'The Racist Legacy in Modern Swedish Saami Policy'. *Canadian Journal of Native Studies*, 14:2 (1994), 203–20.
Lagerlöf, S. *Invisible Links*. Trans. P. Bancroft. Boston, 1909. Project Gutenberg [EBook #14273].
—. 'The Outlaws', in *Invisible Links*, no pagination.
—. *The Saga of Gösta Berling*. Trans. P. Norlen. New York: Penguin, 2009.
Lagerroth, U-B. 'The Troll in Man – A Lagerlöf Motif'. *Scandinavian Studies* 1 (1968) 51–60.
Lagerström, L. 'Tomas – den rätte'. *Film i skolan*, Svenska filminstitutet, November 2008. www.filminstitutet.se/filmiskolan. Accessed 18 September 2017.
Launis, K. 'From Italy to the Finnish Woods: The Rise of Gothic Fiction in Finland', in P. M. Mehtonen and M. Savolainen (eds), *Gothic Topographies: Language, Nation Building and 'Race'*. Farnham: Ashgate, 2013, pp. 169–86.
Leamon, J. S. *Historic Lewistown: A Textile City in Transition*. Produced for the Lewistown Historical Commission, Auburn, Maine, 1976. www.lewistonmaine.gov/DocumentCenter/Home/View/1191. Accessed 25 August 2018.
Leffler, Y. 'The Devious Landscape of Scandinavian Horror', in P. M. Mehtonen and M. Savolainen (eds), *Gothic Topographies: Language, Nation Building and 'Race'*. Abingdon: Routledge, 2013, pp. 141–52.
—. 'Early Crime Fiction in Nordic Literature', in M. Ascari and S. Knight (eds), *From the Sublime to City Crime*. Monaco: Liber Faber, 2015, pp. 161–82.
—. 'Female Gothic Monsters'. *The History of Nordic Women's Literature*, http://nordicwomensliterature.net/article/female-gothic-monsters, Publ. 1 December 2016.
—. 'The Gothic Topography in Scandinavian Horror Fiction', in M. Canini (ed.), *The Domination of Fear*. New York: Rodopi, 2010, pp. 43–53.
—. *Horror as Pleasure: The Aesthetics of Horror Fiction*. Stockholm: Almqvist & Wiksell International, 2000.
—. *I skräckens lustgård: Skräckromantik i svenska 1800-talsromaner*. Göteborg: Göteborgs universitet, 1991.
—. 'Scandinavian Gothic', in W. Hughes, D. Punter and A. Smith (eds), *The Encyclopedia of the Gothic*. Malden: Wiley-Blackwell, 2012.
—. 'Skräckromantik i svensk romantik', in *Nordische Romantik. IASS 19*. Basel and Frankfurt 1991, 134–9.
—. 'Vampyrmotivet och erotiken', in B. Svensson and B. Sjöberg (eds), *Kulturhjälten. Viktor Rydbergs humanism*. Stockholm: Atlantis, 2009, pp. 155–68.
Leine, K. *Prophets of Eternal Fjord*. London: Atlantic Books, 2016.
Lenas, S. 'Damen i skogen'. *Dagens Nyheter*, 18 March 2007. www.dn.se/dn-bok/damen-i-skogen/. Accessed 18 January 2019.
Lewis, M. G. *Tales of Wonder*. Peterborough: Broadview Press, 2010.
Lidström, C. *Sökande, spegling, metamorfos: tre vägar genom Marie Gripes skugg-serie*. Stockholm: Symposion Brutus Östlings bokförlag, 1994.
Lindqvist, J. A. *Handling the Undead*. Trans. E. Segerberg. New York: Thomas Dunne Books/St. Martin's Press, 2011.
—. *Let the Old Dreams Die and Other Stories*. Trans. M. Delargy. London: Quercus, 2012.

—. *Let the Right One In*. Trans. E. Segerberg. London: Quercus, 2009.
—. *Rörelsen. Den andra platsen*. Stockholm: Ordfront, 2015.
Lippe, A. H. von der (ed.). *Dark Cartographies: Exploring Gothic Spaces*. Inter-Disciplinary Press, 2013.
Loftsdóttir, K. and L. Jensen (eds). *Whiteness and Postcolonialism in the Nordic Region*. Farnham: Ashgate, 2012.
Lönngren, A. 'Trolls!! Folklore Literature and "Othering" in the Nordic Countries', in A. Lönngren, H. Grönstrand, D Heede and A Heith (eds), *Rethinking National Literatures and the Literary Canon in Scandinavia*. Newcastle upon Tyne: Cambridge Scholars Publishing, 2015, pp. 205–30.
Loomba, A. *Colonialism/Postcolonialism*. Abingdon: Routledge, 1998.
Lundström, C. *White Migrations: Gender, Whiteness and Privilege in Transnational Migration*. Basingstoke: Palgrave Macmillan, 2014.
Lundström, J. 'John Ajvide Lindqvist: Jag hade zombieskräck sommaren efter min pappas död'. *Dagens Nyheter*, 29 September 2018. www.dn.se/kultur-noje/john-ajvide-lindqvist-jag-hade-zombieskrack-sommaren-efter-min-pappas-dod/. Accessed 3 January 2019.
Magee, S. 'High School is Hell: The TV Legacy of *Beverly Hills, 90210*, and *Buffy the Vampire Slayer*'. *Journal of Popular Culture*, 47:4 (2014), 877–94.
Manker, E. *Fångstgropar och stallotomter. Kulturlämningar från lapsk forntid*. Stockholm: Geber, 1960.
Mäntymäki, H. *Epistemologies of (Un)sustainability in Swedish Crime Series Jordskott*. Green Litters: Studies in Ecocriticism, 2017.
Märak, M. cited in J. Andersson, 'Premiär för SVT:s blodiga morddrama'. *Göteborgsposten*, 23 October 2016. www.gp.se/kultur/tv/premi%C3%A4r-f%C3%B6r-svt-s-blodiga-morddrama-1.3890859. Accessed 31 January 2019.
Masco, J. *The Nuclear Borderlands: The Manhattan Project in Post-Cold War New Mexico*. Princeton: Princeton University Press, 2006.
McClintock, A. *Imperial Leather: Race, Gender, and Sexuality in the Colonial Contest*. New York: Routledge, 1995.
Mehtonen, P. M. and M. Savolainen (eds). *Gothic Topographies: Language, Nation Building and 'Race'*. Farnham and Burlington: Ashgate, 2013.
Mignolo, W. *The Darker Side of Western Modernity: Global Futures, Decolonial Options*. Durham: Duke University Press, 2011.
Miller, C.M. and A. B. Van Riper (eds). *Elder Horror: Essays on Film's Frightening Images of Aging*. Jefferson, North Carolina: McFarland, 2019.
Møller, L. '"They Dance All under the Greenwood Tree": British and Danish Romantic-Period Adaptations of Two Danish "Elf Ballads"', in C. Duffy (ed.), *Romantic Norths: Anglo-Nordic Exchanges, 1770–1842*. New York: Palgrave Macmillan, 2016, pp. 129–53.
Morton, T. *Dark Ecology: For a Logic of Future Coexistence*. New York: Columbia University Press, 2016.
—. *The Ecological Thought*. Cambridge: Harvard University Press, 2010.
—. *Ecology Without Nature: Rethinking Environmental Aesthetics*. Cambridge: Harvard University Press, 2007.
Murphy, B. *The Rural Gothic in American Popular Culture: Backwoods Horror and Terror in the Wilderness*. Basingstoke: Palgrave Macmillan, 2013.
Naum, M. and J. M. Nordin (eds). *Scandinavian Colonialism and the Rise of Modernity: Small Time Agents in a Global Arena*. New York: Springer, 2013.

Nestingen, A. *Crime and Fantasy in Scandinavia: Fiction, Film and Social Change*. Seattle and London: University of Washington Press, 2008.
Niemi, M. *Koka Björn*. Stockholm: Piratförlaget, 2017.
Nilson, M. *Teen Noir: Om mörkret i modern ungdomslitteratur*. Lund: BTJ förlag, 2013.
Norman, T. L. 'Gothic Modernism: Revising and Representing the Narratives of History and Romance'. University of Tennessee, 2012.
Ojala, C.G. and J. M. Nordin. 'Collecting Sápmi: Early modern collecting of Sámi material culture'. *Nordisk Museologi* 2 (2015), 114–22.
O'Malley, P.R. *Catholicism, Sexual Deviance and Victorian Gothic Culture*. Cambridge: Cambridge University Press, 2006.
Omdal, G.K. *Grenseerfaringer. Fantastisk literatur i Norge og omegn*. Bergen: Fagbokforlaget, 2009.
Oxfeldt, E. *Nordic Orientalism: Paris and the Cosmopolitan Imagination 1800–1900*. Copenhagen: Museum Tusculanum Press, 2005.
Patchay, S. 'Not Just a Detective Novel: Trauma, Memory and Narrative Form in *Miss Smilla's Feeling for Snow*'. *JLS/TLW* 26:4 (2010), 17–35. DOI: 10.1080/02564718.2010.529311.
Peacock, S. 'Two *Kingdoms*, Two Kings'. *Critical Studies in Television* 4:2 (2009), 24–36.
Phillips, L. and A. Witchard (eds). *London Gothic: Place, Space and the Gothic Imagination*. London: Continuum Literary Studies, 2010.
Pifer, E. *Demon or Doll: Images of the Child in Contemporary Writing and Culture*. Charlottesville: University Press of Virginia, 2000.
Piper, K. L. 'Inuit Diasporas: Frankenstein and the Inuit in England'. *Romanticism* 13:1 (2007), 63–75.
Punter, D. 'Figuring the Witch', in A. Jackson (ed.), *New Directions in Children's Gothic: Debatable Lands*. New York: Routledge, 2017, pp. 67–80.
––. *The Literature of Terror. A History of Gothic Fiction from 1765 to the Present Day*. London: Longman, 1980.
Qvarsell R. et al. (eds). *I framtidens tjänst: Ur folkhemmets idéhistoria*. Stockholm: Gidlund, 1986.
Reeves, M. 'Matt Reeves Explains How Steven Spielberg Helped Shape *Let Me In*', interview by Peter Hall, *Moviefone*, 5 October 2010. http://news.moviefone.com/2010/10/05/matt-reeves-explains-how-steven-spielberg-helped-shape-let-me-in/. Accessed 27 October 2014.
Redvall, E. 'Skräckmästaren förvånad över framgången'. *Sydsvenskan*, 20 October 2005. www.sydsvenskan.se/2005-10-19/skrackmastaren-forvanad-over-framgangen. Accessed 5 July 2017.
Riquelme, J. P. *Gothic and Modernism: Essaying Dark Literary Modernity*. Baltimore: Johns Hopkins University Press, 2008.
Rouse, R III. 'Match Made in Hell: The Inevitable Success of the Horror Genre in Video Games', in B. Perron (ed.), *Horror Video Games: Essays on the Fusion of Fear and Play*. Jefferson: McFarland, 2009, pp. 15–25.
Royle, N. *The Uncanny*. Manchester: Manchester University Press, 2003.
Saggini, F. *The Gothic Novel and the Stage: Romantic Appropriations*. London: Pickering and Chatto, 2015.
Sandberg McGuinne, J. 'Gunilla Brodrej vet inte hur samer har det'. *Expressen*, 18 November 2016. www.expressen.se/kultur/gunilla-brodrej-vet-inte-hur-samer-har-det/. Accessed 31 January 2019.

Sanders, K. 'A Man of the World: Hans Christian Andersen', in D. Ringgard and M. Rosendahl Thomsen (eds), *Danish Literature as World Literature*. New York: Bloomsbury, 2017, pp. 91–114.
Schmid, A. *The Fear of the Other: Approaches to English Stories of the Double (1764–1910)*. Bern: Peter Lang 1996.
Schön, E. *Troll och människa. Gammal svensk folktro*. Stockholm: Natur och Kultur: 1999.
Scudder, H. E. 'Andersen's Short Stories'. *Atlantic Monthly* 36:217 (Nov. 1875): 598–602. https://babel.hathitrust.org/cgi/pt?id=coo.31924077699977;view=1up;seq=604. Accessed 20 October 2018.
Siegel, C. 'Let a New Gender In? American Responses to Contemporary Scandinavian Gothicism', in C. L. Crow (ed.), *A Companion to American Gothic*. Chichester: Wiley Blackwell, 2014, pp. 547–58.
Sigurðardóttir, Yrsa, *Ashes to Dust*. Trans. P. Roughton. London: Hodder & Stoughton, 2010.
Sinha, M. *Colonial Masculinity: The 'Manly Englishman' and The 'Effeminate Bengali' in the Late Nineteenth Century*. Manchester: Manchester University Press, 1995.
Sinisalo, J. *Not Before Sundown*. Trans. H. Lomas. London: Peter Owen, 2003.
Smith, A. and W. Hughes (eds). *Empire and the Gothic: The Politics of Genre*. London: Palgrave Macmillan, 2003.
Spjut, S. *Stallo*. Trans. S. Beard. London: Faber & Faber, 2015.
––. *Stalpi*. Stockholm: Bonniers, 2017.
Spooner, C. *Post-Millennial Gothic: Comedy, Romance and the Rise of Happy Gothic*. London: Bloomsbury, 2017.
––, and E. McEvoy (eds). *The Routledge Companion to the Gothic*. London and New York: Routledge, 2007.
Stevenson, J. *Lars von Trier*. London: BFI, 2002.
Strandberg, M. *Hemmet*. Stockholm: Norstedts, 2017.
Sugars, C. and G. Turcotte (eds). *Unsettled Remains: Canadian Literature and the Postcolonial Gothic*. Waterloo: Wilfrid Laurier University Press, 2009.
Svalastog, A. and G. Fur (eds). *Visions of Sápmi*. Røros: Arthub Publisher, 2015.
Sveriges nationalparker. www.sverigesnationalparker.se/park/farnebofjardens-nationalpark. Accessed 19 January 2019.
Tangherlini, T. R. 'The Ghost in the Machine: Supernatural Threat and the State in Lars von Trier's *Riget*'. *Scandinavian Studies* 73:1 (2001), 1–24.
Theorin, J. *The Darkest Room*. Trans. M. Delargy. London: Doubleday, 2009.
––. *Echoes from the Dead*. Trans. M. Delargy. London: Doubleday, 2008.
––. *The Quarry*. Trans. M. Delargy. London: Doubleday, 2011.
Thorsen, N. *Geniet Lars von Trier: Liv, Filmer och Fobier*. Trans. T. Andersson. Stockholm: Arkad, 2013.
Tobing, R. F. *The Third Eye: Race, Cinema and Ethnographic Spectacle*. Durham: Duke University Press, 1996.
Troy, M. H. 'Dealing with the Uncanny? Cultural Adaptation in Matt Reeves's Vampire Movie *Let Me In*'. *American Studies in Scandinavia* 48:1 (2016), 25–41.
––. 'Predator and Prey: The Vampire Child in Novels by S. P. Somtow and John Ajvide Lindqvist'. *Edda*, 104:2 (2017), 130–44. DOI: 10.18261/issn.1500-1989-2017-02-05.
Tuan, Y-F. *Landscapes of Fear*. Oxford: Basil Blackwell, 1979.

—. *Space and Place: The Perspective of Experience*. London: Edward Arnold, 1977.
—. 'Space and Place: Humanistic Perspective', in S. Gale and G. Olsson (eds), *Philosophy in Geography*. Dolrecht: cop, 1979, pp. 387–427.
Ullén, M. (ed.). *Våldsamma fantasier: Studier i fiktionsvåldets funktion och attraction*. Karlstad: Kulturvetenskapliga skriftserien 2, 2014.
Walpole, H. *The Castle of Otranto: A Gothic Story*. Ed. with intro. by W. S. Lewis and notes by J. W. Reed, Jr. Oxford, New York: Oxford University Press, 1984.
Wærp, H. H. 'Utover enhver grense – Gotiske trek i Ragnhild Jølsens romancer', in T. Haugen (ed.), *Litterære skygger. Norsk fantastisk litteratur*. Oslo: Cappelen Akademisk Forlag, 1998, pp. 101–21.
Wegner, P. E. *Life between Two Deaths, 1989–2001: U.S. Culture in the Long Nineties*. Durham: Duke University Press, 2009.
Weithz, J. 'Skräckmästaren'. *Flamman*, 18 June 2008. http://flamman.se/a/skrackmastaren. Accessed 5 July 2017.
Wennö, N. 'Låt fulskräcken komma in'. *Dagens Nyheter*, 14 June 2009, www.dn.se/kultur-noje/film-tv/lat-fulskracken-komma-in. Accessed 4 January 2019.
Wheatley, H. *Gothic Television*. Manchester: Manchester University Press, 2006.
Wijkmark, S. 'Ecology, Telepathy, Melancholia in John Ajvide Lindqvist's *Handling the Undead*'. *Edda. Nordisk tidskrift for litteraturforskning*, 104:2 (2017): 145–60. DOI: 101826/issn.1500–1989–2017–02–05.
—. 'Fördömelse från trädkronorna! Ekogotik och mörk ekologi'. *Aiolos* 56:1 (2017): 133–38.
—. *Hemsökelser: Gotiken i sex berättelser av Selma Lagerlöf*. Karlstad: Karlstads Universitet, 2009.
—. 'John Ajvide Lindqvist's Little Star. Gothic Horror and the Remediation of Video Nasties'. *Gothic Studies*, 20:1 (2018): 77–94. DOI: 10.7227/GS.0036.
—. 'Naturen och det kusliga: Nedslag i samtida svensk skönlitteratur'. *Tidskrift för Litteraturvetenskap* 1 (2012), 5–15.
—. Stefan Spjuts *Stallo* som ekogotisk norrlandsskildring', in P. Degerman, A. Johansson and A. Öhman (eds), *Norrlandslitteratur: Ekokritiska perspektiv*. Makadam: Göteborg, 2018, pp. 196–212.
—. 'Trollen i Selma Lagerlöfs "Bortbytingen" och John Ajvide Lindqvists "Gräns"', in M. Karlsson and L. Vinge (eds), *Spår och speglingar*. Hedemora: Gidlunds, 2011, pp. 344–61.
World of Engelsfors. 'FAQ'. www.worldofengelsfors.com/frequently-asked-questions/. Accessed 10 December 2017.
Wright, R. 'Androgyny in Kerstin Ekman's *Rövarna i Skuleskogen* and Virginia Woolf's *Orlando*', in H. Kress (ed.), *Litteratur og kjønn i Norden*. Reykjavik: Háskólaútgáfan, 1996, pp. 676–8.
Wright, R. 'Vampire in the Stockholm Suburbs: *Let the Right One In* and Genre Hybridity'. *Journal of Scandinavian Cinema* 1:1 (2010), 55–70.

Index

Abassi, Ali 108
  Gräns/Border 4
abject, the 130, 132, 136–7, 143–4, 152–5, 164, 180–1
adaptation 4, 6, 9, 21–2, 30, 32, 34, 65, 85–6, 147–68, 190
Alan Wake 9, 170, 172–9, 184, 186–7, 190
Alfredson, Tomas 4, 22, 147, 151–2, 166
Almqvist, Carl Jonas Love 67
  Skällnora kvarn 67
ambiguity 39, 82, 105, 112, 120, 156
American Gothic 8–9, 56, 151, 160, 164, 174, 178
Andersen, Hans Christian 6, 13, 19, 27, 29–36, 44–5
  'De røde sko'/'The Red Shoes' 13
  'De vilde Svaner'/'The Wild Swans' 6, 29–30, 32, 35–6
  'Den lille Havfrue'/'The Little Mermaid' 6, 29, 32–4
  'Dyndkongens datter'/'The Mud-King's Daughter' 19
  Fodreise 31
  'Skyggen'/'The Shadow' 13, 31
  'Snedronningen'/'The Snow Queen' 6, 29, 32, 34
animal 32, 39–42, 51, 104, 106, 109–19, 135
Arctic, the 15, 18–19, 126, 132

Bäck, Madeleine 47
backwoods horror 120, 124
Barker, Clive 4, 20, 152
Bauer, John 117
Bergman, Ingmar 17, 23
  Det sjunde inseglet/The Seventh Seal 17
  Jungfrukällan/The Virgin Spring 17
  Persona 17–18
  Vargtimmen/Hour of the Wolf 18
Bergstrøm, Kåre 19
  De dødes tjern/Lake of the Dead 19
Bjerke, André 19
Björn, Henrik and Anders Engström 25, 66, 108
  Jordskott 25–6, 66, 81, 108–9
Blair Witch Project, The 24, 178
Blicher, Steen Steensen 67
  Præsten i Vejlbye 67
Blixen, Karen 16, 127
  Seven Gothic Tales 16
  'The Supper at Elsinore'/'Et familieskab Helsingør' 16
Blomberg, Erik 18
  Valkoinen peura/The White Reindeer 18
body horror 32, 152, 164
Bornedal, Ole 20
  Nattevagten/The Night Watch 20
Bron/Broen/The Bridge 65, 137, 147–8

cabin 118–19, 124, 139, 176–7, 184, 186
changeling 75, 104–6, 109
Christensen, Benjamin 16
   Häxan/The Witch 16
class 14, 48, 57, 60, 81, 85–6, 92, 97–8, 131, 135
climate change 7, 50, 61, 111–12
Clover, Carol 57, 63, 120, 124
colonialism 8, 125–31, 133–4, 137–9, 141–4
comedy 120, 151–4, 171
Conrad, Joseph 14, 130, 133
consumerism 50–1
Cornell, Jonas 20
   Månguden 20
Craft, The 97–8, 101
Cras, Bengt-Åke 20
crossover fiction 32, 92

Dahl, Gunnar 20
Danielsson, Dagmar 20
dark ecology 8, 103–4, 121
De odöda. Skräckberättelser av John Ajvide Lindqvist, Johan Theorin, Åke Edwardsson 30
decolonisation 17–18, 127
dementia 55–6, 58–9, 178
Dinesen, Isak *see* Blixen, Karen
Disney 6, 16, 30, 33, 35, 45
   Fantasia 16
   Frozen 30, 45
   The Little Mermaid 30, 33, 45
Disneyfication 30, 32
doppelgänger 8, 13, 58, 85, 94–6, 99, 177
double, the 13–15, 17, 37, 43–4, 46, 96, 102, 107, 155, 175
doubling 40, 95, 170, 174, 176–7, 184
Dreyer, Carl Theodor 4, 16, 18
   Vampyr 16
Ducray-Duminil, François 12
   Victor, ou l'Enfant de la Forêt 12

ecogothic 8, 41–2, 103–4, 111, 121–2
ecology 50, 103–4, 110, 121

Ekman, Kerstin 8, 18–19, 41–2, 106–8, 115, 122, 136
   De tre små mästarna/Under the Snow 18, 136
   Händelser vid vatten/Blackwater 19
   Herrarna i skogen 41, 107, 122
   Rövarna i skuleskogen/The Forest of Hours 19, 107, 122
   Eleonora Rosalba, eller Ruinerna i Paluzzi 12
Elfgren, Sara B. and Mats Strandberg 7, 22–3, 84–102
   Cirkeln/The Circle 7, 22, 84, 92–5, 97–9, 101
   Eld/Fire 7, 84, 87–9, 91–2, 95–100
   Engelsfors trilogy, the 84–102
   Nyckeln/The Key 7, 84, 87, 89–90, 93, 98–9
Enlightenment 2, 11, 82, 125, 128, 132–3, 136, 142, 158
environment, the 42, 103–4, 109, 111, 117–18
environmental destruction 103, 111
Ersgård, Joakim 20
   Besökarna/The Visitors 20

Fager, Anders 8, 47, 136, 143
   Svenska kulter/Swedish Cults 137
fairy tale 6, 13, 29–32, 34, 36, 44–5, 117
fantastic, the 6, 12, 29, 31, 38, 151
fantasy 31, 37, 82, 84–5, 100, 110, 122
female Gothic 6, 15, 19
femme fatale 39, 44, 46
fin-de-siècle 6, 14, 30, 36–7, 39, 42, 46
folkhem 48–53, 55, 61
folklore 6, 8, 15, 19, 30, 34, 38–9, 42, 103, 110–11, 115, 185
folktale 13, 23–4, 36, 70–1, 75–6
forest, the 7–8, 24–5, 30, 32–3, 35, 38–44, 66, 72, 90–2, 105–13, 118–19, 121, 139, 154, 162, 178, 185, 187–8
Friday the 13th 20, 176
Friedkin, William 57, 63
   The Exorcist 181

Index

Frost, Mark *see* Lynch, David
Fyhr, Mattias 5, 11, 19, 26

game 1, 3, 6, 9, 11, 21, 25–6, 169–90
   AAA games 170–3, 188
   first-person shooter 173, 188
   third-person survival horror 174, 178, 184
gender 57, 60, 86, 106, 131, 136, 172
geriatric Gothic 7, 55, 57, 60
ghost 13, 15–16, 43, 54, 56, 69–70, 74–5, 92, 95, 104, 140, 141, 156–7, 163, 170, 175, 180, 190
Gothic crime 5, 7, 18, 20, 25, 65–83, 126, 136, 172
Gothic humour 9, 149, 152–6, 164
Gothic space 68, 72–6, 78, 83, 175
Gothic TV 3, 9, 150–1, 160
Greenland 2–3, 17–8, 25, 66, 126, 129–33
Grimm brothers 19
Gripe, Maria 19–20
   Skuggserien/The Shadow series 20
grotesque, the 19, 33, 44, 109, 121, 152–6, 164, 167, 181

Hagberg, Matthias 19
   Rekviem för en vanskapt 19
Halloween 20, 176
Hammerich, Rumle 20
   Svart Lucia/Black Lucia 20
Hansen, Mauritz Christopher 67
   Mordet på Maskinbygger Roolfsen 67
Hatwig, Hans 20
   Blödaren/The Bleeder 20
haunted house 13, 20, 56, 157, 170
haunting 2, 38, 43, 58
Hellberg, Amanda 47
Hoffmann, E. T. A. 3, 12–14, 31
home 7, 17, 55–61, 69–70, 119
horror film 6, 18, 20, 22–4, 57, 63, 81, 95, 120, 134, 137, 165, 180, 185–6
hulder 25, 183, 185, 190
humanity 41, 59, 97, 113, 119, 186
humankind 8, 15, 39, 41, 49, 104, 106, 108

Høeg, Peter 8, 25, 126, 130–2, 137, 142–3, 172
   Frøken Smillas fornemmelse for sne/Miss Smilla's Feeling for Snow 25, 126, 128, 130–2, 137–8, 142, 145
Höglund, Panu Petteri 17
Hutcheon, Linda 148–9, 157, 165

Ibsen, Henrik 15
   Gengangere/Ghosts 15
Imperial Gothic 127, 136, 144
incest 13, 16, 119–20
indigeneity 132, 137, 143–4
Ingemann, Bernhard Severin 12
   Varulven/The Werewolf 12
   Sphinxen/The Sphinx 12
insanity 17, 108, 176
Inuit 66, 129–32, 144

Jensen, Caroline L. 23
   Vargsläkte 23
Jølsen, Ragnhild 15, 17, 27
   Rikka Gan 15

Kaaberbøl, Lene 23, 84, 100
   Vildheks/Wild Witch 23, 84, 100
Kalla kårar 20
Kandre, Mare 19
   Aliide, Aliide 19
   Bestiarium 19
   Bübins unge/Bübin's Kid 19
Kastbjerg, Kirstine 5, 11, 30–2, 45
Kemp, Julius 23
   Reykjavik Whale Watching Massacre 23
Kindblom, Johan and Thomas Tivemark 25, 66
   Ängelby 25, 66
King, Stephen 4, 9, 20–1, 56, 63, 92, 147–9, 151–2, 155–64
   Carrie 155
   Kingdom Hospital 9, 21, 92, 147–9, 151–2, 155–64, 167
kitchen-sink fantasy 85, 90
Kivinen, Albert S. 17
Koontz, Dean R. 20, 56, 63

Kranz, Leif 20
Kullamannen 20

lady of the forest, the 38–9
Lagercrantz, David 148
  Det som inte dödar oss/The Girl in the Spider's Web 148
Lagerkvist, Per 16
  Dvärgen/The Dwarf 16
  'Far och jag'/'Father and I' 16
  Onda sagor/Evil Tales 16
Lagerlöf, Selma 6–8, 15, 17, 23, 27, 29, 30, 36–46, 105, 110, 121
  'Bortbytingen'/'The Changeling' 30, 105, 110, 121–2
  'De fågelfrie'/'The Outlaws' 6, 30, 42–6
  En Herrgårdssägen/From a Swedish 'Frid på jorden' 15, 37
  Gösta Berlings saga/The Saga of Gösta Berling 6, 30, 37–42
  Herr Arnes Penningar/Herr Arne's Hoard 15, 27, 37
  Homestead 37
  Körkarlen/Thy Soul Shall Bear Witness 16, 37
  Nils Holgerssons underbara resa genom Sverige/The Wonderful Adventures of Nils 36
  'Stenkumlet'/'The King's Grave' 6, 15, 30, 42, 46
Larsson, Stieg 65, 85, 100
  Män som hatar kvinnor/The Girl With the Dragon Tattoo 65, 148
  Millenium trilogy 65, 85, 148
Leine, Kim 25, 128, 132, 143
  Profeterna i evighetsfjorden/Prophets of Eternal Fjord 25, 128, 132–3
Lewis, Matthew 12, 26, 169
  Monk, The 12, 169
Lindberg, Rolf 118
Linderholm, Helmer 20
  De ulvgrå 20
Lindqvist, John Ajvide 3–4, 6–7, 9, 22, 30, 47–53, 60–1, 85, 100, 108, 126, 143, 147–53, 162–4, 166, 172, 181

'Gräns'/'Border' 4, 22, 108–9, 122, 143
Hanteringen av odöda/Handling the Undead 7, 22, 47–8, 50, 52–3, 61–2
Låt den rätte komma in/Let the Right One In 3–4, 6, 9, 22, 47, 49, 50, 85–6, 147–9, 151–2, 162, 164
Lilla stjärna/Little Star 22
Människohamn/Harbour 22, 30
Rörelsen. Den andra platsen 7, 48, 53–4, 61
Little Nightmares 9, 170, 178–82, 184, 186–9
Livijn, Clas 12–13
'Samwetets fantasi' 12
Ljungstedt, Aurora 13
'Harolds skugga' 14
Hin ondes hus 13
ludology 170, 174, 189
Lynch, David 5, 66, 150, 175
  Twin Peaks 5, 66, 84, 101, 143, 149, 150–1, 165, 175

madness 24, 37–8, 40, 108
Mårlind, Måns and Björn Stein 25, 137–8
Idjabeaivváš/Jour Polaire/Midnight Sun/Midnattssol 126, 128, 137–43
Maryatt, Florence 14, 27
mermaid 32–3, 35, 44, 46
Middle Ages, the 34, 42, 106, 133
Million Programme 52, 61, 162
modernism 14, 16, 31
modernity 11, 16, 79, 80–2, 137, 143, 158, 163–4, 172, 189
monster 6, 18, 21, 24, 49, 51, 79, 81, 95–6, 109, 122, 126, 132, 150, 153, 184–6
Morton, Timothy 103–4, 119, 121

Nature/nature 5, 8, 15, 21, 23–4, 38, 41, 66, 68, 80–2, 103–4, 106, 111–13, 117–18, 121, 137, 188
Niemi, Mikael 19, 126
  Fallvatten 19
  Koka björn 19, 126
non-human 103, 105, 107, 119

Index

Nordaas, Alexander L. 24, 108
  Thale 24–5, 81, 108–9, 185
Nordic mythology 7, 20, 25, 66, 103, 178, 182–3
Nordic Noir 5, 7, 25, 65–6, 100, 137, 147–8, 172, 188

Ohlmarks, Åke 20
  Gengångare 20
  Slottsspöken 20
Øie, Pål 24
  Villmark/Dark Woods 24
old age 7, 51, 56, 59, 60–1
Otherness 120, 125–7, 135
Øvredal, André 24, 108
  Trolljegeren/Troll Hunter 24, 81, 108–9, 137, 185

Palme, Olof 7, 53–4, 61–2
Poe, Edgar Allan 14
Polidori, John 12
possession 56–7, 60

race 24, 41, 131, 136, 143, 172
Radcliffe, Ann 12–13, 15, 42
  Italian, The 12
Raimi, Sam 25
  Evil Dead 20, 25
realism 30–1, 36, 68, 85, 117, 150, 166
Reeves, Matt 9, 22, 148
  Cloverfield 149
  Let Me In 9, 22, 148–9, 154, 163–4
Refn, Nicolas Winding 24
  Valhalla Rising 24
romanticism 30–1, 37
Rydberg, Viktor 12, 27
  Vampyren 12
  Rymdinvasion i Lappland/Terror in the Midnight Sun 18, 126

Sámi, the 2–3, 18–19, 49, 116–7, 126–9, 135–43
Sápmi 2–3, 17–9, 128–9, 134–43
Scandinavian Noir/Scandi Noir 65
sexuality 44, 58, 60, 136
shapeshifter 23, 104, 120
Shelley, Mary 126

Frankenstein 104, 126, 132, 144–5, 169
Sigurðardóttir, Yrsa 8, 25, 66, 81
  Auðnin/The Day is Dark 25, 66
  Þóra Guðmundsdóttir/Ashes to Dust 66
Sinisalo, Johanna 8, 30, 108–13, 172
  Ennen päivänlaskua ei voi/Not Before Sundown 30, 108–12
Six Feet Under 154, 156
Sjöström, Victor 16–17, 37
  Körkarlen/The Phantom Carriage 16–17
slasher 20, 23, 134, 155, 175
social criticism 37, 50, 52, 66
Social Democrat 31, 48–55, 161
social realism 3, 7, 47, 85, 90
species 8, 24, 103–21
Spjut, Stefan 8, 19, 30, 108, 113, 126, 128, 136, 143
  Stallo 19, 30, 108, 113–21
  Stalpi 108, 113–14, 116–17, 120–1
Stagnelius, Erik Johan 13
  Riddartornet 13
Stoker, Bram 14, 136
  Dracula 14, 136, 144
Strandberg, Mats *see also* Elfgren, Sara B. 7, 47–9, 55–61, 172
  Hemmet 7, 55–8, 61, 63
Strindberg, August 15, 27
  Spöksonaten/Ghost Sonata 15, 27
  Tschandala 15, 27
Sue, Eugène 12
supernatural, the 3, 5, 7, 13, 19–20, 25, 31, 37–9, 41–2, 47, 49, 53, 56–9, 61, 66–8, 75–80, 82, 85, 89, 97, 106–7, 130, 136–7, 155, 157–9, 164, 186

terror 1, 11, 14, 16–17, 19, 25, 73, 75, 79–81, 130, 133, 139, 163
Texas Chainsaw Massacre, the 23, 120
Theorin, Johan 7, 25, 30, 67–83
  Blodläge/The Quarry 67, 69, 71–2, 76, 78
  Nattfåk/The Darkest Room 25, 67, 69–71, 74, 76–8, 80

Rörgast/The Voices Beyond 67, 69–70, 75–6, 78–81
Skumtimmen/Echoes of the Dead 25, 67, 69, 71, 73, 76–9
Through the Woods 26, 170, 184–8
Topelius, Zacharias 67
  'En natt och en morgon' 67
transgression 18, 71, 78, 80–1, 94, 96
Trier, Lars von 9, 22, 92, 139, 147, 149–52, 155, 161
  Antichrist 22
  Riget/The Kingdom 3–4, 9, 10, 21–2, 92, 139, 147–68
troll 4, 8, 19, 24, 34, 41, 44, 69, 75–6, 103–24, 136–8, 143, 185, 187
Trotzig, Birgitta 19
  Dykungens dotter: En barnhistoria 19
Tuan, Yi-Fu 7, 68, 72–3, 82
TV horror 9, 150–1

uncanny, the 8, 16, 40–1, 43, 49–50, 52, 58–61, 69, 75–77, 104, 106–8, 112–21, 126, 132, 139–40, 149, 156–64
undead, the 7, 47, 51–2, 61, 153–4
Uthaug, Roar 24
  Fritt Vilt/Cold Prey 24

vampire 4, 16–17, 22, 49, 50, 85, 94, 101–3, 137, 147, 151, 153–4, 162–3

Walpole, Horace 11, 13, 42, 68, 82, 169
  The Castle of Otranto 11, 13, 68, 82, 169
welfare profiteering 7, 55, 59, 61
welfare state 7, 47–63, 66, 86, 136, 163, 167, 172
Whedon, Joss 92, 101
  Buffy the Vampire Slayer 84–6, 89–95, 97, 99, 101
whimsical macabre, the 155–6, 164
wilderness, the 5, 15, 23–5, 68, 72, 103, 117, 119, 178, 188
Wirkola, Tommy 24
  Død snø/Dead Snow 24
witch 7–8, 16, 23, 32–3, 35–6, 39–40, 44, 84–102, 143
witchcraft 8, 18, 40, 85, 90–4, 136
woods, the 18, 22, 60, 111, 114–15, 118, 124

Year Walk 9, 170, 182–4, 186–9

zombie 7, 24, 47, 49–52, 59, 62, 75, 103, 170, 173

EU authorised representative for GPSR:
Easy Access System Europe, Mustamäe tee 50,
10621 Tallinn, Estonia
gpsr.requests@easproject.com